Troubleshooting Guide

D1608748

FRAMEMAKER® 4 FOR UNIX® SOLUTIONS

Helena Fernandez Jerney
and John Jerney

John Wiley & Sons, Inc.
New York · Chichester · Brisbane · Toronto · Singapore

Associate Publisher: Katherine Schowalter
Editor: Tim Ryan
Associate Managing Editor: Jacqueline A. Martin
Editorial Production & Design: Publication Services, Inc.

Library of Congress Cataloging-in-Publication Data:
Jerney, Helena Fernandez
    FrameMaker 4 for UNIX solutions / by Helena Fernandez Jerney and
John Jerney.
        p.   cm.
    Includes index.
    ISBN 0-471-59076-2 (pbk. : alk. paper)
    1. FrameMaker (Computer file)   2. Desktop publishing.   3. UNIX
(Computer file)   I. Jerney, John, 1963-   . II. Title.
III. Title: FrameMaker four for UNIX solutions.
Z253. 532.F7J47 1994
686.2ʹ25445365–dc20   93-38410
                                                                CIP

  Printed in the United States of America
  10 9 8 7 6 5 4 3 2 1

Introduction

This Solutions book is a complete reference to FrameMaker 4 and is written so that you can find quick, complete answers to your questions and problems. Start by looking up your question in the Troubleshooting Guide at the front of the book. The shortcut keys listed next to your question are there in case you only need a quick reminder. If you have a more complicated problem or are trying something for the first time, turn to the page listed in the Troubleshooting Index for a detailed solution.

On each page you'll find a "task" devoted to answering your specific question, so you won't have to read a lot of extra text that doesn't apply. The Solutions Series is designed to answer your questions quickly so you can get on with your work. Each task has a brief introduction, a list of Assumptions and Exceptions that tells you how to set up your computer and software to make sure you will complete the task successfully, and clear, concise steps that get right to the point. In case there is a glitch, the What To Do If section tells you how to fix it.

The Solutions Series doesn't just tell you the mechanics of using FrameMaker 4; it also gives you tips on savvy things to do with the software, such as how to locate your data quickly, how to produce reports with a minumum of fuss, and how to customize FrameMaker 4 so it works the way you want it to.

FrameMaker 4 for UNIX Solutions is full of the answers you need to keep your business going.

Conventions

The Solutions Series uses the following conventions to make instructions clear:

Key combinations are written in bold. "**Esc g r**" means press the **Esc** key and, then the **g** key, and then press the **r** key.

File menus are written in bold so you can find them easily within the text.

Acknowledgments

We would like to thank the following people for their contributions to this project:

Jennifer Atkinson, Lee Taylor, and PDR Information Services, for their continued support of this project, and their encouragement and advice concerning numerous endeavors over the past several years.

Sophia Moustakas, for her keen eye and willingness to read our chapters early and thoroughly. Sophia's editing skills and to-the-point questions about the topics and organization of the book helped to make this a better resource for FrameMaker users.

Lisa Braz, for always listening and providing us with constant support, good advice, and a reality check through the project. Lisa was always there to help when doubt set in, when important content and organization decisions had to be made, or when we simply needed someone to talk with. Thanks Lis!

Paul Bailey, for his support and encouragement through this project, and for always guiding us in the right direction when we needed information. Paul's enthusiasm for this project and his strong belief in FrameMaker helped us gain valuable insight into the product, as well as some very useful information.

We would also like to thank Frame Technology for their co-operation in providing us with timely product information and software releases. Thanks to Jolana Leinson, Craig Yappert, and Carol Kaplan, for taking time from their busy schedules to deal with our questions and requests.

We have worked with the people at Waterside Productions on several other projects and are always impressed with the friendly and efficient environment they create for completing complex projects like this. Special thanks to our agent, Carole McClendon, for her tremendous energy and great work, especially through the early stages of the project.

We were happy to have the opportunity to work with Tim Ryan, Alison Roarty, and others at John Wiley & Sons. Tim created a very pleasant environment for producing a book about an exciting product like FrameMaker. He has a way of always bringing the best out of people, even when faced with the usual deadlines and other minor crises that are part of every book. Thanks Tim, it was a real pleasure.

Finally, we would like to dedicate this book to our parents, Janos and Amalia Jerney, Helena Fernandez Lathrop, and Carlos P. Rojas.

Contents

Chapter
1

Opening a Document

Navigating a Document

Manipulating Objects

Saving a Document

Printing a Document

GETTING
STARTED

Opening a Document

FrameMaker keeps all the information you write in a document. When you use FrameMaker on a workstation, it displays the contents of the document in a window on the screen. This window contains not only the information you are writing, but also menus, buttons, and a status bar, which gives you the tools and commands to manipulate your document. Before you can start writing, you must open a new document.

1 Starting FrameMaker

Before you can enter information into a document, you have to start FrameMaker on your workstation. You can start FrameMaker by entering a command in an xterm window. When you do this, FrameMaker shows that it's running by displaying the Frame-Maker main window, which contains five buttons labeled New, Open, Help, Info, and Exit. Your first interaction with FrameMaker will be through this window, by which you can open new or existing documents (see Figure 1.1).

Assumptions

- This section assumes that your system administrator has installed a licensed copy of FrameMaker that is accessible from your workstation. The system administrator is the person in

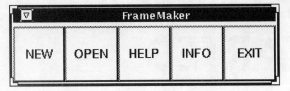

Figure 1.1 The FrameMaker main window.

your organization who installs and maintains hardware and software on your workstations.

_____ **Exceptions**

- None.

_____ **Steps**

1. Open an xterm window on your workstation.
   If you already have an xterm window open or iconized, you can use this window.
2. Enter the command **maker** in the xterm window.

The command **maker** will start the United States version of Frame-Maker.

_____ **What To Do If**

- If you enter the FrameMaker command in an xterm window and you don't see FrameMaker's main window, please contact the system administrator in your organization.
- If you want to exit FrameMaker and close all documents, click Exit in the main FrameMaker window.

_____ **See Also**

- Opening a Blank Page, below.

TIP
If you want to run an international version of Frame-Maker, you should use the following command:
imaker -l <language>
For example,
imaker -l spanish

TIP
If you want to open several documents, you need to run FrameMaker only once.

Opening a Blank Page   2

You have two choices when you want to create a new document using FrameMaker. If you are creating something that will be part of a series or already has a predefined layout and appearance, you can use a template. Many times, however, you will want to open with a blank sheet of paper and design the structure and appearance of your document from scratch.

Starting with a blank piece of paper has the advantage of allowing you to completely specify the layout of the document as you feel appropriate, but it is also time-consuming and takes certain skills. By using a suitable template, you can get a starting point that has much of this work already completed.

FrameMaker supplies three types of blank paper: Portrait, Landscape, and Custom. This section deals with Portrait and Landscape orientations; the next section will describe opening custom documents. Portrait and Landscape refer to the orientation of the paper. They are named after two common styles of paintings and are easy to remember when you think of it this way. A painted portrait is usually taller than it is wide, while a painting of a landscape is generally wider than tall. The same is true for documents. Portrait is the way you normally read a book, whereas landscape describes the book turned on its side.

Assumptions

- None.

Exceptions

- None.

Steps

1. Click on **New** in the main FrameMaker window (or press **Esc f n**).
   The main FrameMaker window is the one displayed after you start FrameMaker from the xterm window. After you click New, FrameMaker displays a dialog box from which you ll select the type of blank paper to use. See Figure 1.2.
2. Click **Portrait** or **Landscape**.
   FrameMaker opens a new document and assigns it the temporary name of NoName.

What To Do If

- None.

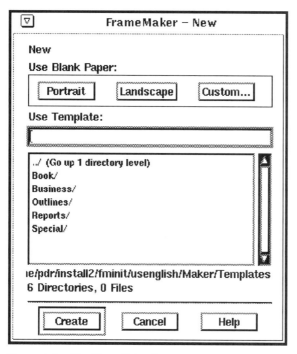

Figure 1.2   The New dialog box.

_____ **See Also**

- Opening a Custom Document, below.
- Opening a Template, p. 8.
- Opening an Existing Document, p. 11.
- Saving a FrameMaker File, p. 26.

Opening a Custom Document   3

Using a custom document enables you to create a new document and specify the general page layout upfront. Creating a custom document can save you time when you know the layout of your document and can't find a matching template.

When opening a custom document, you can specify the page size along with the width of the margins. You can also define the number of columns the page will contain and specify the spacing between them. A custom document also enables you to control whether the document is single- or double-sided and to specify the unit of measurement for the document.

Assumptions

- There is no existing template that meets your needs. You want to create a customized document.

Exceptions

- None.

Steps

1. Click on **New** in the main FrameMaker window (or press **Esc f n**).
   The main FrameMaker window is the one displayed after you start FrameMaker from the xterm window. After you click New, FrameMaker displays a dialog box with options to create a Portrait, Landscape, or Custom document.

2. Click **Custom** in the New dialog box.
   FrameMaker displays a dialog box where you'll specify the general page layout of the new document (see Figure 1.3).

3. Select a page size from the pop-up menu of preset page size.
   Selecting some of the page sizes in the pop-up menu may cause some of the other options in the dialog box to change. Continue on and modify any of the settings as required.

4. Enter a width and height for the document pages.

5. Enter the number of columns that you want on the page and the gap value.
   The gap value is the space that separates the columns.

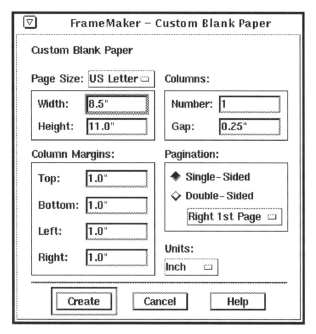

Figure 1.3 The Custom Blank Paper dialog box.

6. Enter the column margins.
   The margins refer to the distance from the edge of the document page, not the text column.

7. Select a pagination.
   You can select Single-Sided or Double-Sided. When you select Double-Sided, you should also specify whether the first page of your document starts on the left page or the right page. Choosing Double-Sided also causes the text boxes for the Left and Right column margins to change to Inside and Outside column margins. The Inside margin refers to the space in between two facing pages when you open a book. The Outside margin refers to the space closest to the outside of the book, and farthest from the spine.

   > **TIP**
   >
   > When creating a double-sided document, make the inside margin slightly larger than the outside to accommodate the binding.

8. Select the units of measurement for the document.
   FrameMaker will use the units of measurement you select to display the distances in your document. Normally, these

distances will appear in dialog boxes and in the status bar of the document window.

What To Do If

- None.

See Also

- Opening a Blank Page, p. 3.
- Opening a Template, below.
- Opening an Existing Document, p. 11.
- Saving a FrameMaker File, p. 26.

4   Opening a Template

A template is a FrameMaker document that contains information controlling the layout and structure of a document. Templates can also help you create professional-looking publications. They contain settings for paragraph, character, and table formats as well as information about how the pages are laid out in the document. The layout information describes how to set margins, spacing, headers, and footers and how to number the pages. Templates can include reference pages that contain graphics and formatting information that you can use in the document. It can also contain cross-references, variable definitions, and conditional text formats and settings.

Most templates already contain text to help you visualize how the page layout and formatting looks. Most times, you can simply delete this text and enter your own. However, you can create templates that already contain some of the text you need in the document, in which case you can simply edit and enhance the document. FrameMaker includes many different templates, which you'll find in the Templates directory in the FrameMaker installation.

Assumptions

- You want to create and save a template that you can use again.

Exceptions

- None.

Steps

1. Click on **New** in the main FrameMaker window (or press **Esc f n**).
   The main FrameMaker window is the one displayed after you start FrameMaker from the xterm window. FrameMaker responds by displaying a dialog box showing the contents of the Templates directory, or your home directory if it can't find the templates directory (see Figure 1.4).

2. Navigate through the directories until you find the template you want.
   You can display the contents of a directory by double-clicking on its name in the list. If you want to go back outside a directory, double-click on the entry "../(Go up 1 directory level)."

3. Select the template in the list and click **Create.**
   FrameMaker will open a new document called NoName, copying the formats from the template you selected. You can now modify the text already in the document, or you can delete all the text and enter your own. Either way, you should use the Save As command to save the document to disk and give it a new name.

> **TIP**
> Selecting a template that matches your new document requirements can save you a lot of work.

What To Do If

- If FrameMaker can't find the templates directory and displays your directory in the New dialog box, you can help it out by entering the following in the text box labeled Use Template:

  $FMHOME/fminit/usenglish/maker/Templates

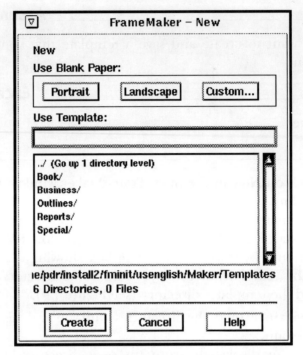

Figure 1.4 The list of templates in the New dialog box.

If you are using an international version of FrameMaker, enter the name of the language in place of "usenglish" in the above example.

- If you want to delete all the text in the document, click anywhere in the text and choose Select All in Flow in the Edit menu. This causes all the text in the document to be highlighted. Press Delete to remove all the highlighted material.

See Also

- Opening a Blank Page, p. 3.
- Opening a Custom Document, p. 5.
- Opening an Existing Document, p. 11.
- Saving a FrameMaker File, p. 26.

Opening an Existing Document **5**

You can open not only documents created with FrameMaker, but also documents created using some other applications. If FrameMaker realizes that the file was created using some other program, it will try to convert it into the FrameMaker format while it is opening it. You can then store the document in Frame-Maker's native format, enabling you to save time whenever you work with the document in the future.

Assumptions

- You want to work with a document that already exists.

Exceptions

- FrameMaker displays a warning if someone else is editing the file you are trying to open. When this happens, you can either cancel the open, open the file for view-only, or open a copy of the file for editing. This will create a new version of the file.

Steps

1. Click on **Open** in the main FrameMaker window (or press **Esc f o**).
   FrameMaker displays the Open dialog box, which you can use to select the file you would like to open (see Figure 1.5). This dialog box also includes such important information as the current directory name and the number of files and directories in the list.

2. Navigate through the directories to find the file you want to open.
   You can use the scrollable file and directory list to navigate through the file system until you find the document. You can move back out of any directory by selecting the parent directory (one directory level up)—the "../"entry in the list.

TIP

FrameMaker lets you specify this file name pattern using special characters called wildcards. The two most common wildcard characters are the asterisk "*" and the question mark "?". You can use the "?" to match any single character in a file name, while the "*" will match any series of characters. Here are several examples to illustrate the use of wildcards:

*.doc displays all files that end with the characters *.doc*.

chap* displays all files that begin with *chap*.

TOC displays all files that have the letter combination TOC somewhere in the name. The case of the letters is important; this pattern will only match capital T, O, and C.

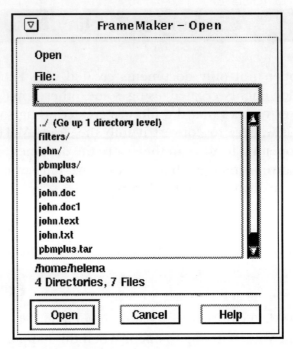

Figure 1.5   The Open dialog box.

3.   Select the file name when it appears in the current directory.

   If there are many files in the current directory, or if there are several files with similar names but different extensions, you can restrict the file names that are displayed in the scrollable list by entering a pattern in the File text box.

4.   Click **Open** to open the highlighted file.

   You can also open a file in the list by double-clicking on the name. Alternatively, you can enter the name of the file in the space provided in the File text box.

5.   If you do not want to open a document, click **Cancel.**

What To Do If

- If FrameMaker finds an unavailable font in the document, it will display an alert "Document uses unavailable fonts.

OK to continue?" If you choose to continue, FrameMaker substitutes new fonts and reformats the document.

- If you want to open an ASCII text file, open the file as usual. When FrameMaker realizes that the file contains ASCII text, it will display a dialog box asking you how to treat the paragraphs. You have the choice of treating each line in the text as a separate paragraph or merging nonblank lines into paragraphs. In the latter case, blank lines in the text serve as paragraph breaks.

- If you can't find a file, there are several utility programs (such as find and grep) that you can use to find a file based on its name or its ASCII text contents. These programs must be run from the UNIX shell you are using (such as the Bourne shell, or the C shell). For more information about these programs, consult the UNIX manuals that came with your workstation.

- If you accidentally open the wrong document, select Close in the File menu of the document window.

See Also

- Opening a Blank Page, p. 3.
- Opening a Custom Document, p. 5.
- Opening a Template, p. 8.
- Saving a FrameMaker File, p. 26.

Navigating a Document

Most of the documents you create in FrameMaker will consist of more than one page. In fact, FrameMaker is ideally suited for creating large and complex publications that not only contain many pages, but can also span several documents. To help you move from one location to another, FrameMaker provides several methods to navigate through a document, including leafing and thumbing. When you scroll up or down a document, you are performing the electronic equivalent of leafing from page to page in a printed book. Likewise, by moving up the marker in the scroll bar, you are doing roughly the same as thumbing into a particular location in a book. Of course, FrameMaker enables you to scroll both vertically and horizontally if the document page is too large to fit on your workstation screen.

6   Displaying a Specific Page

The ability to go to a specific page is as important in a FrameMaker document as it is in a printed book. FrameMaker gives you several options to accomplish this, and you should become familiar with all of them and then select the most convenient or easiest to remember.

Assumptions

- You are in a large document and want to go to a specific page.

Exceptions

- None.

Steps

TIP

You can make FrameMaker display pages faster by turning off the graphics display.

1. Click in the Page Status Area (see Figure 1.6) to move to a specific page (or press **Esc v p** or **Control + g**).
   FrameMaker displays the Go to Page dialog box (see Figure 1.7). To move to a specific page, select Page Number and type the number in the text box. If you want to move to the page where the insertion point is located, select Page

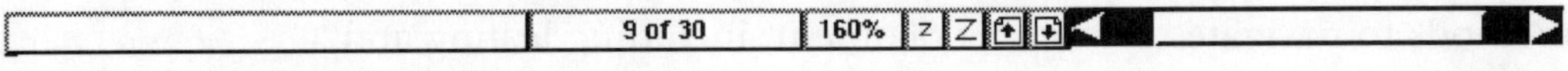

Figure 1.6   The Page Status area.

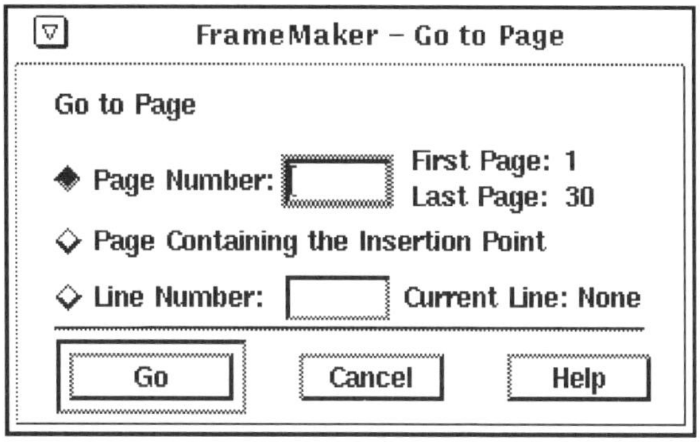

```
┌─────────────────────────────────────────────┐
│ ▽    FrameMaker – Go to Page                  │
│ ┌───────────────────────────────────────────┐│
│ │ Go to Page                                 ││
│ │                                            ││
│ │ ◆ Page Number: ▢       First Page: 1       ││
│ │                        Last Page: 30       ││
│ │ ◇ Page Containing the Insertion Point      ││
│ │                                            ││
│ │ ◇ Line Number: ▢       Current Line: None  ││
│ │ ┌─────────┐  ┌─────────┐  ┌─────────┐      ││
│ │ │   Go    │  │ Cancel  │  │  Help   │      ││
│ │ └─────────┘  └─────────┘  └─────────┘      ││
│ └───────────────────────────────────────────┘│
└─────────────────────────────────────────────┘
```

Figure 1.7   The Go to Page dialog box.

Containing the Insertion Point. Finally, if you want to move to particular line number in the document, select Line Number and enter the number in the text box.

2.   Click **Go** to move to the selected page.

_____ **What To Do If**

• If you prefer to use the document window menus, you can display the Go to Page dialog box by selecting Go to Page in the View menu.

• If you want to turn off the graphics display to enable FrameMaker to display pages faster, select Options in the View menu, turn off Graphics, and click Set.

_____ **See Also**

• Setting the Scroll Options, below.

Setting the Scroll Options   7

Scrolling using the mouse or keyboard is a handy way to navigate through a document. FrameMaker gives you even more control by enabling you to specify how the pages are displayed when you scroll. For example, you may be used to setting out your pages horizontally on your desk when you are preparing or editing a publication. In this case, you can have FrameMaker match the way you work by setting up the pages so you can scroll through them horizontally.

Assumptions

- You want to view the document in a specialized way.

Exceptions

- None.

TIP

You can make the document window fit the page you are working on by selecting Fit Window to Page in the Zoom pop-up menu.

Steps

1. Select Options in the View menu.
   FrameMaker displays the View Options dialog box, in which you can specify the page scrolling mode (see Figure 1.8).
2. Select one of the options in the Page Scrolling pop-up menu.

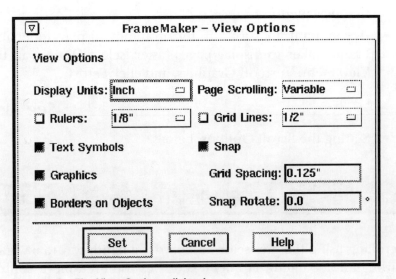

Figure 1.8   The View Options dialog box.

The four options are Vertical, Horizontal, Facing Pages, and Variable. Vertical is the mode that you will probably be most familiar with, since nearly all word processors use this scrolling model. When you select Horizontal, the pages are ordered from left to right. To scroll from one page to the next, you use the horizontal scroll bars at the bottom of the document window instead of the vertical scroll bars.

Facing Pages pairs up the pages in the document and displays them as pairs on the screen. To make the best use of this option, you will probably need a large screen, or else you will be scrolling around a lot or displaying the pages zoomed-down.

The Variable setting displays as many pages as will fit on the screen from left to right. In some workstation screens, this means only a single page, which makes it appear much like the Vertical setting. However, on larger screens, you can have several pages displayed at once.

3. Click **Set.**

_____ **What To Do If**

• None.

_____ **See Also**

• None.

Manipulating Objects

The advantage of using a program such as FrameMaker to produce your documents is the flexibility that it provides when it comes to modifying and editing the content. No matter how carefully you produce something, it's rarely just the way you want it on the first try. Fortunately, FrameMaker supplies some powerful tools to help you massage your document until you are satisfied.

In this section, you'll learn how to use a few basic FrameMaker tools for selecting and moving text and objects within the document. While these operations are simple to master, they constitute the core skills that you need to efficiently manipulate the content in your document.

8   Selecting Text

Before you can manipulate anything in FrameMaker, you must first select it. This informs FrameMaker of the object on which you plan to perform an operation. For example, if you want to change the weight of a group of characters from regular to bold, you first need to select the text before you can apply the change on the characters.

Assumptions

- FrameMaker displays text that you select in reverse video. This lets you know if you've selected the desired region.

Exceptions

- None.

Steps

1. Drag through the text to select a continuous range.
    You can also select a range of text by clicking at the start of the text, positioning the insertion point at the end of your desired selection, and Shift-clicking.

2. See Table 1.1 to find out how to select the piece of text you want. Be careful, because this could select all the text in your document, and the next operation that you perform will apply to this selection.

TIP

If you prefer to use the keyboard, there is still another way to select a range. Position the insertion point at the start of the text and press Shift+Right Arrow on the keyboard. This selects one character at a time.

Table 1.1 Keyboard Shortcuts

Command	Shortcut
To select the next character	Shift+right arrow
To select the previous character	Shift+left arrow
To select the current word, then next	Esc h w
To select the current word, then previous	Esc H W
To select the current sentence, then next	Esc h s
To select the current sentence, then previous	Esc H S
To select the current paragraph, then next	Esc h p
To select the paragraph, then previous	Esc H P

What To Do If

- If you want to unselect or change a selection, simply click anywhere in the document.

- If you want to delete the selected text, press the Delete key. This will permanently remove the text from the document. However, you can undo the delete operation by selecting Undo from the Edit menu.

TIP

After double-clicking to select a word, you can extend the selection a word at a time by Shift-clicking.

See Also

- Cutting, Copying, and Pasting Text, p. 22.

Selecting and Moving Objects   9

FrameMaker can display many different types of objects, including drawings, graphics, and scanned images imported from other applications. When you are preparing the layout of your document, you will probably have to move these objects around to create the best effect. The tools that FrameMaker provides are designed to help you manipulate objects as easily as manipulating text.

FrameMaker includes two tools on the Tools palette that you can use to select objects in a document: the Smart Selection tool and the Object Selection tool. By default, FrameMaker offers you the Smart Selection tool because it is the most flexible. When you use this tool, the pointer changes its shape depending on the type of object you are moving the cursor over.

Assumptions

- None.

Exceptions

- None.

Steps

TIP

You can select several objects by clicking in the first one and Shift-clicking the others.

1. Click on the selection tool that you want to use in the Tools palette (or press **Esc g T**). See Figure 1.9.
   Normally, FrameMaker highlights the Smart Selection tool which is the one you are likely to use the most.

2. Click on the object to select it.
   If the object only has a frame, like a rectangle or circle, click on its border to select it.

3. To select more than one object, start outside any object and drag the mouse through the other objects.

4. Select a frame and choose Select All in Frame in the Edit menu to select all the objects in a frame.

5. Click outside any object or text, and choose Select All on Page in the Edit menu to select all the objects on a page.

6. Drag the mouse starting from a selected object to move the object.

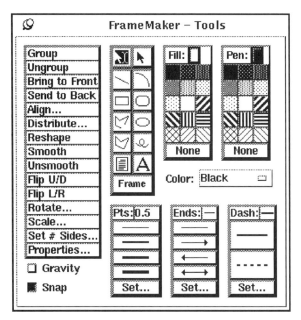

Figure 1.9 FrameMaker's object selection tools.

If several objects are selected, dragging any of the objects will move them all.

What To Do If

- If you want to manipulate text columns as objects instead of as text, you should use the Object Selection tool. This will enable you to move or resize a text column as a whole.

- If you want to deselect all the objects, click outside of the objects.

- If you move an object by mistake, release the mouse button and select Undo in the Edit menu immediately.

See Also

- Cutting, Copying, and Pasting Objects, p. 23.

10   Cutting, Copying, and Pasting Text

Moving text within a document is one of the most basic editing operations, and it's also the task that you're more likely to perform than any other. When you want to move a block of text from one place to another, you select the text and use the Cut or Copy command. FrameMaker places this text in an electronic clipboard, from which you can insert it in your document using the Paste command.

Assumptions

- FrameMaker uses only one clipboard for all windows and documents that are open at any time. Also, the clipboard can only hold one selection at a time. When you cut or copy something onto the clipboard, the new content replaces anything that was already on the clipboard.

Exceptions

- None.

Steps

> **TIP**
> You can quick-copy text into a new location that is visible by selecting the text and then clicking the middle mouse button where you want the text to appear.

1. Select the text you want to move or copy.
2. Select Cut in the Edit menu to move the text (or press **Esc e x**).
   Cutting removes the text from the document and places it on the clipboard. You should not cut the text if you want it to appear in the original location as well as the new location.
3. Select Copy in the Edit menu to copy the text (or press **Esc e c**).
   Copying leaves the selected text intact in its original location while also placing it on the clipboard.

4. Position the insertion point where you want to paste the text.

5. Select Paste in the Edit menu (or press **Esc e p**).

The text will retain its paragraph format if the text you are pasting contains paragraph symbols. If it doesn't, the text will assume the format of the paragraph into which it's pasted.

_____ **What To Do If**

- If you want to paste the same text in several locations, you don't need to cut or copy each time. This is because the clipboard retains its content after you paste, enabling you to paste the same text over and over until you copy something else onto the clipboard.

- If you want to replace some text with new typing, simply select the text and type the new text. The selection will be deleted and the new text will be put in its place.

- If you want to undo a cut or paste, press **Esc e u**.

_____ **See Also**

- Selecting Text, p. 18.
- Cutting, Copying, and Pasting Objects, below.

Cutting, Copying, and Pasting Objects | 11

Cutting and pasting objects is very similar to performing these operations on text. FrameMaker uses a clipboard to keep a temporary copy of the object while you transfer it to the new location in the document. This clipboard also enables you to move objects between FrameMaker documents displayed in separate windows.

Assumptions

- None.

Exceptions

- None.

Steps

1. Select the object you want to move or copy.

2. Select Cut in the Edit menu to move the object (or press **Esc e x**).
   Cutting removes the object from the document and places it on the clipboard. You should not cut an object if you want to duplicate it in both the new and original location.

3. Select Copy in the Edit menu to copy the object (or press **Esc e c**).
   Copying leaves the object in place while putting a copy of it on the clipboard.

4. Position the insertion point where you want to paste the object.
   If you want to paste the object into an existing frame, select the frame by clicking on the frame border. You can also click in text to position the object there. If you want to place the object on the current page in the document, click in the page margin.

5. Select Paste in the Edit menu (or press **Esc e p**).

What To Do If

- If you want to paste the same object in several locations, you don't need to cut or copy each time. This is because the clipboard retains its content after you paste, enabling you to paste the same object over and over until you copy something else onto the clipboard.

_____ **See Also**

- Selecting and Moving Objects, p. 19.
- Cutting, Copying, and Pasting Text, p. 22.

Saving a Document

One of the most important operations in FrameMaker is saving the document to the computer disk. The golden rule is simply stated: "Save early and save frequently." Until you save a document to disk, your newly entered work hangs on the stability of your workstation and its power supply. If there is a glitch in either, you have lost your new work forever! FrameMaker can help you with this by giving you the option to instruct it to save your work periodically without your intervention.

You can also set FrameMaker to create a backup file each time your document is saved. This is helpful when you are unhappy with your new changes and want to revert to a previous copy. Since this happens more often than anyone cares to admit, FrameMaker even provides a command enabling you to return to the most recent previous version of the document.

To make your information as transportable as possible, Frame-Maker can save your file in the following formats: Normal, View Only, Interchange (MIF), and Text Only.

Normal is the regular FrameMaker format and the one FrameMaker can manipulate the fastest. View Only is also a FrameMaker format, however, readers can open the file only to read, not to edit.

The Maker Interchange Format (MIF), or Interchange for short, is an ASCII format that contains statements that completely describe all the text and graphics in a FrameMaker document.

Finally, FrameMaker can save a document in ASCII Text Only format. This format is nearly universal, and when all else fails, you can import ASCII text into almost any application.

Saving a FrameMaker File

FrameMaker provides two commands for saving information: Save and Save As. You can use the Save As command when you want to specify or change the documents file name or location in the directory system. You can also use the Save As command when you want to change the format that FrameMaker uses to save the file. For example, you would use the Save As command if you wanted to change the file name of the document or to give it a name just after creating it. The Save As command enables you to save the document with a new file name, in any directory for which you have the proper permissions.

In contrast, use the Save command after you've already saved and named the document using the Save As command. Since the Save command doesn't require any additional information, it doesn't display a dialog box.

Assumptions

- The document you want to save is open.

Exceptions

- None.

Steps

TIP
FrameMaker reminds you that you need to save new changes to the document by displaying an asterisk next to the page number in the Page Status Area.

1. Select Save in the File menu to save the open document. If this is a new document and has never been saved before, FrameMaker will display the Save dialog box requesting you to enter the name of the file and the directory in which to store it. You can also specify the format FrameMaker should use when storing the file (see Figure 1.10).

   If the document has already been saved and named before, the Save command stores the document using its current file name and directory.

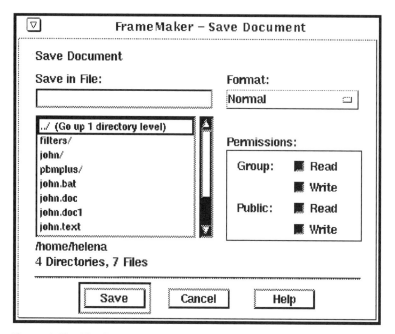

Figure 1.10   The Save Document dialog box.

2.   Select a directory and enter a file name in the text box.

3.   Select a format for the document.
     In most cases, you will want to save the document in
     the Normal format, which is the standard FrameMaker
     format. However, you can create a read-only version of
     your document by selecting the View Only format. Selecting
     the Text Only format creates a file containing ASCII text
     without any formatting or graphics. You can also save the
     document using the Maker Interchange Format (MIF).

4.   Select the permissions for the file.
     You can select the group and public permissions for the file
     by clicking on the read and write check boxes. The group
     permissions specifies whether members of a group can
     read or write the document, while the public permissions
     determines whether everyone can read or write the file.

5. Click **Save.**
   FrameMaker saves the document in the file you specified.

6. To save all open documents, hold down the Shift key and select Save All Open Files in the File menu.

7. Select Save As in the File menu if you want change the file's name, location, or format.
   You can change the file name of the document, along with the directory in which it's stored. You can also select the new format FrameMaker should use to save the file.

What To Do If

- If you accidentally save a document in View Only format, you can unlock it by pressing **Esc F l k** when the mouse pointer is inside the FrameMaker document window. After unlocking the document, you can use the Save As command to save it in Normal format.

- If you made some unwanted changes to the document, but haven't saved it yet, you can easily revert to the last saved version of the document by selecting Revert to Saved in the File menu. Click **OK** to complete the operation when FrameMaker displays a dialog box asking you to confirm. Note: This command will not revert your document to an autosaved version of the document.

See Also

- Saving a MIF File, below.
- Saving a Text Only File, p. 30.
- Saving Automatically, p. 33.

13 | **Saving a MIF File**

FrameMaker has two native formats for saving documents to disk as files: Normal and Maker Interchange Format (MIF). Generally, when you save a document, FrameMaker uses the Normal format, which enables it to store the document in the most compact form and speeds up loading and saving. However, the Normal format uses special codes that are not part of the ASCII text characters to specify formatting and layout information.

FrameMaker's Maker Interchange Format also encodes all the formatting and layout information of a document, but whereas files stored in the Normal format contain non-ASCII text characters, MIF files are pure ASCII text. This can be very advantageous, especially if you need to work with other applications that can accept only ASCII text. What's more, all the formatting and layout information is preserved intact when you save using this format, making MIF a very useful file format.

Assumptions

- You need to save your open document as ASCII text but with current formats.

Exceptions

- None.

Steps

1. Select Save As in the File menu.
   FrameMaker displays the Save Document dialog box.

2. Select a directory and enter a file name in the text box.
   You should change the name of the file to reflect that it is being stored in the MIF format. This preserves your existing file stored in the regular format for day-to-day use. You can also change the location in the directory structure where the new file should be stored.

3. Select Interchange in the Format pop-up menu to store the file in the MIF format (or press **Esc f a**).

4. Click **Save.**
   FrameMaker stores the file as you named it in the dialog box, using the MIF format.

TIP

To help distinguish a MIF file, you should save the document using the regular file name with the .MIF extension.

What To Do If

- None.

See Also

- Saving a FrameMaker File, p. 26.
- Saving a Text Only File, below.

14 ▽ Saving a Text Only File

FrameMaker prefers to save files using its own format, because this enables the program to store and manipulate the document more efficiently. However, this format, which is called Normal, is understood only by FrameMaker. If you need to move the document between different applications, you will have to save it using a more widely understood format.

Perhaps the most universal format for encoding computer files is ASCII text. FrameMaker enables you to save your documents in this format, making it easy to move information around a wide range of application programs. For example, you can edit ASCII text files using the standard vi text editor that is available with most UNIX systems.

In contrast, a MIF file stores all the text, graphics, formatting, and layout information as ASCII text. FrameMaker does this by including extra formatting information interspersed in the file. This has the advantage of maintaining the format of your document, and it is very useful when you need to send an ASCII file to another FrameMaker user.

An ASCII text file, on the other hand, strips all the formatting information away and leaves the pure text. This too has its uses, especially when you are transferring the content to an application that doesn't understand FrameMaker formats and would simply get confused by them.

Assumptions

- When you save a document as Text Only, you can instruct FrameMaker to put a carriage return at the end of each line or only at the end of each paragraph.

- You can also instruct FrameMaker to convert tables to text by reading across the rows or down the columns.

Exceptions

- Saving as Text Only does not save format selections.

Steps

1. Select Save As in the File menu.
   FrameMaker displays the Save Document dialog box.

2. Select a directory and enter a file name in the text box.
   You should use a file name that reflects that this is an ASCII text file. This preserves your existing file stored in the regular format for day-to-day use. You can also change the location in the directory structure where the new file will be stored.

3. Select Text Only in the Format pop-up menu to store the file as ASCII text (or press **Esc f a**).

4. Click **Save.**
   FrameMaker displays the Save As Text dialog box requesting information on how to break up the lines and how to convert the tables into text in the ASCII file. See Figure 1.11.

   You can elect to put a carriage return at the end of each line in the FrameMaker document or only at the end of each paragraph. Your choice will depend on how you intend to use the new ASCII file. You can also specify how FrameMaker should convert the tables in the document into text—by rows or by columns.

> **TIP**
>
> To help distinguish an ASCII text file, you should save the document using the regular file name with the .txt extension.

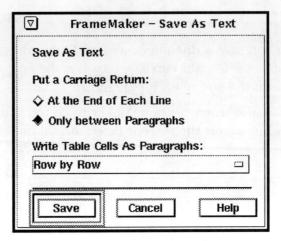

Figure 1.11   The Save As Text dialog box.

What To Do If _____

- Saving a document as an ASCII text file should not be confused with saving the document in the Maker Interchange Format (MIF), which also uses ASCII text. The difference may appear subtle, but is very important. An ASCII text file contains all the content of your document without any of the formatting, graphics, or layout information. Only the text is saved to the file.

- If you plan to use the new ASCII text file with applications that have difficulty handling long lines, you should instruct FrameMaker to put a carriage return at the end of each line, using the Save As Text dialog box.

See Also _____

- Saving a FrameMaker File, p. 26.
- Saving a MIF File, p. 28.

Saving Automatically | 15

You should take every reasonable precaution to prevent errors from costing you time, effort, and money. In the case of FrameMaker, this means saving your file with a certain regularity. FrameMaker enables you to set two Preference options that are related to saving documents on your workstation. The first option enables you to force FrameMaker to save your document automatically after a certain amount of time has passed. You can specify this time interval as an option. This will protect you in case of a system failure or if you forget to manually save your document.

The second option enables you to specify whether a backup copy should be made each time you manually save your document using either the Save or Save As commands.

Assumptions

- None.

Exceptions

- FrameMaker won't bother to save your document automatically unless you've made a change to it.

Steps

1. Select Preferences in the File menu (or press **Esc f P).**
   FrameMaker displays the Preferences dialog box (see Figure 1.12). You can set both features using this dialog box.

2. Click **Automatic Backup on Save** to force a backup copy to be stored.
   FrameMaker creates the backup copy before it saves the new version of your document. FrameMaker does this to

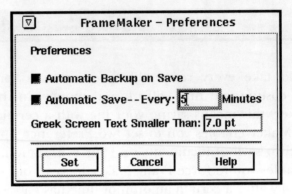

Figure 1.12   The Preferences dialog box.

enable you to restore your document to a previous version
if you need to.

3. Click **Automatic Save** and specify an interval to force
   FrameMaker to regularly save your work. FrameMaker
   will save your document automatically after the number
   of minutes you specified in the interval.

4. Click **Set** to save your preferences.

What To Do If

- If your workstation crashes before you can save the document, you may still be able to recover it. When you restore
  the system, open the document as usual. FrameMaker will
  display a message if it is able to recover your file. If the
  file is recovered, check to make sure your recent changes
  are in place and save the file using the original file name.
  You should then check the current directory and remove
  any files that have your document's filename along with the
  .recover or .auto extension.

  For example, if your document was called chapter4.doc,
  you can use the following UNIX commands in an xterm
  window to remove the recover and auto files:

```
rm chapter4.recover
rm chapter4.auto
```

Remember to do this only after you've already recovered and saved the document using its original name!

_____ **See Also**

- Saving a FrameMaker File, p. 26.

Printing a Document

Though we've all dreamed of the paperless office, most people still like to see their final work output on a printer. Even during the document-editing process, many people still feel more comfortable annotating and highlighting on paper. FrameMaker provides you with all the options you need to print any type of document.

For example, using FrameMaker you can print an entire document or only a select range of pages containing some particular information. You can print a document as single-sided or double-sided, and you can print a single copy or multiple copies at once.

FrameMaker also enables you to control when and where your output will be printed. If your workstation is attached to several printers on a network, you can monitor how many people are queued on each one and send your print job to the least congested. Likewise, if some printers are more powerful than others, you can direct your document to print where you believe it will be completed faster.

Printing a FrameMaker Document | 16

One option to keep in mind is printing a double-sided document. People expect certain publications to be double-sided, including books, manuals, product proposals, and fancy newsletters. The good news is that printing a double-sided document is easy, since many of the steps are the same as for printing any other type of document.

Assumptions

- Either your workstation must be directly attached to a printer, or the workstation and the printer must be connected by means of a network.

Exceptions

- If you want to print the document to a file instead of a printer, click Print Only to File in the Print dialog box and enter the name of the file.

Steps

TIP

Printing can be time-consuming and wasteful, so perform operations such as spell-checking before you send something to the printer.

1. Select Print in the File menu (or press **Esc f p**).
    FrameMaker displays the Print dialog box, which looks quite overwhelming at first. Fortunately, you will only need to set a few options to print your document (see Figure 1.13).

2. Click an option in the Print Page Range area.
    Selecting Click All prints the entire document, while clicking Start Page and entering a value for this and the End Page will only print the pages falling in this range. To help you print from the current page, the Start Page displays the current page by default.

3. Check the Printer Name to see whether the document is going where you intend.
    Your system administrator at your organization will have a list of all the valid printer names to which you can send a document.

4. Check the Printer Page Size to make sure it matches the paper in the printer.

5. Click **Print.**

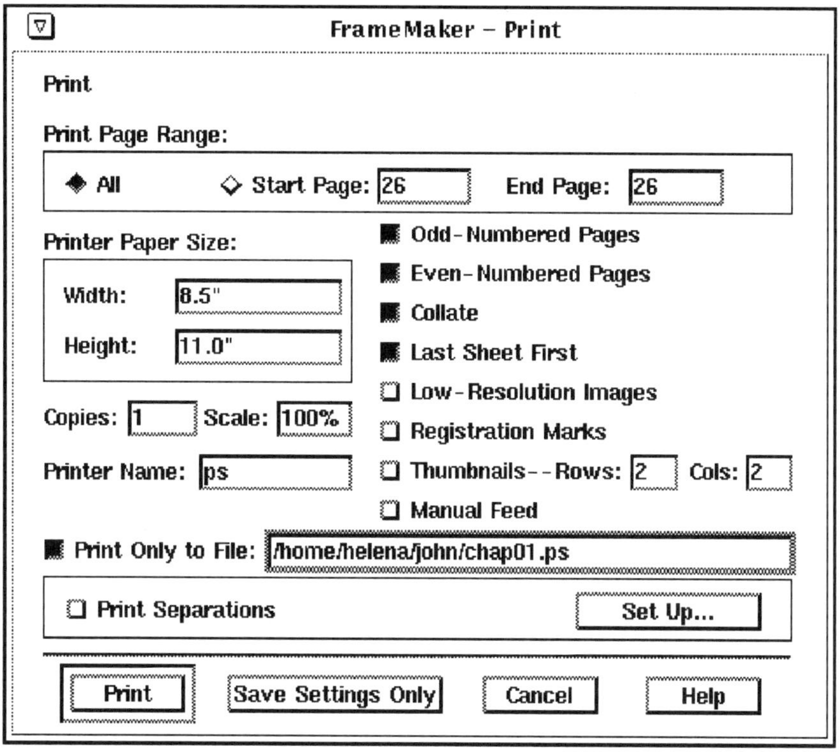

Figure 1.13   The Print dialog box.

FrameMaker submits the document to be printed on the printer. FrameMaker will then return you to the document window so that you can continue any additional work with the document.

What To Do If

• None.

See Also

• Managing the Printer Queue, p. 38.

Managing the Printer Queue

FrameMaker uses many of the standard services of the UNIX operating system to print a document. Both FrameMaker and UNIX use a program called lpr to print a file. Since several people may be attempting to send output to the same printer, lpr doesn't send the file directly to the printer, but instead stores it in a printer queue until the printer is available. You can take a look at which files are in the printer queue and, if necessary, remove a print job from the queue, using UNIX commands.

You may want to do this if, for example, you notice an important error in your document just after issuing the Print command with FrameMaker. In this section, you'll read about the commands for displaying and managing the UNIX printer queues.

Assumptions

- You need to enter all the UNIX printer queue commands from an xterm window on your workstation.

Exceptions

- You can delete only your own print jobs from the printer queue.

Steps

1. Enter **lpq** at the command line in an xterm window to list the jobs in the printer queue for the default printer.

2. Enter **lpq -Pprinter_name** to display the printer queue for the printer called printer_name.
   Substitute the name of the printer for "printer_name" in the foregoing command. You can get a list of the names of printers on your network from your system administrator. Also, be sure to use a capital P in the command and

don't insert any extra spaces around the command parameters.

For example, if you want to examine the print jobs on printer laser1, enter the following command in an xterm window:

lpq -Plaser1

3. Enter **lprm job_number** to remove a print job from the default printer queue.

    Replace "job_number" with the actual print job number. You can get a list of the print job numbers using the lpr command as described earlier. After entering this command, the print job will be removed from the queue and the document will not be printed.

4. Enter **lprm -** to remove all your print jobs from the default printer queue.

5. Enter **lprm -Pprinter_name -** to remove all your print jobs from the printer called printer_name.

    Replace "printer_name" with the name of the printer. As before, you can safely use this command, because UNIX will only permit you to remove your own print jobs.

What To Do If

*   None.

See Also

*   Printing a FrameMaker Document, p. 35.

Chapter

2

Using Special Text Features

Searching and Replacing

Using the Spell Checker and Thesaurus

EDITING
TEXT

Using Special Text Features

As you edit and revise your documents, you will find a variety of places where you want to add content or change details of the characters and punctuation you use throughout. You can save some time by getting to know the keystrokes for the most commonly used characters in your document, by specifying global settings to handle spacing and quotes, and by leveraging existing material.

18 ▽ Using Special Characters

FrameMaker allows you to use special characters and fixed-width spaces not available on the keyboard by typing key combinations. You can also use these characters in a dialog box by using a backslash equivalent. The key combinations make it easy to type in special characters without having to use the standard ASCII mappings. The dialog box backslash equivalents enable you to use special characters and spaces for searching and replacing, use them in paragraph numbering specifications, or on marker text.

Assumptions

- Caps Lock is turned off.

Exceptions

- You cannot use the backslash equivalents within the main document—only in dialog boxes.
- You cannot use the standard key combinations in dialog boxes—only the backslash equivalents.

Steps

1. Consult Table 2.1 to find the special character you need.

Table 2.1   Commonly Used Special Characters

Character	Key Combination	In Dialog Box, Type
Em dash (—)	Control + q Q	\m
En dash (–)	Control + q P	\ =
Bullet (•)	Meta + period	\b
Em space ( )	Esc space m	\sm
En space ( )	Esc space n	\sn
Numeric space[1]	Esc space one	\s#
Thin space ( )	Esc space t	\st
Nonbreaking space ( )	Control + space	\space
Nonbreaking hyphen (-)	Meta + hyphen	\¬
Discretionary hyphen	Control + hyphen	\ -

[1] This space is based on the width of the current font's digits.

What To Do If

- If you insert the wrong special character, simply delete it and try again.

- If you want a fixed-width space, use an em or en space. An em space is the width of the letter "m" in the font you are using. An en space is half of an em space.

- If you want to align numbers in a column without using tabs, use a numeric space. The numeric space is based on the width of the current font's digits.

- If you want to use a tiny space between characters, such as between a number and its measurement unit, use a thin space. A thin space is one-sixteenth the width of an em space.

See Also

- None.

19   Using Smart Quotes and Smart Spaces

One of the most difficult aspects of copy editing is performing a search on spaces between words, because spacing is proportional, which means searching does not always catch every instance of extra spacing.

However, you can minimize your spacing problems by using Smart Spaces. For example, if you know you only want a single space between words, turning Smart Spaces on prevents you from entering more spaces. If your style requires two spaces after a period, you can use Smart Spaces while you write to avoid errors. Then you can turn them off and search and replace the single spaces after periods with double spaces.

Using the right type of quotation marks is also a frequent task in editing. It is difficult and time-consuming to find all the quotation marks that are used incorrectly, even when searching electronically. You can decide which style of quotation marks is most used in your document and then set Smart Quotes accordingly.

Assumptions

- You want to set the spacing between words before you begin your document.
- You want to set what type of quotation marks you are going to use before you begin your document.

Exceptions

- Turning Smart Spaces on will not change already-existing multiple spacing into single spaces.
- Turning Smart Quotes on will not change already-existing straight quotes into curly quotes.

Table 2.2 Using Smart and Straight Quotes

Type of Quote	Smart Quotes Turned On	Smart Quotes Turned Off
Straight single quote	Control + '	'
Curly single quotes	' and '	Control + ' and Control + '
Straight double quote	Control + "	"
Curly double quotes	" and "	Meta + ' and Meta + '

Steps

1. Select **Document** from the Format menu.
2. Turn Smart Spaces, Smart Quotes, or both on.
3. Click **Set**.

What To Do If

- If you want to use a space between words that is larger than the spacing provided by a single proportional space, use an em space or a tab setting.
- If you want to override the Smart Quotes setting, use the key combinations shown in Table 2.2.

See Also

- None.

Importing Text 20

You can import non-FrameMaker documents and spreadsheets directly into your document. Supported formats include MML, MIF, ASCII text, WordPerfect, Microsoft Word, troff, and Interleaf. FrameMaker also reads some versions of Excel and Lotus.

Check the conversion list that opens when you try to import a file to see if your file type is supported.

Assumptions

- The file you want to import is in a supported format.
- The cursor is positioned where you want to insert the imported file.

Exceptions

- You cannot import text files using Import by Reference.

Steps

1. Select **Import:File** from the File menu (or press **Esc f i f**). Figure 2.1 shows the Import File dialog box.
2. Select the file you want to import.
3. Turn on Copy into Document.
4. Click **Import**.
   Another dialog box opens. The content of this dialog box depends on the kind of file you are importing.
5. Fill in the appropriate information.
6. Click **Read**.

What To Do If

- If you are importing an ASCII text file, you have the options listed in Table 2.3 to read the file.
- If you are importing text in another format, the dialog box allows you to pick the format from which you are importing the text. If the format is not listed in the dialog box, then it is not available. For more information on supported formats, consult with your system administrator.

See Also

- Opening an Existing Document, p. 11.

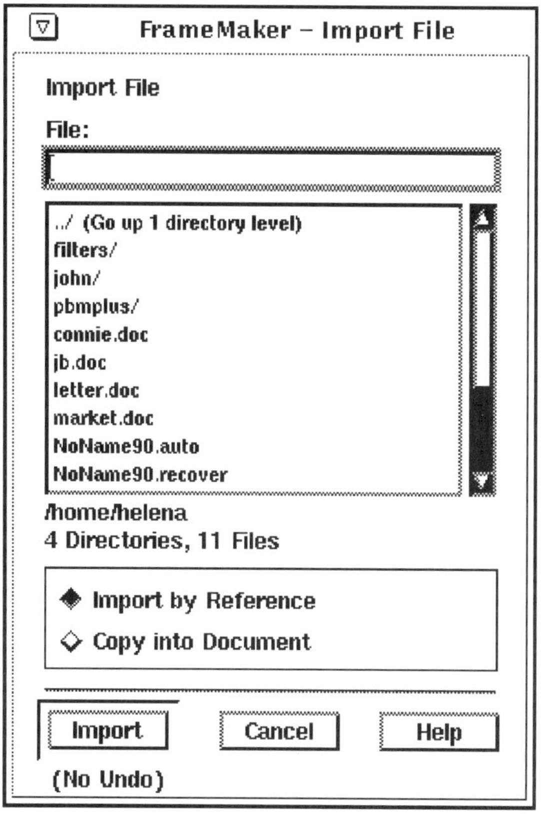

```
┌─────────────────────────────────────────────┐
│ ▽    FrameMaker – Import File                │
├─────────────────────────────────────────────┤
│  Import File                                 │
│  File:                                       │
│  ┌─────────────────────────────────────────┐ │
│  │                                         │ │
│  └─────────────────────────────────────────┘ │
│  ┌───────────────────────────────────────┬─┐ │
│  │ ../ (Go up 1 directory level)         │▲│ │
│  │ filters/                              │ │ │
│  │ john/                                 │ │ │
│  │ pbmplus/                              │ │ │
│  │ connie.doc                            │ │ │
│  │ jb.doc                                │ │ │
│  │ letter.doc                            │ │ │
│  │ market.doc                            │ │ │
│  │ NoName90.auto                         │ │ │
│  │ NoName90.recover                      │▼│ │
│  └───────────────────────────────────────┴─┘ │
│  /home/helena                                │
│  4 Directories, 11 Files                     │
│  ┌─────────────────────────────────────────┐ │
│  │ ◆ Import by Reference                   │ │
│  │ ◇ Copy into Document                    │ │
│  └─────────────────────────────────────────┘ │
│  ┌──────────┐  ┌──────────┐  ┌──────────┐    │
│  │  Import  │  │  Cancel  │  │   Help   │    │
│  └──────────┘  └──────────┘  └──────────┘    │
│  (No Undo)                                   │
└─────────────────────────────────────────────┘
```

Figure 2.1   The Import File dialog box.

Table 2.3   Importing ASCII Text

Option	Action
Merge Lines into Paragraphs	Merges lines into paragraphs. Breaks text into paragraphs at blank lines.
Treat Each Line As a Paragraph	Breaks text into paragraphs at the end of each line.
Convert to Table	Converts the text into a table according to the parameters you specify in the Convert to Table dialog box. For more information, see "Converting Text to Tables."

Searching and Replacing

An important aspect of electronic editing is the ability to search and replace text and objects as you develop or apply a style or standard wording to your documents. FrameMaker has powerful search and replace tools that enable you to go beyond normal text search and replace. You can search for just about any type of text, tag, object, or marker you create.

Searching and replacing is a task that is performed similarly for the different types of objects for which FrameMaker allows you to search. The differences in handling some of these objects are outlined in this section. In most cases, it is a matter of simple search and replace, while some items require extra work.

21   Searching and Replacing Any Item

You have several options for searching and replacing items. For example, you may search for something without replacing it; you might search and replace items automatically; or you can choose whether or not to replace an item as FrameMaker finds each occurrence.

Assumptions

- The insertion point is placed where you want to begin the search.

Exceptions

- These steps apply to most, but not all, cases of search and replace operations. For information on searching and replacing items that require additional steps, see the appropriate sections in this chapter.

_____ **Steps**

1. Select **Find/Change** from the Edit menu (or press **Esc e f**). Figure 2.2 shows the Find/Change dialog box.

2. Select the kind of item to find from the Find pop-up menu.

3. Type the item in the Find text box.

4. Select the kind of item to replace it with from the Change pop-up menu.

5. Type the item to replace with in the Change text box.

6. Choose one of the actions in Table 2.4 (also see Table 2.5 for wildcards that you can use in your search).

> **TIP**
>
> If you want to search and replace in the master pages or reference pages, switch to master or reference pages before you start the operation. FrameMaker does not include master and reference pages when you are searching in body pages.

_____ **What To Do If**

- If you want to search for, or replace with, any of the characters used as wildcards, type a backslash before the character. For example, to find an asterisk when Use Wildcards is turned on, type \ * in the Find text box.

- If you want to specify words with spaces between them, type the spaces between those words in the text box.

- If you want to give replacement text the same capitalization as the text you are replacing, turn on Clone Case.

- If you want to find a complete word, turn on Whole Word. If Whole Word is turned off, FrameMaker finds all words

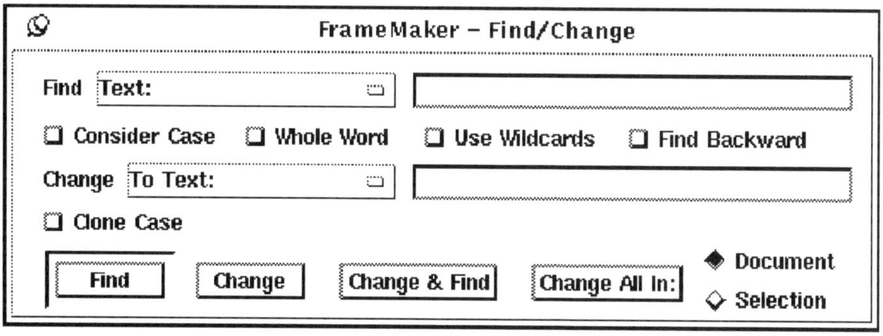

Figure 2.2   The Find/Change dialog box.

Table 2.4 Searching and Replacing Actions

For Action	Click	Results
Search only	Find	Looks for the next instance of the object you specify to find.
Replace only	Change	Replaces the instance it finds with the object you specify to replace it with.
Search and replace	Change and Find	Replaces the last found instance and then looks for the next instance of the object you specified to find.
Replace all found instances of an object	Change All In	Replaces all instances of the specified object in a document or selection.

Table 2.5 Wildcards Used in Searching

Wildcards	Searches
*	Zero or more characters
?	One character
|	Spaces and punctuation characters that end a word
[xy]	Any character inside the bracket (here "x" or "y")
[ˆ xy]	Any character not inside the bracket (here any character except "x" or "y")
[h-x]	Any character in a range (here any character from "h" through "x")
ˆ	The beginning of a line
$	The end of a line

containing the string you specified. For example, if you search for "any" when Whole Word is turned off, FrameMaker finds all words containing "any," such as "any," "anything," "many," and "banyan."

- If you want to specify special characters in the text boxes, use their backslash equivalents to type them in. Table 2.6 lists the most commonly searched-for special characters.

_____ **See Also**

- None.

Table 2.6 Commonly Searched Special Characters	
Character	**In Text Box, Type**
Space	\s
Tab	\t
Forced return	\r
End-of-Paragraph	\p
Start-of-Paragraph	\P
Start-of-word	\<
End-of-Word	\>
Em dash	\m
En dash	\=
Bullet	\b
Em space	\sm
En space	\sn
Numeric space	\s#
Thin space	\st
Non-breaking space	\space
Non-breaking hyphen	\¬
Discretionary hyphen	\-
Suppress hyphenation	_
End-of-flow	\f

22 — Searching for Text with a Specific Format

You can perform a search to find a specific text string that is formatted in a certain way. For example, you can look for the phrase "the quick brown fox jumps over the lazy dog" and specify that the search find it only if it is 14-point Helvetica Narrow. You can then replace the text, the formatting of the text, or both.

Assumptions

- You want to find a specific string of text formatted with a specific look.

Exceptions

- You cannot search for any paragraphs formatted with a specific look.
- You cannot search for a specific character tag using these steps.
- FrameMaker uses only the first 126 characters it finds stored in the clipboard to search.

Steps

1. Select the text you want to find which uses a specific character format.
2. Select **Copy** from the Edit menu.
3. Select **Find/Change** from the Edit menu. Do not type anything in the Find text box.
4. Select **Text & Character Formats on Clipboard** from the Find pop-up menu.
5. Click **Find**.

What To Do If

- None.

_____ **See Also**

- Searching and Replacing a Character Format, below.
- Searching and Replacing Any Item, p. 48.

Searching and Replacing a Character Format 23

You can search for any paragraph containing text with specific formatting. For example, if you search for text that is 14-point Helvetica Narrow, FrameMaker finds the next instance of text formatted that way. This is useful when you didn't use a paragraph or character tag to format text and you need to find it, or when you don't remember the name of the tag you used to make text look a certain way.

_____ **Assumptions**

- You want to find any paragraph formatted with a specific look.

_____ **Exceptions**

- You cannot search for a specific character tag using these steps.
- You cannot search for specific text formatted with a specific look using these steps. For information on searching for specific text and format, see Searching for Text with a Specific Format, p. 52.

_____ **Steps**

1. Select text that uses the character format you want to find.
2. Open the Find/Change dialog box.
3. Select **Character Format** from the Find pop-up menu.

The Find Character Format dialog box will open (see Figure 2.3).

TIP

To set your search to look for only a few format properties, set the Find Character Format dialog box to As Is, then set only the specific properties for which you are searching. To limit your change to replace only a few format properties, set the Change to Character Format dialog box to As Is by pressing Shift+F8, then set only the specific properties you want to change.

4. Check the Find Character Format dialog box to ensure that the settings for the Character Format you are looking for are correct. Change the settings to match what you are looking for at this point.

5. Click **Set**.

6. Select **Character Format** from the Change pop-up menu. The Change To Character Format dialog box will open.

7. Change the settings to the character format you want to apply.

8. Click **Set**.

9. Choose the search action you want to execute.

What To Do If

- None.

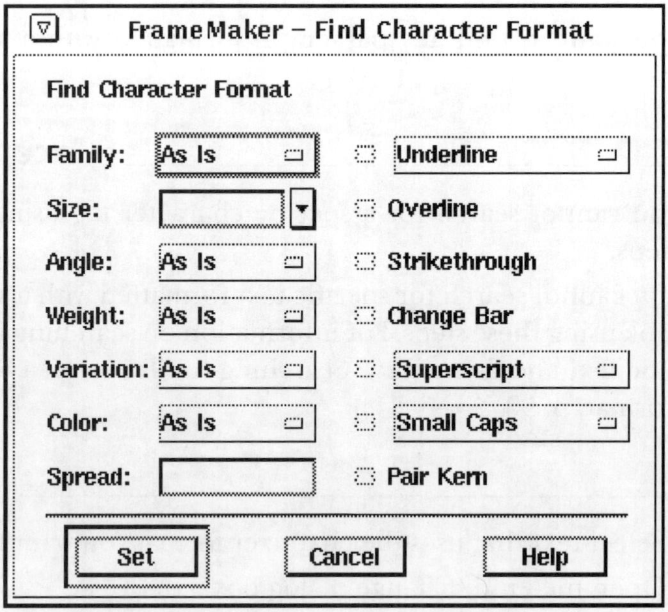

| FrameMaker – Find Character Format |

Find Character Format

Family: As Is   ☐ Underline
Size: ☐ Overline
Angle: As Is   ☐ Strikethrough
Weight: As Is   ☐ Change Bar
Variation: As Is   ☐ Superscript
Color: As Is   ☐ Small Caps
Spread: ☐ Pair Kern

[Set]   [Cancel]   [Help]

Figure 2.3   The Find Character Format dialog box.

See Also

- Searching and Replacing Any Item, p. 48.

Searching for Conditional Text   24

You can search for the next instance of text tagged with a condition tag. This is particularly useful when you have conditional documents that use more than two condition tags. Although you have an option to view just the conditional text for which you are searching, you may find instances where you want to view the whole document to compare or verify that you tagged the document correctly or that there are no pieces missing. Also, you may have a conditional document where you use more than one condition per logical document.

Assumptions

- The conditional text for which you are searching is displayed.

Exceptions

- You cannot search for a specific character string using these steps. FrameMaker finds the next instance of text that contains a specific conditional tag.

Steps

1. Open the Find/Change dialog box.
2. Select **Conditional Text** from the Find pop-up menu.
   The Conditional Text dialog box will open (see Figure 2.4).
3. Place the condition tags of the text you want to find in the In list.
4. Click **Set**.
5. Click **Find** in the Find/Change dialog box.

> **TIP**
> If you want to find text that is not conditional, place the condition tags in the Not In scroll list. If you want to find all text that is conditional, without specifying a condition tag, place all condition tags in the As Is scroll list.

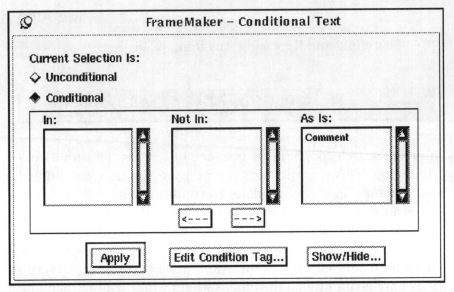

Figure 2.4   The Conditional Text dialog box.

What To Do If _____

- If the conditional text for which you are searching is not visible, choose Conditional Text from the Special menu and set it to show.

See Also _____

- Choosing the View of a Conditional Document, p. 444.

25   Searching for Markers

Searching for markers is a very useful tool when you edit a generated file, such as a table of contents or index. Once you mark up the generated file, you have to make the changes to the marker text to update the file. Instead of looking for each marker manually, you can perform a search on either the kind of marker you need or on the marker text itself. If you want to check the types of markers or how many different types you have in a document, you may search for any marker.

Assumptions

- You want to find a marker or text contained in a marker.

Exceptions

- You cannot edit the marker or its content from the Find/ Change window. Once you find the marker, open the specific marker window and make any modifications to the marker or its text there.

Steps

1. Open the Find/Change dialog box.
2. Select the type of marker search you want to perform from the Find pop-up menu.
3. Type the marker name or text in the Find text box.
4. Click **Find**.

> **TIP**
> You can search for marker text that is not visible in the document.

What To Do If

- If you are searching for a specific type of marker, select **Marker of Type** and enter the type in the Find text box.
- If you are searching for specific marker text, select **Marker Text** and type the text in the Find text box.
- If you are searching for any or all markers in a document, select **Any Marker**.

See Also

- Searching and Replacing Any Item, p. 48.

26 ▽ | Using the Clipboard to Replace

You can use the contents saved in the FrameMaker clipboard to replace text or objects in your document. This is useful when the object you are inserting is not something you can place in the Change text box, or when you are using objects from other documents.

Assumptions

- You want to replace several instances of the same object in a document.

Steps

TIP
If you want to copy a Paragraph or Character format, or condition tag to the Clipboard, use the Copy Special commands on the Edit menu.

1. Select the existing object you want to use to replace.
2. Copy the object to the Clipboard.
3. Open the Find/Change dialog box.
4. Define an item to find.
5. Select **By Pasting** from the Change pop-up menu.
6. Click **Find**.
7. Click **Change**.

What To Do If

- None.

See Also

- Cutting, Copying, and Pasting Text, p. 22.

Using the Spell Checker and Thesaurus

FrameMaker includes a powerful Spell Checker for correcting spelling as well as a Thesaurus for helping you express the same thought in different ways and find opposite words.

Checking for Spelling and Typing Errors | 27

FrameMaker enables you to check for both spelling and typing mistakes while performing a spell check. The Spelling Checker allows you to specify the kinds of words and typing errors to find or to ignore, and to build dictionaries to suit your personal, project, or specific document needs. It provides you with a variety of options with which to perform and control your check and corrections.

Assumptions

- The dictionaries that FrameMaker uses are installed in your system.

Exceptions

- You cannot add or delete words from the system dictionary. Any additions or deletions of words to the dictionaries is performed to either the personal or document dictionaries.

- A paragraph with a tag that has the language set to None is not checked during a spell check.

- If you are checking for spelling in a language other than the default language you are using, check with your system administrator to ensure that the appropriate dictionaries for that language are installed as well.

TIP

You can spell check in a language other than the one you are currently using by opening the Paragraph Designer Window and selecting Use the Advanced properties.

If you want to spell check text lines created with the Graphics tools, use the Language pop-up menu in the Properties.

If you want to limit the types of words to check, click **Options** in the Spelling Checker window. Turn on the appropriate options and click set.

Steps

1. Select **Spelling Checker** from the Edit menu.
    Figure 2.5 shows the Spelling Checker window.

2. Select the text you want to spell check.

3. Click **Start Checking**.

4. When FrameMaker finds a misspelled word, correct or confirm the spelling.
    Correcting the word changes it in your document; confirming the word adds it to one of the dictionaries.

5. Click **Start Checking** to find the next misspelled word.
    When you finish spell checking, close the Spell Checker window by double-clicking on the left top corner of the window.

What To Do If

*   None.

See Also

*   Managing Your Personal Dictionaries, p. 61.
*   Defining Hyphenation, p. 117.

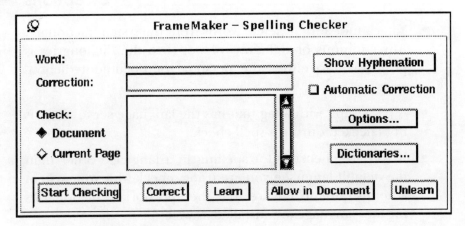

Figure 2.5   The Spelling Checker window.

Managing Your Personal Dictionaries 28

FrameMaker uses four dictionaries to perform a spelling check: the Main dictionary, a Site dictionary, your Personal dictionary, and a Document dictionary. The Main dictionary is the dictionary provided with FrameMaker. It contains the most common words in the language you are using and is based on a standard dictionary. This dictionary is read-only.

The Site dictionary is the dictionary maintained for your specific site. It is generally maintained by a system administrator and usually contains site-specific or company-specific terms, such as your company or product name.

The Personal dictionary is the dictionary to which you add when you "Learn" new words. This dictionary is used across all your documents. You can specify a different dictionary file to use as your personal dictionary, perhaps according to project or product line.

The Document dictionary contains the words you decide to "Allow in Document" without adding them to your Personal dictionary. The words added to the Document dictionary are specific to the document where they were added. This is useful when you have terms, acronyms, or strings that would be misspellings or typographical errors under any other circumstance, and you don't want your Personal dictionary to recognize the words otherwise.

Assumptions

- You already know how to insert and delete words from the dictionary.

- You want to add words to the dictionaries directly rather than as you go.

Exceptions

- You cannot add or delete words from the Main Dictionary. Any additions or deletions of words to the dictionaries take place either in the Personal or Document dictionaries.

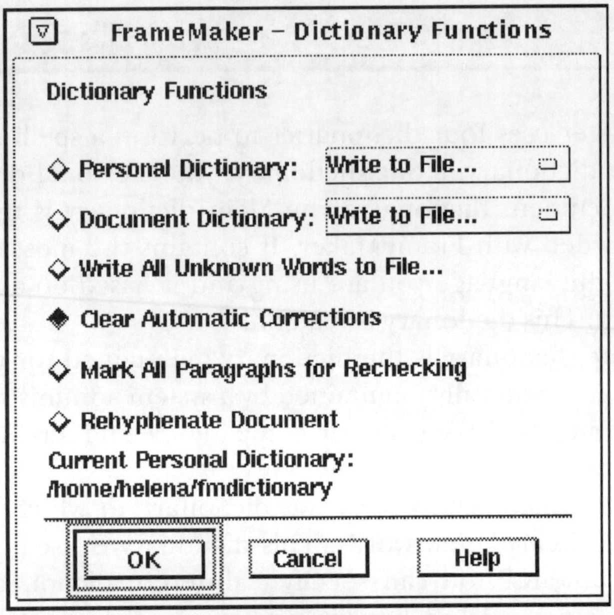

Figure 2.6 The Dictionary Functions window.

> **TIP**
>
> If you use FrameMaker to edit a dictionary file, read it in to treat line endings as paragraphs. Then save it as Text Only with Only Between Paragraphs turned on.
> To create other personal dictionaries, create a file with the words you want in that dictionary and save it as Text Only with Only Between Paragraphs turned on. Before you save the file, make sure that the words hyphenate where you want them to, and make the first line of the file the following:
>
> <MakerDictionary 2.0>

Steps

1. Click **Dictionaries** in the Spelling Checker window.
   Figure 2.6 shows the resulting Dictionary Functions window.
2. Turn on Write All Unknown Words to File and click **OK**.
3. Select the name of the file where you want to put the new words in, or type a new name.
   FrameMaker places all the unknown words in the document in this dictionary file.
4. Edit the file to contain just the words you want FrameMaker to recognize and accept.
   You can use either FrameMaker or a standard editor to modify the file.
5. Go back to the Dictionary Functions dialog box.

6. Select **Merge** from File in either the Personal or Document Dictionary pop-up menu.

7. Type the name of the file you just created and click **OK**.

_____ **What To Do If**

- None.

_____ **See Also**

- Checking for Spelling and Typing Errors, p. 59.

| Using the Thesaurus | **29**

The thesaurus provides you with a quick way of finding synonyms, antonyms, and related words for a word you select or specify. Synonyms are words that have the same meaning; related words have a similar meaning; and antonyms have the opposite meaning.

_____ **Assumptions**

- You are looking for a synonym, antonym, or related word for a specific word.

_____ **Exceptions**

- None.

_____ **Steps**

1. Decide on the word you want to look up.

2. Select **Thesaurus** from the Edit menu.
   Figure 2.7 shows the Thesaurus windows.

3. Click **Look Up**.

Figure 2.7   The Thesaurus window.

4. Click the word you choose to replace the selected word.

5. Click **Replace** (or press **Esc T r**).

What To Do If

- If you want to look up a word displayed in the Thesaurus dialog box, click the word.

- If you want to look up a word that is not in your document or in the Thesaurus dialog box, click **Look Up**, type the word in the Look Up dialog box, and click **Look Up**. If you want to specify a different language to look up a word, choose the language before clicking Look Up in the Look Up dialog box.

Chapter

3

FORMATTING
TEXT

Changing the Look of a Text Range

The majority of the text you format is defined through the Paragraph Catalog according to each paragraph's function. However, when you want to format words or characters individually, you can also apply specific formats without changing the rest of the paragraph.

You can change specific format characteristics as you go or by using predefined formats. The Format menu contains items that enable you to select the font, size, and style of selected text. The Character Catalog contains a list of tags, with predefined format characteristics associated with each tag.

You can also change any other character format characteristic by using the Character Designer. For more information see Chapter 4, "Creating the Formats."

30 ▼ Applying a Predefined Character Tag

Using character tags saves you the time you would spend formatting text as you go along. Each character tag contains formatting information specific to the type of text range you need.

You can apply a predefined character tag by opening the Character Catalog in one of two ways:

- By opening the Character Catalog in your desktop.

- By selecting Character from the Format menu and displaying the list.

Assumptions

- A text range is selected for formatting.

- A character tag with the format you want already exists.

Exceptions

- You cannot format a character created with FrameMaker's autonumbering capabilities using these steps. For information on autonumbering, see Chapter 5, "Using Writing Tools."

Steps

1. Open the Character Catalog by selecting **Catalog** from the Format:Character menu (see Figure 3.1).
2. Select a tag.

What To Do If

- If, after you tag a text range, you decide to add or change one of its characteristics, use the Format menu. When you select a format, it will either add it to the existing ones or override them. For example, if you apply a tag that keeps the size and font family of the current paragraph and adds italics only, you can manually make the text bold and underlined, and it will remain in italics. However, if you choose a new size or font family, the new settings will override the existing size or family and apply the new one.

> **TIP**
> You can return the text range to the format of the rest of the paragraph by selecting **Default Font** from the Character Catalog (or press **Esc o c p**).
> You can also use these steps to format text created using the graphics tools.

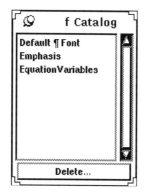

Figure 3.1   The Character Catalog.

- If you apply a tag to text you just typed and then continue typing, the text that follows will be tagged the same way. To avoid this, finish typing before you tag the text range.

See Also

- Creating and Updating Format Tags, p. 104.

31 ▽ Applying a Font and Size

If you decide to change the font or size of a text range and don't have a character tag to match, you can apply them manually by using the Format menu. However, if you decide to use these same characteristics frequently, you should consider creating a character tag.

Assumptions

- A text range is selected for formatting.
- A character tag with the formats you want does not exist.

Exceptions

- You cannot format a character created with FrameMaker's autonumbering capabilities using these steps. For information on autonumbering, see Chapter 5, "Using Writing Tools."

Steps

1. Select **Font** or **Size** from the Format menu.
   Figure 3.2 shows the Font menu.
2. Select the characteristic you want to apply.

What To Do If

If you decide to apply a character tag to a text range you formatted manually, the character tag will override the manual formatting.

TIP

You can return the text range to the format of the rest of the paragraph by selecting the text and selecting **Default Font** from the Character Catalog. You can also use these steps to format text created using the graphics tools.

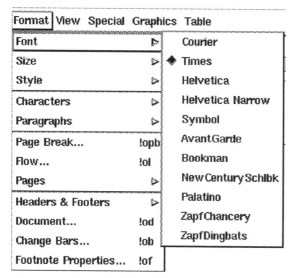

Figure 3.2   The Font menu.

If you want to have both the tag and the manual formats remain, apply the tag first and the manual formats later. For example, if you apply a new font family and size to a text range, and then decide you want to apply an emphasis tag that adds italics, the other formatting information in the tag—that is, the font family and size—will override the tags you applied earlier. Generally, a character tag is set to keep the format of the current paragraph for all characteristics except those that make that tag different, such as italics.

_____ **See Also**

• Applying a Predefined Character Tag, p. 66.

Applying a Font Style   32

If you decide to change the font style of a text range and don't have a character tag to match, you can apply it manually by using the Format menu. However, if you decide to use these same characteristics frequently, you should consider creating a character tag.

Assumptions

- A text range is selected for formatting.
- A character tag with the formats you want does not exist.

Exceptions

- You cannot format a character created with FrameMaker's autonumbering capabilities using these steps. For information on autonumbering, see Chapter 5, "Using Writing Tools."

TIP

You can return the text range to the format of the rest of the paragraph by selecting **Default Font** from the Character Catalog.

Steps

1. Select **Style** from the Format menu.
   The Style menu, shown in Figure 3.3, will appear.
2. Select the characteristic you want to apply to the text range.

Format	View	Special	Graphics	Table		
Font			▷	Body		
Size			▷	3 ... 4 ... 5		
Style			▷	■ Plain	!cp	
Characters			▷	☐ Bold	!cb	
Paragraphs			▷	☐ Italic	!ci	
Page Break...			!opb	☐ Underline	!cu	
Flow...			!ol	☐ Double Underline	!cd	
Pages			▷	☐ Strikethrough	!cs	
Headers & Footers			▷	☐ Overline	!co	
Document...			!od	☐ Change Bar	!ch	
Change Bars...			!ob	☐ Superscript	!c+	
Footnote Properties...			!of	☐ Subscript	!c-	

Figure 3.3   The Style menu.

_____ **What To Do If**

- If you want to apply more than one format characteristic to a text range, follow the previous steps for each characteristic. You can combine as many styles as you choose. For example, you can define the text range to be bold, italic, and underlined.

_____ **See Also**

- Applying a Predefined Character Tag, p. 66.

Changing the Look of a Paragraph

Most paragraph level formatting is done using paragraph tags. However, with FrameMaker you can override or add to the format of the paragraph tag you are using to fit your immediate needs.

You can change the alignment, spacing, tab settings, margins, and indents of specific paragraphs manually. For example, if you are using a paragraph tag that is aligned left and is single-spaced, you can change it to be aligned center and double-spaced by using the ruler, which is shown in Figure 3.4.

Applying a Predefined Paragraph Tag | 33

Using paragraph tags saves you the time you would spend formatting every paragraph as you go along. Each paragraph tag contains

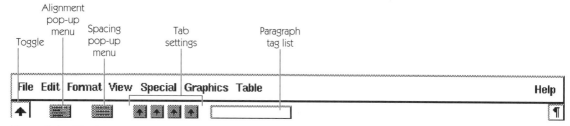

Figure 3.4   The FrameMaker formatting ruler.

formatting information specific to the type of paragraph you need. For example, if you need a numbered list, the Paragraph Catalog can contain tags for the first and subsequent steps in the list. These tags would include indents, tabs, line spacing, paragraph spacing, and automatic numbering as well as the font, size, style, and color of both the text and the auto-numbering properties.

The Paragraph Catalog contains a list of predefined tags with formatting characteristics associated with the tags. See Figure 3.5.

Assumptions

- You want to format the one paragraph the insertion point is in, or a whole range of paragraphs that is selected.

- A paragraph tag with the function and format you want already exists.

Exceptions

- You cannot change the format of text created with the graphics text tool using these steps.

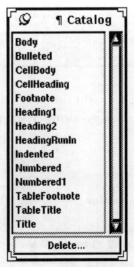

Figure 3.5   The   Paragraph
Catalog.

_____ **Steps**

1. Go to the **Paragraph Catalog.** You can access it in one of
   four ways:

   • By pressing **Esc o p c**.

   • By clicking on the **Paragraph Catalog** button to open it
     in your desktop.

   • By displaying the **Paragraph Format** pop-up menu in
     the ruler.

   • By displaying the **Paragraph Format** list in the Format:
     Paragraph menu.

2. Select a tag.

_____ **What To Do If**

• If you accidentally change a paragraph, repeat the previous
  steps for that paragraph, and select the previous tag.

• If you accidentally change a paragraph but don't remember
  the tag it had, select **Undo** from the Edit menu.

_____ **See Also**

• None.

TIP
If you are doing heavy formatting, the best way to use the Paragraph Catalog is to have the catalog open at a convenient place on your desktop. Usually you want to place it close to your cursor so that you can keep your mouse movement to a minimum.

Choosing the Alignment | 34

FrameMaker allows you to choose text alignment on a paragraph-
by-paragraph basis. Generally, alignment is determined by the
tags you apply to each paragraph. If you are not using tags for
a specific paragraph, or if you need to override the alignment
set by the tags you are using, you can select the new alignment
manually by using the formatting part of the ruler.

Note that alignment determines the position of a paragraph
within the left and right indents, not within the margins.

Assumptions

- You want to format the one paragraph the insertion point is in, or a whole range of paragraphs that is selected.
- The formatting part of the ruler is visible.

Exceptions

- You cannot set the alignment manually if you are not displaying the ruler.
- You cannot make text align with the margins using the alignment settings if the indents are set at different places from the margins.
- You cannot use these steps to align text created with the graphics text tool.

TIP

If you are center aligning a paragraph but you want its width to be less than the rest of the column, readjust the indents for that paragraph.
If you are justifying a paragraph, you can avoid white space running through your text by adjusting the character and word spacing. For more information on these tasks, see Chapter 4, "Creating the Formats."

Steps

1. Click on the alignment pop-up menu on the ruler.
   You have the options shown in Figure 3.6.

2. Select the alignment option you want.

What To Do If

- If you want to find out the current alignment of a paragraph, place the insertion point within the paragraph and look at the alignment pop-up menu on the ruler. It will graphically show you the alignment of the paragraph.

ALIGNMENT
◆ Left   !jl
   Center   !jc
   Right   !jr
   Justify !jf

Figure 3.6   Possible Alignments
for a paragraph.

- If you accidentally change the alignment of a paragraph, repeat the foregoing steps, only select your original setting.

- If you accidentally change the alignment of a paragraph but don't remember the previous alignment, reapply its paragraph tag or select **Undo** from the Edit menu.

See Also

- Applying a Predefined Paragraph Tag, p. 71.

Changing the Line Spacing 35

FrameMaker allows you to change the line spacing within a paragraph. Generally, the line spacing is determined by the tags you apply to each paragraph. If you are not using tags for a specific paragraph, or if you need to override the line spacing set by the tags you are using, you can select the new line spacing manually by using the formatting part of the ruler.

The line spacing is measured from baseline to baseline. The default line spacing is two points greater than its font size. If you change the font size, FrameMaker adjusts the line spacing automatically.

Assumptions

- You want to change the line spacing of the one paragraph the insertion point is in, or of a whole range of paragraphs that is selected.

- The formatting part of the ruler is visible.

Exceptions

- You cannot set the line spacing manually if you are not displaying the ruler.

- You cannot set line spacing by using the Space Between option in the spacing pop-up menu.
- You cannot use these steps to set the line spacing for text created with the graphics text tool.

Steps

1. Click on the **Spacing** pop-up menu on the ruler.
   You have the options shown in Figure 3.7.
2. Select the line spacing option you want.

What To Do If

- When you select Custom from the spacing pop-up menu, the Custom Line Spacing dialog box opens. Type the line spacing you want and click **Set.**
- If you want to set a fixed line spacing, turn on the **Fixed** setting in the Custom Line dialog box and click **Set**. If you specify fixed line spacing, FrameMaker will not create extra space to accommodate larger font sizes in the paragraph.
- If you accidentally change the line spacing of a paragraph but don't remember the previous line spacing, reapply its paragraph tag or select **Undo** from the Edit menu.

See Also

- Applying a Predefined Paragraph Tag, p. 71.

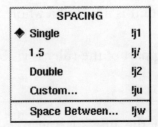

Figure 3.7   The Spacing menu.

Adjusting the Paragraph Spacing   36

FrameMaker allows you to adjust the space between paragraphs. Generally, the paragraph spacing is determined by the tags you apply to each paragraph. If you are not using tags for specific paragraphs, or if you need to override the space above or below set by the tags you are using, you can select the new paragraph spacing manually by using the formatting part of the ruler.

Paragraph spacing is applied based on the Space Below of the first paragraph and Space Above of the following paragraph. FrameMaker selects the larger of the two spaces when it determines the space between two paragraphs.

Assumptions

- You want to adjust the paragraph spacing of the selected range of paragraphs or the one paragraph the insertion point is in.

- The formatting part of the ruler is visible.

Exceptions

- You cannot set paragraph spacing manually if you are not displaying the ruler.

- You cannot set paragraph spacing by using the Custom option in the spacing pop-up menu.

- FrameMaker ignores any Space Above setting if the paragraph is at the top of a column.

- FrameMaker ignores any Space Below setting if the paragraph is at the bottom of a column.

- You can use these steps to set paragraph spacing between paragraphs only.

- You cannot specify whether the space is above or below a paragraph; FrameMaker sets one or the other automatically.

- You cannot use these steps to set the paragraph spacing for text created with the graphics text tool.

Steps

1. Click on the **Spacing** pop-up menu on the ruler.
2. Select the **Space Between** option.
   Figure 3.8 shows the Space Between dialog box.
3. Select the paragraph spacing option you want and click **Set**.

What To Do If

- When you select Custom from the Space Between Paragraphs dialog box, the Custom Spacing dialog box opens. Type the paragraph spacing you want and click **Set.**
- If you accidentally change the spacing between paragraphs, reapply their paragraph tags or select **Undo** from the Edit menu.

See Also

- Creating and Updating Format Tags, p. 104.

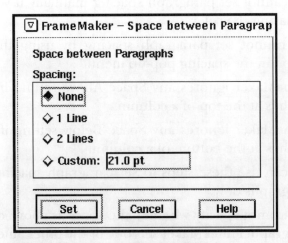

Figure 3.8 The Space Between dialog box.

Adjusting the Tab Settings   37

FrameMaker has four tab settings: Left, Center, Right, and Decimal. The Left and Right tab settings align text at the left and right edges of the tabbed text, the Center setting aligns the tabbed text at the center of the tabbed text, and the Decimal setting aligns the text on the decimal character of the tabbed text.

You can set the tab stops visually by using the ruler, or manually by using the Edit Tab Stop dialog box. Tab stops are set from the left edge of the column as opposed to the page. Tab stops are also set within paragraph tags.

Assumptions

- You want to adjust tab settings for the whole selected range of paragraphs or the one paragraph the insertion point is in.
- The ruler is visible.

Exceptions

- You cannot set tab stops this way if the ruler is not visible.
- You cannot use these steps to set tabs for text created with the graphics text tool.

Steps

1. Select a tab setting from the formatting part of the ruler (see Figure 3.9).
2. Drag the tab symbol to the position you want on the ruler.

What To Do If

- If you want to access the Edit Tab Stop dialog box, double-click on an existing tab stop.
- If you want to edit or specify characteristics for a specific tab, double-click on it to open the Edit Tab dialog box.

TIP

FrameMaker tab stops are absolute. For example, the second tab on a line moves the insertion point to the second tab stop, not to the next available tab stop.

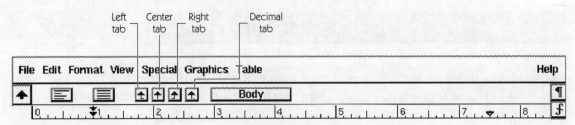

Figure 3.9   The tab stop selections on the formatting ruler.

- If you place a tab accidentally or want to delete one, drag it off the bottom of the ruler.

- If you want to make sure the tabs align with the ruler markings, turn on **Snap** on the Graphics menu.

- If you want to change the alignment of a tab, double-click on it to open the Edit Tab Stop dialog box, and choose a different alignment.

- If you want to set a tab leader character, double-click on the tab to open the Edit Tab Stop dialog box and choose a tab leader. You can also type your own custom tab leader. Leader characters can be anything you define; they don't have to be dots or punctuation marks.

See Also

- Creating and Updating Format Tags, p. 104.

Adjusting the Indents

FrameMaker has three indents: First, Left, and Right. The First indent left-aligns the first line of a paragraph; the Left indent left-aligns the rest of the paragraph; and the Right indent aligns the right edge of the whole paragraph.

You can set the indents visually by using the indent symbols on the ruler. Indents are measured from within the column, not the page. For example, even though an indent will be set at the ruler setting of 2.5″, its actual value is a 1.5″ indent, because it is measured from the edge of the column, not the page. The indents are also set within paragraph tags.

Assumptions

- The insertion point is in the paragraph where you want to set indents.
- The ruler is visible.

Exceptions

- You cannot set indents this way if the ruler is not visible.
- You cannot use these steps to adjust indents for text created with the graphics text tool.

Steps

- Drag the indent symbol to the position you want on the ruler (see Figure 3.10).

What To Do If

- If you create an indent for a list, such as a numbered or bulleted list, where the first line is indented less than the

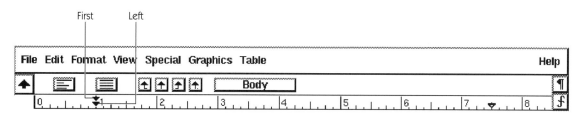

Figure 3.10   The indent markers in the formatting ruler.

rest of the paragraph, use a tab stop to align the text in the first line with the rest of the paragraph.

- If you want a numbered list to align the numbers to the right, set a right tab; then set the left indent; then set the left tab to line up with the left indent. This will align the number and then allow the text to line up.

See Also

- Creating and Updating Format Tags, p. 104.

Specifying the Color of Text

You can specify the color of text at the paragraph level and at the text range level. The default color for text is black; this is defined as the default for all paragraph and character tags. You can override the default by changing the color with the Paragraph Designer and Character Designer to fit your specific needs. Note that you can change any paragraph or character specification using similar steps.

39   Changing the Color of a Text Range

In FrameMaker you can specify the color of specific characters, words, or text ranges of any size. This enables you to integrate color right into the page design at your desktop. Color can be useful at the character level to create emphasis or attract attention to a specific area in your document.

Assumptions

- You can access the Character Designer.
- You have a color model selected for your file.
- The color you want exists within your color model.

- You have access to a color printer, are going to print color separations, or are planning to display color online.

_____ **Exceptions**

- If you want, you can use color on the screen only for printed documents. Light colors will print as shades of gray. Dark colors will print solid.
- You cannot set the color for conditional text using these steps.
- You cannot set the color for graphics using these steps. However, you can set the color of text that has been entered as graphic text.

_____ **Steps**

1. Select the text range you want to change.
2. Open the Character Designer.
3. Select a color from the Color pop-up menu.
4. Click on **Apply To Selection**.

_____ **What To Do If**

- If the color you want does not exist, check the color model associated with your file and change it to something else. For information on color models, see "Using Color."
- If, by accident, you change the color of your text to white on a white background, the text will disappear. To correct this, select **Undo** from the Edit menu, or double-click on the area where the text is, to select it, and choose **Black** from the Color pop-up menu. This should bring the text back.

_____ **See Also**

- Using Color, p. 339.

Changing the Color of a Paragraph

In FrameMaker you can specify the color of text for whole paragraphs. This enables you to integrate color in the page design at your desktop. Color can be useful at the paragraph level to create headings or attract attention to a specific area in your document.

Assumptions

- You want to change the color of an entire paragraph.
- You can access the Paragraph Designer.
- You have a color model selected for your file, and the color you want exists within your color model.
- You have access to a color printer, are going to print color separations, or are planning to display color online.

Exceptions

- If you want, you can use color on the screen only for printed documents. Light colors will print as shades of gray. Dark colors will print as solids.
- You cannot set the color for conditional text using these steps.
- You cannot set the color for graphics using these steps.
- You cannot reverse the color of text (for example, white text on black background) automatically. The background has to be done separately from the text.

Steps

1. Select the paragraph you want to change.
2. Open the **Paragraph Designer**.
3. Select **Default Font** from the Properties pop-up menu.
4. Select a color from the **Color** pop-up menu.
5. Click on **Apply To Selection**.

TIP

. Find out the colors available on your monitor and printer to make sure you are making decisions based on your resources. Not all printers and monitors have all colors available.

. Decide your color model before you decide to use color throughout your document.

. Once you decide to use color in your document, assign the color through the character tags. This ensures consistency and makes it easier to change the color throughout your document.

_____ **What To Do If**

- If the color you want does not exist, check the color model associated with your file and change it to something you can use. For information on color models, see "Using Color."

- If, by accident, you change the color of your text to white on a white background, the text will disappear. To correct this, select **Undo** from the edit menu, or double-click to select the text and choose **Black** from the Color pop-up menu. The text should reappear.

_____ **See Also**

- Using Color, p. 339.

Controlling Text Flow

You can control text flow by using line and page breaks to control the flow of a column, or you can create separate text flows for different parts of a document that you don't want interfering with each other.

For example, if you want a page or a line to end at a specific point, you can use the manual page or line break to enforce the formatting you choose for that page or line. On the other hand, if you are writing a document that has several articles or sections that are unrelated to each other but are part of the same page, such as articles in a newsletter, you can create separate text flows for each article or section.

Controlling Page Breaks | 41

If you want to force the flow of text from one page to the next, you can insert a page break manually. Usually you will have paragraph tags that will force a new page if needed consistently for a specific paragraph, such as for specific headings, or for paragraphs that should stay together but don't fit on one page together.

Assumptions

- You are not going to modify your document after you put in hard page breaks.

Exceptions

- You cannot modify your document after inserting hard page breaks.

Steps

1. Place the insertion point in the paragraph that you want to force to the next page.
2. Choose **Page Break** from the Format menu (or press **Esc o p c**).
3. Choose where the paragraph starts from the **At Top of Next Available** pop-up menu (see Figure 3.11).
4. Click **Set**.

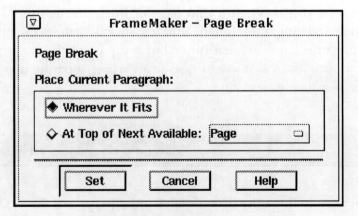

Figure 3.11   The Page Break dialog box.

_____ **What To Do If**

- If you change your document, and your page break is now wrong, select **Wherever It Fits** from the Page Break dialog box.

- If you have more than one column in a page and you want the text to start at the next column, select **Top of Column,** not **Top of Page**.

_____ **See Also**

- Creating and Updating Format Tags, p. 104.

Controlling Line Breaks ▽ 42 ▽

Text wraps automatically where the right indent is set for a specific paragraph. However, for those occasions when you don't want the text to wrap at the regular right indent, FrameMaker provides a few ways to force the flow from one line to another manually.

_____ **Assumptions**

- You want the text to continue on the next line.

_____ **Exceptions**

- None.

_____ **Steps**

To force a line break:

- Place the insertion point where you want the line to break and press **Meta + Return** or **Shift + Return.**

TIP

Create a list of words that require nonbreaking spaces and place them as you go along. This will save time in checking whether you have them everywhere you need them.
Be sure that you are not going to have any major changes to your document before you force line breaks manually. It will be less time-consuming to update the document if you introduce the line breaks when you know you won't be making many more changes to it.

To keep two words together:

- Place the insertion point between the two words and press **Control + Space.**

To allow line breaks after specific nonalphabetic characters (FrameMaker's default is not to break after any nonalphabetic character):

- Choose **Document** from the Format menu, type the characters in the **Allow Line Breaks After** text box, and click **OK.**

What To Do If

- If you accidentally force a line break, you can delete it by placing the insertion point after it and pressing **Backspace.** Then you can type a regular space.
- If you need to check whether you have nonbreaking spaces throughout your document, use **Find/Change** in the Edit menu. Then find and replace the words that need the nonbreaking spaces but don't have them. Conversely, if you want to delete all nonbreaking spaces in your document, use **Find/Change** to find and replace them with regular spaces. For information on searching and replacing, see Chapter 2, "Editing Text."

See Also

- Adjusting the Indents, p. 80.

43 Controlling Text Flows

FrameMaker enables you to create different text flows for content that you don't want connected to each other. For example, if you are creating a newsletter, you can assign each article in the

import all the settings from one document to the next. This is usually the way a template is applied to an existing document.

FrameMaker also allows you to import individual format tags or master pages by using functions in the Edit menu. This is useful if there's a limited number of formats you want to copy from one document to another.

Copying Individual Character Tags 44

You can copy individual character tags when you find that you only want to use a few tags contained in a document, or if you do not want to override anything in your document by accident. FrameMaker provides a special Copy menu item for copying character tags. Once the tags are in the new document, however, you have to make sure you save them.

Assumptions

- The document from which you are copying the character tags is open.

- The existing document doesn't have tags that you might override by copying formats.

- You saved the document to which you are copying before performing these steps.

Exceptions

- You cannot specify more than one character tag to copy at a time.

Steps

1. Place the insertion point in a text range that has the tag you want to copy.

TIP

To avoid overriding an existing tag, rename the tag you are copying before you add it as a new tag to the catalog.

2.   Select **Copy Special:Character Format** from the Edit menu (or press **Esc e y c**).

3.   Go to the document to which you are copying.

4.   Select **Paste** from the Edit menu (or press **Esc e p**).

5.   Open the **Character Designer**. The name in the Character Tag box should be the one you want to copy.

6.   Select **New Format** from the Command pop-up menu. The name in the New Format dialog box should be the one you want to copy.

7.   Turn on **Store in Catalog**.

8.   If you want to apply the tag to the characters you selected, turn on **Apply to Selection**.

9.   Click **Create**.

What To Do If

- If you accidentally override a tag, select **Revert to Saved** from the File menu (or press **Esc f r**).

See Also

- Importing All Format Specifications, p. 99.

45   Copying Individual Paragraph Tags

You can copy individual paragraph tags when you find that you only want to use a few tags contained in a document, or if you do not want to override anything in your document by accident. FrameMaker provides a special Copy menu item for copying paragraph tags. Once the tags are in the new document, however, you have to make sure you save them.

Assumptions

- The document from which you are copying the paragraph tag is open.

- The existing document doesn't have tags that you might override by copying formats.

- You saved the document to which you are copying before performing these steps.

_____ **Exceptions**

- You cannot specify more than one paragraph tag to copy at a time.

_____ **Steps**

1. Place the insertion point in a paragraph that has the tag you want to copy.

2. Select **Copy Special:Paragraph Format** from the Edit menu (or press **Esc e y p**).

3. Go to the document to which you are copying.

4. Select **Paste** from the Edit menu (or press **Esc e p**).

5. Open the **Paragraph Designer**. The name in the Paragraph Tag box should be the one you want to copy.

6. Select **New Format** from the Command pop-up menu. The name in the New Format dialog box should be the one you want to copy.

7. Turn on **Store in Catalog**.

8. If you want to apply the tag to the paragraph you are on, turn on **Apply to Selection**.

9. Click **Create**.

> **TIP**
>
> To avoid overriding an existing tag, rename the tag you are copying before you add it as a new tag to the catalog.

_____ **What To Do If**

- If you accidentally override a tag, select **Revert to Saved** from the File menu (or press **Esc f r**).

_____ **See Also**

- Importing All Format Specifications, p. 99.

Copying Individual Conditional Text Tags

You can copy individual conditional text tags when you find that you only want to use a few tags contained in a document, or if you do not want to override anything in your document by accident. FrameMaker provides a special Copy menu item for copying conditional text tags. Once they are in the new document, however, you have to make sure they are saved.

Assumptions

- The document from which you are copying the conditional text tag is open.
- The existing document doesn't have tags that you might override by copying formats.
- You saved the document to which you are copying before performing these steps.

Exceptions

- You cannot specify more than one conditional text tag to copy at a time.
- You cannot copy the color and format settings for a conditional text tag using these steps.

Steps

TIP
To avoid overriding an existing tag, rename the tag you are copying before you add it as a new tag to the catalog.

1. Place the insertion point in the text that has the conditional tag you want to copy.
2. Select **Copy Special:Conditional Text Settings** from the Edit menu (or press **Esc e y d**).
3. Go to the document to which you are copying.
4. Select **Paste** from the Edit menu (or press **Esc e p**).
5. Select **Conditional Text** from the Special menu. You should now have the new tag in your list.

What To Do If

- If you accidentally override a tag, select **Revert to Saved** from the File menu (or press **Esc f r**).
- If you want to set the format and color for a conditional tag after you copied it, select **Conditional Text** from the Special menu, then edit the tag.

See Also

- Importing All Format Specifications, p. 99.

Copying Individual Master Page Specifications

47

Although FrameMaker enables you to merge the master pages of one document with the master pages of another document, you may not want to override your master pages, or you may just want to add very specific aspects of a master page to your document. In these cases, you can copy and paste the objects from one document to another, just as you would for text or figures.

Assumptions

- The document from which you are copying the layout is open.
- You saved the document to which you are copying.

Exceptions

- You cannot specify more than one master page to copy at a time.

Steps

1. Go to the master page that contains the object you want to copy.

TIP

If you have to rearrange the page after you copy, be sure to save before you make any changes, and save often while you rearrange. This will ensure that you can revert to the last saved version if you need to go back to the previous version.

2. Select the objects. You can select specific objects, or you can select **Select All in Page** from the Edit menu (by pressing **Esc e a**).

3. Select **Copy** from the Edit menu.

4. Go to the master page in the document to which you are copying.

5. Select **Paste** from the Edit menu (or press **Esc e p**).

What To Do If

- If Select All in Page is not available in the Edit menu, click outside of the text column and try again. The Select All in Page menu item is available when there is no insertion point present in the text column.

See Also

- Importing All Format Specifications, p. 99.

48

Copying Individual Reference Page Specifications

Although FrameMaker enables you to merge the reference pages of one document with the reference pages of another document, you may not want to override your reference pages, or you may just want to add very specific aspects of a reference page to your document. In these cases, you can copy and paste the objects from one document to another, just as you would for text or figures.

Assumptions

- The document from which you are copying the reference specifications is open.

- You saved the document to which you are copying.

_____ **Exceptions**

- You cannot specify more than one master page to copy at a time.

_____ **Steps**

1. Go to the reference page that contains the layout or back-ground object you want to copy.
2. Select the objects. You can select specific objects, or you can select **Select All in Page** from the Edit menu (by pressing **Esc e a**).
3. Select **Copy** from the Edit menu.
4. Go to the reference page in the document to which you are copying.
5. Select **Paste** from the Edit menu (or press **Esc e p**).

> **TIP**
>
> If you have to rear-range the page after you copy, be sure to save before you make any changes, and save often while you rearrange. This will ensure that you can revert to the last saved version if you need to go back to the previous version.

_____ **What To Do If**

- If Select All in Page is not available in the Edit menu, click outside of the text column and try again. The Select All in Page menu item is available when there is no insertion point.

_____ **See Also**

- Importing All Format Specifications, p. 99.

Copying Individual Table Formats | 49

FrameMaker enables you to import table formats from one docu-ment to another. However, if you want to add just one format to your Table Catalog, you can copy and paste a table that contains the table format you want, then save the format in the Catalog.

Assumptions

- The document from which you are copying the table formats is open.

- The existing document doesn't have table formats that you might override by copying formats.

- You saved the document to which you are copying before performing these steps.

Exceptions

- You cannot specify more than one format to copy at a time.

Steps

1. Select a table that has the formats you want to copy.

2. Select **Copy** from the Edit menu (or press **Esc e c**).

3. Go to the document to which you are copying.

4. Select **Paste** from the Edit menu (or press **Esc e p**).

5. Select **Table Format** from the Table menu. The format settings should be the same as the table you have selected.

6. Type a new name for the table formats.

7. Select **New Format** from the Command pop-up menu. The name in the New Format dialog box should be the one you want to copy.

8. Turn on **Store in Catalog**.

9. If you want to apply the tag to the table you are on, turn on **Apply to Selection**.

10. Click **Create**.

What To Do If

- If you accidentally override a table format, select **Revert to Saved** from the File menu.

_____ **See Also**

- Importing All Format Specifications, below.

Importing All Format Specifications   50

FrameMaker enables you to import formats from one document to another selectively or at once. You can import these format specifications:

- Paragraph formats
- Character formats
- Page layouts
- Table formats
- Color definitions
- Reference pages
- Variable definitions
- Cross-reference formats
- Conditional text settings
- Math definitions

You can import any combination of these format definitions. This merges with and overrides your existing formats. When you choose the format definitions you want to import, you cannot choose specific formats, such as one paragraph tag or master page; you import whole catalogs or sets of pages.

Assumptions

- The document from which you are importing the formats is open.
- The existing document doesn't have tags you want that you might override by importing formats.

- You are in the document into which you want to import formats.
- You saved the document to which you are importing before performing these steps.

Exceptions

- You cannot specify exactly which tags or specific master pages to import using these steps. Once you select to import the paragraph tags, for example, the whole Paragraph Catalog is imported onto your document.
- You cannot import the content of a document using these steps.

Steps

1. Select **Import:Formats** from the File menu (or press **Esc f i o**).
   Figure 3.13 shows the Import Formats dialog box.
2. Turn on the Format Specifications you want to import.
3. Turn the format overrides on or off as appropriate.
4. Click **Import**.

TIP

Names are case-sensitive, so if you are importing tags or other formats with the same name, but different case, your document will contain both. For example, you can have a "Body" tag and a "body" tag.

What To Do If

- If you accidentally override a format, select **Revert to Saved** from the File menu.
- Importing formats causes the imported tags, pages, and settings to merge with the existing ones. If the names of the formats in your document are the same as the ones being imported, they will be replaced by the imported ones.
- If you import Paragraph Formats, the settings imported also include the footnote properties, the Allow Breaks After setting, and the Feather settings.
- If you import Page Layouts, the settings imported also include the character properties, the First Page properties, and the View option settings.

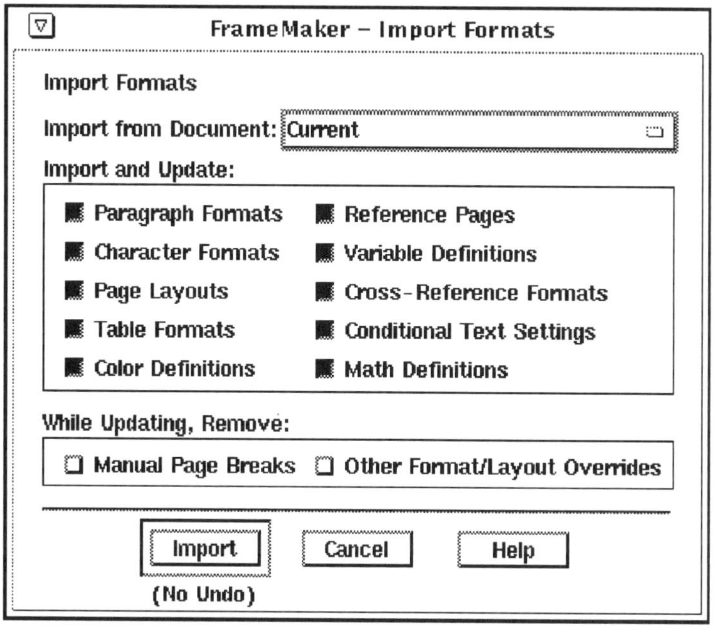

Figure 3.13   The Import Formats dialog box.

- If you import Table Formats, the Table Catalog and Ruling Styles merge with the existing ones.
- If you import Reference Pages, FrameMaker removes any reference frames with a name different from the imported ones.
- If you import Cross-references, FrameMaker updates the internal cross-references.
- If you import Conditional Text, the Show/Hide settings are also imported.
- If you import Math Definitions, FrameMaker copies the equation size and font settings into your document.

See Also

- Creating and Updating Format Tags, p. 104.
- Chapter 8, "Creating the Page Layout."

Chapter
4

CREATING
THE FORMATS

103

Creating and Updating Format Tags

Although you can easily format text as you go along, FrameMaker emphasizes defining format tags to match the function of text. Creating predefined formats enables you to

- Define the look and feel of text such as for headings, lists, and captions.
- Define a structure for the document.
- Change the look and feel of text without affecting its function.

One advantage to predefined formats is that if you decide to change the way something is defined in your list, such as the font and size of the numbers, you need only change to the format definition rather than go through the whole document, find every instance of the list, and then change every list item manually.

There are two types of format tags that you can define with FrameMaker: character tags and paragraph tags. Use character tags to define properties that you want to apply to a word or text range but not to a whole paragraph. Character tag characteristics include font family, size, and style. You apply character tags by selecting the text and then clicking on the name of the tag in the Character Catalog.

Paragraph tags contain the format specifications for whole paragraphs. This includes properties such as indents, tabs, alignment, font properties, auto-numbering, heading style, and spacing between paragraphs, lines, words, and letters. You apply paragraph tags by clicking on the paragraph to which you want to apply the tag and then clicking on the name of the paragraph tag in the Paragraph Catalog.

Note that you cannot use paragraph tags to format text created with the graphics tool, but you can use character tags to format it.

Defining New Tags | 51

When you create a new tag, you need to give it a name and the characteristics you want for the tag. Naming tags for their function makes it easier to use the catalogs and to make formatting changes to the documents later on.

You can define new tags based on existing ones, or from scratch. If you have a format that's similar or contains some of the characteristics you want for a new format, use it as a base from which to start. Also, it is a good idea to tag the current paragraph or text to see if the new characteristics have the look and feel you intended.

Assumptions

- The catalog does not contain any tags that you could modify to fulfill the function you need. For example, if you don't like how the "Emphasis" character tag looks, you could modify it instead of creating another tag to perform the same function.

- The Paragraph or Character Designer window is open.

Exceptions

- None.

Steps

1. Select **New Format** from the Commands pop-up menu.
2. In the New Format dialog box (see Figure 4.1), type a name in the **Tag** text box.
3. Turn on **Store in Catalog**.
4. To apply the format to the current paragraph or selected text range, turn on **Apply to Selection**.

TIP

Modify your new paragraph tags visually. For example, use the ruler to set First, Left, and Right indents and tabs. This way you can see what your changes look like, as the current paragraph takes on some of these characteristics, before you actually update the tag in the catalog.
Try not to create too many tags or duplicate functions. Too many tags or too many formats for essentially the same function make the catalog confusing to use.

Figure 4.1   The New Format dialog box.

5. Click **Create**.
    If you have the appropriate catalog open, you will see the new tag name added to the list.

6. Modify the properties you need to make the text look the way you want.
    If you are in the Character Designer, modify the font and character settings and click **Update All**.
    If you are in the Paragraph Designer, go to a specific Properties window using the **Properties** pop-up menu, modify the settings, and click **Update All**. Move on to the next Property window and repeat this step.

What To Do If

*   If you create a new tag and forget to apply it to the current text, click on **Apply to Selection** on the Designer window.

*   If you want to create a tag that is similar to an existing paragraph or text range, click on the text. The Designer window will reflect the format of the current text. Create a new tag and modify the properties to create the new look.

See Also

*   Updating Tags, p. 107.

Updating Tags | 52

Occasionally you will want to update the formats to match new styles or changed formatting specifications or to correct settings. FrameMaker gives you tremendous power to make extensive changes to the look of your documents in a reasonable amount of time and with relatively minimum effort. To update the formats of your documents, you only update the tags—you don't need to change each paragraph manually.

You can also change the function of certain paragraphs by retagging them with a different tag automatically. For example, if you have a type of heading, instead of captions, preceding figures, you can specify that all paragraphs tagged with that type of heading be changed to a figure caption tag.

Assumptions

- You are not going to override a tag with settings you want to keep, even if it has the same or similar function. For example, for a "Heading1" paragraph tag set to start anywhere, if you want some to start on a new page, create a new tag specifically to perform that function instead of modifying the existing tag.

- The Paragraph Designer window is open in the Basic properties.

Exceptions

- You cannot selectively exclude or include groups of tags to update. You must modify all tags.

Steps

1. Click on a paragraph or text range that has the tag you want to update, or select the name of the tag from the **Tag** pop-up menu in the Designer window.

TIP

To modify specific text ranges or paragraphs, make the changes manually, or apply the changes to the selection only, click **Apply To Selection**.

2. Modify the properties to create the new look.

3. Specify which tags you want to modify by selecting **Global Update Options** from the Commands pop-up menu. Figure 4.2 shows the Global Update Options dialog box. You can choose to update all tags in the document; all text or paragraphs tagged with the tag of the current text; or all text or paragraphs tagged with another tag.

   The default setting is All Matching Tags in Selection. The Use Properties is not present in the Character Designer, because it doesn't have property groups.

4. Click **Update All** to make the changes to the tag permanent before you move on to the next property group you want to modify.

What To Do If

- If you want to update specific settings, such as the font or size, for all tags in the document without affecting the rest

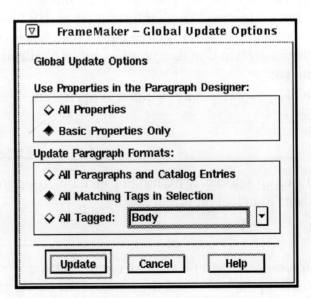

Figure 4.2   The Global Update Options dialog box.

of the tags' settings, select **Set Window to As Is** from the Commands pop-up menu and set the property you want to modify. Then, choose **All Paragraphs** (or **Characters**) and **Catalog Entries** in the Global Update Options and click **Update**.

- If you want all paragraphs or text with a specific tag to take another tag, choose **All Tagged** and pick the tag name from the pop-up menu.

See Also

- Changing the Look of a Text Range, p. 66.
- Changing the Look of a Paragraph, p. 71.

Deleting a Tag | 53

FrameMaker provides a set of default tags for the Character and Paragraph Catalogs that you can use. However, if you are creating a new set of paragraphs, you may want to delete these tags from the catalog. Also, when you merge templates, or apply a new template to existing documents with their own set of tags, you may want to delete tags that you won't be using.

You can access the Delete Formats dialog box (see Figure 4.3) by clicking **Delete** at the bottom of the Catalog window or by selecting **Delete** from the Commands pop-up menu in the Designer window.

Assumptions

- The Delete Formats dialog box is open.

Exceptions

- You cannot select multiple tags to delete at once. You have to delete each one explicitly. However, you can delete multiple tags in one deleting session.

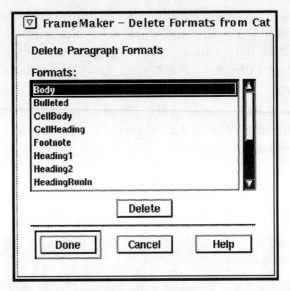

Figure 4.3   The Delete Formats dialog box.

Steps

TIP

If you decide not to delete the tags you selected, click **Cancel**.

1. Select the tag you want to remove and click **Delete**. Repeat for each tag you want to delete.

2. Click **Done**.
    All the tags you deleted will be gone from the catalog. Note that once you click Done, Framemaker does not allow you to Undo.

What To Do If

- If you want to replace a tag with another, consider modifying the existing tag before deleting it.

- If you are going to import the formats from a template or another document, you may want to delete the existing tags first.

- If you delete a tag that is already in use, the text ranges or paragraphs with the tag retain that tag.

_____ **See Also**

• Updating Tags, p. 107.

Defining the Position of Text

The position of a paragraph can determine its function and its readability. For example, if you define paragraphs to run from margin to margin, and do not differentiate in paragraph alignment between body text and other types of paragraphs such as bulleted lists, then your documents will be very hard to read.

You can use indents and tabs to differentiate between types of lists. You can use alignment to establish a pattern for certain types of information; to allow for enough white space to make your documents readable; and to add other types of information, such as callouts or icons.

Don't be afraid to use white space when establishing the position of text. The readability of your documents is imperative to get your information or point across to the readers, and in some cases it can affect how people do business with your company.

For example, products that lack understandable guides or manuals might not sell as well as comparable products that provide users with a better guide. Also, proposals or reports that a reader cannot easily scan or read, because of the formatting, can cost the deal or approval you or your company needs to succeed in business.

You can always offset the possible use of extra paper by manipulating spacing for paragraphs and lines, as you create your catalog. (However, this tends to be a perception problem, rather than a real one.)

Indenting a Paragraph | 54

FrameMaker allows you to indent paragraphs without changing your document's margins. FrameMaker measures the indents from the edge of the text column, except when you are using side heads. You can specify the indent for the first line of a paragraph separately from the indent for the rest of the paragraph. This makes it easy to format lists or definitions, such as glossaries.

You can use indents to make paragraphs stand out or to create a consistent look for specific types of information.

Assumptions

- The Paragraph Designer window is open in the Basic Properties.

- The format is already created.

- The indent settings are generally relative to the edge of the text column.

Exceptions

- You can use these steps for text that is not tagged, or if no tag exists, by clicking **Apply To Selection** instead of **Update All**.

Steps

TIP

Set the indents visually by using the ruler. This modifies the current paragraph before you update the tag, and allows you to see if that is the setting you want for the tag.

1. Select the tag you want to indent from the **Paragraph Tag** pop-up menu.

2. Set the first, left, and right indents for the paragraph tag using the Indents area of the Basic Properties window (see Figure 4.4).

3. Click **Update All** to make the settings permanent to the tag.

What To Do If

- If you are using side heads, the indents are relative to the normal-text area, not the edge-of-text column. The normal-text area starts at a specified point: after the heading for a left side head, and before the heading for a right side head.

Indents area

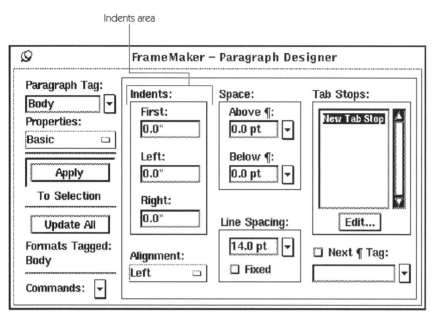

Figure 4.4   The Indents area of the Basic Properties window.

- For bulleted or numbered lists, set the first indent at the normal indent setting for your document, and the left indent aligned with the tab setting where the text starts. This aligns all the lines in the paragraph with the text on the first line, not with the bullet or number. You can use this technique to simulate side heads within the normal-text area.

_____ **See Also**

- Adjusting the Indents, p. 80.
- Defining Headings, p. 140.

Defining the Alignment of a Paragraph   55

There are four types of alignment you can specify for a paragraph: Left, Center, Right, and Justified.

Left aligns the text along the left indent and leaves a ragged right. Center aligns the text on each line's center. Right aligns the text along the right indent and leaves a ragged left. Justified aligns the text along both the left and right indents, creating space between letters and words if necessary.

Left alignment is the most common and is argued to be the most readable of the settings. Justifying text can create white space and readability problems, although it can be used effectively once those issues are resolved.

Assumptions

- The Paragraph Designer window is open in the Basic Properties.

- The format is already created.

Exceptions

- You can use these steps for text that is not tagged, or if no tag exists, by clicking **Apply To Selection** instead of **Update All**.

Steps

TIP

Select the alignment visually, using the formatting part of the ruler. This modifies the current paragraph before you update the tag, and it allows you to see whether that is the setting you want for the tag.

1. Select the format you want to align from the **Paragraph Tag** pop-up menu.

2. Click on the Alignment pop-up menu and select the alignment for the paragraph format.

3. Click **Update All** to make the settings permanent to the tag.

What To Do If

- If you want to have left-justified and right-justified text within the same paragraph, select left justification for the paragraph and set a right-aligned tab stop in the position where you want text to be right-justified.

- If you are center aligning a paragraph, but you want its width to be less than the rest of the text column, adjust the indents of the tag.
- If you are justifying a paragraph, you can avoid white space running through the text by adjusting the character and word spacing. For more information, see "Specifying Spacing" in this chapter.

See Also

- Choosing the Alignment, p. 73.

Specifying the Position and Alignment of Tabs   56

There are many uses for tabs in paragraphs. From creating a simple table of information to aligning numbers and creating lists, tab stops are a better alignment tool for text within paragraphs than spaces. In this day of proportional fonts and spaces, tab stops have replaced using spaces to align, even for relatively small distances between text.

You can use tabs to align text on the left, center, and right of a paragraph, such as for letterhead or for headers and footers. There are four types of tab alignments you can use: Left, Center, Right, and Decimal. Left and Right align text on the left or right side of the tabbed text. Center aligns along the center of the tabbed text. Decimal aligns along the decimal character of a number.

Assumptions

- The Paragraph Designer window is open in the Basic Properties.
- The format is already created.

Exceptions

- You can use these steps for text that is not tagged, and if no tag exists, by clicking **Apply To Selection** instead of **Update All**.

Steps

TIP

Select the tab settings visually, using the ruler. This modifies the current paragraph before you update the tag, and it allows you to see whether those are the settings you want for the tag.

1. Select the format for which you want to set tab stops from the **Paragraph Tag** pop-up menu.
2. Select a tab setting from the formatting part of the ruler.
3. Click on the position you want the tab stop on the ruler. For an exact location, specify the position in the **Edit Tab Stop** dialog box, as described in the following three steps.
4. Select the tab stop in the Paragraph Designer and click **Edit** to access the Edit Tab Stop dialog box, shown in Figure 4.5.
5. Specify characteristics such as leaders for the tab stop.
6. Click **Continue**.
7. Repeat these steps for each tab you want to add to a format.
8. Click **Update All** to make the settings permanent to the tag.

What To Do If

- If you want to delete a tab, drag it off the bottom of the ruler.
- If you want to move a tab, drag it to a new position, or click on it in the Edit Tab Stop dialog box and change its position.
- If you want to add tabs at regular intervals, type the interval in the **Repeat Every** text box.
- If you want to make sure the tabs align with the ruler markings, turn on **Snap** on the Graphics menu.
- If you want to set a tab leader character, choose one of the tab leaders available on the Edit Tab Stop dialog box, or type your own.

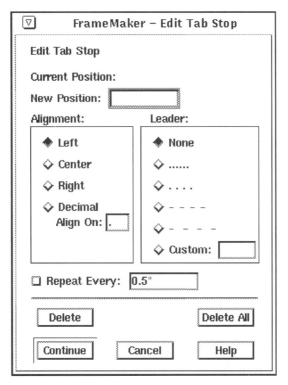

Figure 4.5   The Edit Tab Stop dialog box.

- If you want to change the decimal character for decimal tab stops, type the character in the **Align On** text box.

See Also

- Adjusting the Tab Settings, p. 79.

Defining Hyphenation   57

FrameMaker is very flexible in how it allows you to set hyphenation. Each language version of FrameMaker contains hyphenation guides for words, so that automatic hyphenation is generally correct according to the specific language's rules and guidelines. You can also customize hyphenation for specific words if you like, or suppress hyphenation altogether.

Hyphenation should be used sparingly. You can set FrameMaker not to allow hyphenation on consecutive lines, or to allow hyphenation only at intervals that you define.

Assumptions

- The Paragraph Designer window is open in the Advanced Properties.

- The format is already created.

Exceptions

- You can use these steps for text that is not tagged, or if no tag exists, by clicking **Apply To Selection** instead of **Update All**.

Steps

1. Select the format for which you want to set hyphenation from the **Paragraph Tag** pop-up menu.

2. Turn on **Hyphenate**.

3. Specify the characteristics of hyphenated words, using the Automatic Hyphenation area in the Advanced Properties window see (Figure 4.6).

4. Click **Update All** to make the settings permanent to the tag.

What To Do If

- If you want to specify the number of consecutive lines in a paragraph that can end with a hyphen, type the number in the **Max. # Adjacent** text box.

> **TIP**
>
> Use the Spelling Checker to define hyphenation points for a specific word. Define hyphenation for specific words by defining the hyphenation through the Dictionaries. Define hyphenation properties for specific instances of a word by placing discretionary hyphens (**Control + hyphen**) or suppressing hyphenation (**Shift + Meta + hyphen**).

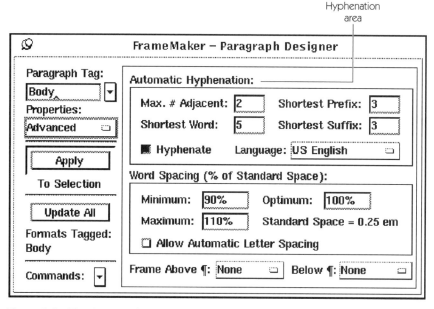

Figure 4.6   The Automatic Hyphenation area in the Advanced Properties window.

- If you want to specify the length of the shortest word that can be hyphenated in a paragraph, type the number of letters in the **Shortest Word** text box.

- If you want to specify the minimum number of letters that precede or follow a hyphen, type the number in the **Shortest Prefix** or **Shortest Suffix** text boxes.

- If you want to hyphenate words based on a language other than U.S. English, select a different language from the **Language** pop-up menu.

    This hyphenation style will apply only to paragraphs tagged with the tag you are presently defining. To set the whole document to this hyphenation style, update all tags in the document.

- If you do not want to hyphenate the paragraph, turn **Hyphenation** off.

- If you do not want to hyphenate or spell-check the paragraph, set the Language to **None**.

See Also

- Checking for Spelling and Typing Errors, p. 59.

Specifying Spacing and Pagination

The spacing and pagination patterns you establish for your documents will affect their length and readability. Very evenly spaced paragraphs and lines do not allow paragraphs to stand out enough to guide the eye or scan through a document. By the same token, documents that are spaced or paginated erratically can be confusing.

In general, FrameMaker enables you to do just about anything in terms of spacing between paragraphs, lines, words, and letters. It also allows you to specify characteristics that affect the pagination of your document, such as allowing a specific number of widow and orphan lines for paragraphs, or always having a specific paragraph kept together with the following one.

58　Specifying the Space Between Lines

The spacing between lines in a paragraph is called the "leading," pronounced "ledding," based on terminology used when type was set on lead. FrameMaker allows you to set as much space between lines as you want. The default leading is proportional to the size of the font, and FrameMaker changes it automatically whenever you modify the size.

Assumptions

- The Paragraph Designer window is open in the Basic Properties.
- The format is already created.

Exceptions

- You can use these steps for text that is not tagged, or if no tag exists, by clicking **Apply To Selection** instead of **Update All**.

Steps

1. Select a format from the **Paragraph Tag** pop-up menu.

2. Set the line spacing for the paragraph using the Line Spacing area of the Basic Properties window (see Figure 4.7). The line spacing is measured from baseline to baseline.

3. Click **Update All** to make the settings permanent to the tag.

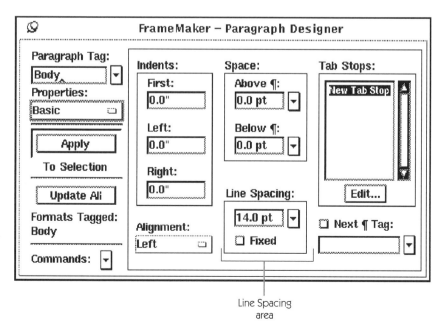

Line Spacing
area

Figure 4.7   The Line Spacing area of the Basic Properties window.

What To Do If

- If you turn the Fixed check box on, FrameMaker does not adjust the line spacing to accommodate larger characters, subscripts, or superscripts within a line.
- If you change the font size for a paragraph tag, FrameMaker updates the line spacing automatically.

See Also

- Changing the Line Spacing, p. 75.

59 Defining the Space Between Paragraphs

FrameMaker provides you with two settings to specify the spacing between paragraphs: Above and Below. Consecutive paragraphs take the largest number for the spacing between them. For example, for a heading with a Below setting of 12 points, followed by a Body text paragraph with an Above setting of 6 points, FrameMaker sets the paragraph spacing between them to 12 points.

In general, be consistent in the use of paragraph spacing. Create less space between a heading and the text that follows it than between the heading and the text that precedes it. Also, you may want to set less space between list items than between body paragraphs.

Assumptions

- The Paragraph Designer window is open in the Basic Properties.
- The format is already created.

Exceptions

- You can use these steps for text that is not tagged, or if no tag exists, by clicking **Apply To Selection** instead of **Update All**.

- Framemaker ignores the Space Above setting if the paragraph is at the top of a column.

- FrameMaker ignores the Space Below setting if the paragraph is at the bottom of a column.

Steps

1. Select a format from the **Paragraph Tag** pop-up menu.

2. Set the space above and below for the paragraph format using the Space area of the Basic Properties window (see Figure 4.8). When subsequent paragraphs have a different Above and Below setting, FrameMaker uses the largest.

3. Click **Update All** to make the settings permanent to the tag.

TIP

To start the paragraph at the top of a column in a specific position below the margin, Space Above does not work. Instead, move the top of the column down to the position where you want the text to start.

Paragraph
spacing area

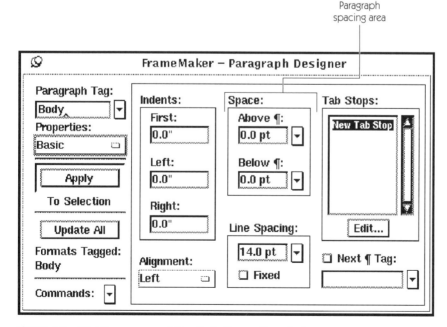

Figure 4.8   The Space area of the Basic Properties window.

What To Do If

- None.

See Also

- Adjusting the Paragraph Spacing, p. 77.

Specifying the Space Between Words

Each font has a standard default spacing between words. If you want to pack the words more tightly or loosely, you can specify the spacing you want FrameMaker to achieve in filling lines with text. The range of values you set for word spacing are a percentage of the standard space of the font you are using. Making the range between the maximum and minimum word spacing larger allows FrameMaker to make more adjustments to fill a line more evenly. This can be particularly useful for justified text.

FrameMaker enables you to specify the maximum space allowed, the minimum space allowed, and the optimum space you want to achieve between words.

Assumptions

- The Paragraph Designer window is open in the Advanced Properties.
- The format is already created.

Exceptions

- You can use these steps for text that is not tagged, or if no tag exists, by clicking **Apply To Selection** instead of **Update All**.

_____ **Steps**

1. In the Word Spacing area specify the minimum, optimum, and maximum space between words.

2. Click **Update All** to make the settings permanent to the tag.

_____ **What To Do If**

*   If you want to add extra space between letters in justified text to avoid too much spacing between words, turn on **Allow Automatic Letter Spacing**.

_____ **See Also**

*   None.

Specifying the Space Between Characters   61

FrameMaker defines the space between characters in two ways: how you can set certain letters together, and how you can define how close or apart characters are.

Pair kerning refers to the space between two characters brought closer together to improve their appearance and to avoid unnecessary space between them. For example, the letter combinations "We" or "To," where parts of the larger letter overlap the vertical space of the smaller letter, are set to kern.

Spread refers to the distance between all characters. FrameMaker enables you to set tighter or looser text, based on a percentage of the regular spread for a specific font. Note that setting a paragraph too loosely can blur the difference between words, as the space between letters becomes more like the space between words.

Assumptions

- The Paragraph Designer window is open in the Default Font properties or the Character Designer window is open.
- The format is already created.

Exceptions

- You can use these steps for text that is not tagged, or if no tag exists, by clicking **Apply To Selection** instead of **Update All**.

Steps

1. Select a format from the **Tag** pop-up menu.
2. Select the **Pair Kern** check box.
3. Type the character spread percentage in the **Spread** text box.
4. Click **Update All** to make the settings permanent to the tag.

> **TIP**
>
> If you apply a spread to a word, do not select the last character. Otherwise, the space between words is changed as well.

What To Do If

- If you want to apply these settings to a paragraph, use the Paragraph Designer. If you want to apply it to a word or text range, use the Character Designer.
- If you want to increase the space between characters, and thus make the text looser, use a percentage larger than zero.
- If you want to decrease the space between characters, and thus make the text tighter, use a negative percentage.
- If you select Pair Kerning and a Spread setting for a paragraph, the pair kern brings pairs of characters closer together than the spread you selected. This might cause text to look uneven in a loose spread setting.

See Also

- Specifying the Space Between Words, p. 124.

Controlling Pagination | 62

The ability to control where your pages break automatically can be a powerful and time-saving feature. As you develop your document, FrameMaker enables you to take care of widows, orphans, and stray headings.

The settings you specify for each paragraph tag control how a paragraph breaks at the end of a page. You can specify if a paragraph starts at the top of a column, page, or a specific page side. This allows you to create paragraphs, such as section headings, that always start on a new page.

You can specify that a paragraph be kept with the paragraph preceding or following it. For example, if you want to make sure you don't have stray headings at the end of a page, set it to be kept with the next paragraph.

You can also specify how many widow and orphan lines a paragraph can have. If you set all regular paragraph tags to have two or more, then you never have to check your document for widows and orphans. However, if you set the number of lines too high, you may force small paragraphs onto the next page or column without intending to do so.

Assumptions

- The Paragraph Designer window is open in the Pagination Properties.

- The format is already created.

Exceptions

- You can use these steps for text that is not tagged, or if no tag exists, by clicking **Apply To Selection** instead of **Update All**.

Steps

You can control where a paragraph starts, ends, or breaks when the paragraph is at the end of a column or page.

To specify where a paragraph starts:

- Select where you want paragraphs with the current tag to start from the **Start** pop-up menu.

To keep paragraphs with the current tag together with the previous or next paragraph:

- Turn on **Next Paragraph** or **Previous Paragraph** in the Keep With area.

To specify the number of widow and orphan lines allowed for paragraphs with the current tag:

- Type the minimum number of lines to leave as widow or orphan lines in the **Widow/Orphan Lines** text box.

What To Do If

- If you are setting properties for a heading, choose **Keep With Next**. This prevents the heading from staying at the bottom of a page.

- If you set too many tags to Keep With Next or Previous, you may find that the settings force paragraphs together and move them to a new page, leaving you with some nearly empty or halfway filled pages or columns. To prevent this, make sure you use this setting sparingly—only when necessary.

- If you set the widow and orphan lines to a number that is too large, you may find large gaps at the end of pages or columns. Keep the number relatively low, depending on the length you expect your paragraph to be.

TIP

Using a combination of these settings throughout your paragraph helps you avoid forcing page breaks once your document is complete.

_____ **See Also**

- Controlling Text Flows, p. 88.

Freezing Pagination to Insert Revision Pages

63

When your documents are updated very frequently, you might want to use revision pages rather than replace the whole document. In this case, it is important to maintain the pagination of the original document. Revision pages should not affect the pagination, since the table of contents and index may not be updated with every revision of a document.

For this purpose, FrameMaker enables you to freeze the pagination of a document and to specify a numbering style for revision pages.

_____ **Assumptions**

- Your document has a single text flow.
- There are no body page overrides of the master page layouts anywhere in your document.

_____ **Exceptions**

- Do not insert revision pages in a multipage table.
- Do not insert a revision page when a paragraph breaks at the end of a page and continues in another. The portion of a paragraph that is in the revision page becomes its own paragraph, and FrameMaker cannot merge both portions when you unfreeze the pagination.

_____ **Steps**

1. Press **Esc p z**. FrameMaker displays the Freeze Pagination dialog box.

2. Choose a numbering style for the revision pages from the **Point Page # Style** pop-up menu.

3. Click **Freeze**.

What To Do If

- If you want to unfreeze the document, press **Esc p z** to display the Unfreeze Pagination dialog box, and click **Unfreeze**.

- If you want to change the numbering style without unfreezing pagination, display the Unfreeze Pagination dialog box, choose a different numbering style, and click **Set Point Page # Style**.

Specifying Page and Paragraph Numbering

With FrameMaker you can specify the numbering style, the number with which a document begins, and the starting page side of a document. You can specify these settings, for each file that composes a document, from within the document by using the Document Properties dialog box. However, with the exception of the numbering style, you can override them with the settings you give each file within a book.

Assumptions

- None.

Exceptions

- If a document is part of a book, the page and paragraph numbering is established from the book settings. The book settings override the document settings for numbering.

- You cannot set numbering-by-folio numbering style using these steps. For page numbering that follows that convention, use the book numbering settings. For paragraph numbering, use the numbering properties in the appropriate paragraph tag.

_____ **Steps**

1. Select Document from the Format menu. Figure 4.9 shows the Document Properties dialog box.

2. Type a page number in the **1st Page #** text box. You can specify negative numbers if you want.

3. Select a numbering style from the **Page # Style** pop-up menu.

4. Set **Restart Paragraph Numbering**.

5. Click **Apply**.

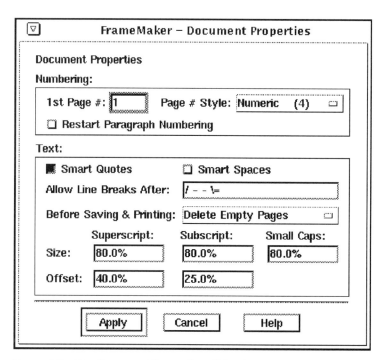

Figure 4.9   The Document Properties dialog box.

What To Do If

- If you want to make the second page in your document be number 1, set the first page to start at 0. If you want the third page to be number 1, set the first page to start at −1.
- If you want to have a part of your document, such as the front matter, be paginated separately from the rest of your document, create two files, one for each set to be paginated. Then create a book file for all the files in your document.
- If you want the paragraph numbering, such as section numbering or table and figure caption numbering, to restart for each document, turn **Restart Paragraph Numbering** on.

See Also

- Setting Page Numbering for Each File in a Book, p. 389.
- Setting Paragraph Numbering for Each File in a Book, p. 390.

65 Specifying the Page Count in a Document

Setting the page count in your document to odd, even, or anything else, depends upon such factors as whether you are producing a double-sided or single-sided document, or whether you are specifying page count settings for a stand-alone file or for a file that is part of a book.

Setting the page count for each file in a book is important in order to keep the pagination of the book correct. For example, if you have files in the middle of the book that are set to make the page count even, FrameMaker adds pages where necessary so that it turns out even. The result may be empty pages in the middle of the document where you may not want them. Be sure that whatever strategy you choose for page count is consistent with how you want to paginate your document.

Steps

1. Select **Document** from the Format menu.
2. Select a document page count setting from the **Before Saving & Printing** pop-up menu.
3. Click **Apply**.

What To Do If

- If you want to allow FrameMaker to base the page count of your document on where the text ends, select **Delete Empty Pages**.
- If you want the page count to be even or odd, select **Make Page Count Even** or **Make Page Count Odd** as needed.
- If you want to keep the number of pages you have, regardless of full or empty pages, select **Don't Change Page Count**.
- If you want to allow FrameMaker to add extra pages to adjust the pagination in a book, select **Delete Empty Pages**. FrameMaker deletes the extra pages when it saves the document, but it adds a page if necessary when processing the document as part of a book.

See Also

- Setting the Starting Page Side for Each File in a Book, p. 387.

> **TIP**
>
> - For a document that is double-sided and starts on the right page, select **Make Page Count Even**.
>
> - For a document that is double-sided and starts on the left page, select **Make Page Count Odd**.
>
> - Set the document page count to **Delete Empty Pages** if the document is part of a book. The document settings override the book settings for page count, which can cause problems when paginating a book.

Defining Font Properties

Using the appropriate font and size is very important for defining the presentation of documents you prepare. There are many font families, sizes, and styles from which to choose, and your choices affect how professional your documents will look, how readable they will be, and how they will be perceived by your readers.

In making these decisions, given the flexibility that FrameMaker gives you, there are two general rules to keep in mind: Use fonts and styles sparingly and consistently, and use serif fonts, such as

Palatino, for large blocks of text, such as body text. Sans-serif fonts are well suited for headings or callouts, but it is difficult to read blocks of text that use sans-serif fonts such as Helvetica.

FrameMaker enables you to apply the font properties to paragraphs and text ranges. The properties you apply are the same in either case, the main difference is in the range of text that the settings affect. In the case of paragraph tags, font property changes affect whole paragraphs. In the case of character tags, font property changes affect only the selected text.

Defining the Font Properties of a Paragraph or Text Range

The most basic properties you need to choose when designing the look of your document are the font family, size, angle, and weight. Font families are determined by the fonts your system has installed. For information on the fonts available, contact your system administrator. In addition, some font families have variations of the font, such as Helvetica, Helvetica Narrow, and Helvetica Condensed. If variations exist for a font family, they will be listed in the Variations pop-up menu.

The Angle pop-up menu generally lists italics or oblique options for the font you are using, and the Weight pop-up menu lists whether there are bold or light options for it.

Assumptions

- The Paragraph Designer window is open in the Default Font Properties, or The Character Designer window (see Figure 4.10) is open.
- The format is already created.

Exceptions

- You cannot select a font family not installed by your system. If you need a font other than those FrameMaker lists, contact

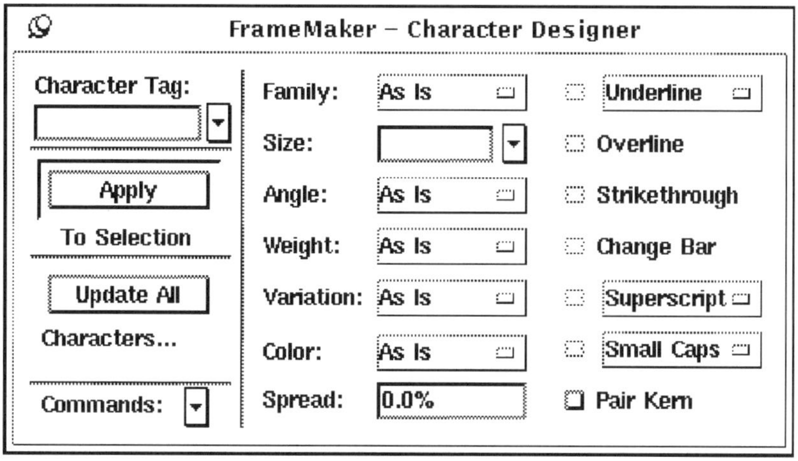

Figure 4.10   The Character Designer window.

your system administrator to install it and to confirm that
FrameMaker supports it.

- You can use these steps for text that is not tagged, or if no
  tag exists, by clicking **Apply To Selection** instead of **Update
  All**.

Steps

1. Select a format from the **Tag** pop-up menu.

2. Select the family and size of the font you want to use for
   the format.

3. Select the angle, weight, and variation of the font.

4. Click **Update All** to make the settings permanent to the
   tag.

What To Do If

- If you want to specify a different size from the ones listed
  already, click on the **Size** text box and type the number.

- If angle, weight, or variation do not list any options, there are none available for the font family you chose. The pop-up menus list only the characteristics available to the font family you chose.

- If you want to use a different color for the text in a paragraph or text range, select the color from the **Color** pop-up menu.

See Also

- Applying a Font and Size, p. 68.
- Specifying the Color of Text, p. 82.
- Using Color, p. 339.

67 Specifying Special Character Styles

Special character styles allow you to make your text stand out or perform a specific function in your document. For example, you can use revision or change bars to show new or changed content in a document draft.

You can use underline, overline, strikethrough, change bar, outline, and shadow in whole paragraphs or in text ranges. You can use more than one style if you want.

Assumptions

- The Paragraph Designer window is open in the Default Font Properties, or the Character Designer is open.

- The format is already created.

Exceptions

- You can use these steps for text that is not tagged, or if no tag exists, by clicking **Apply To Selection** instead of **Update All**.

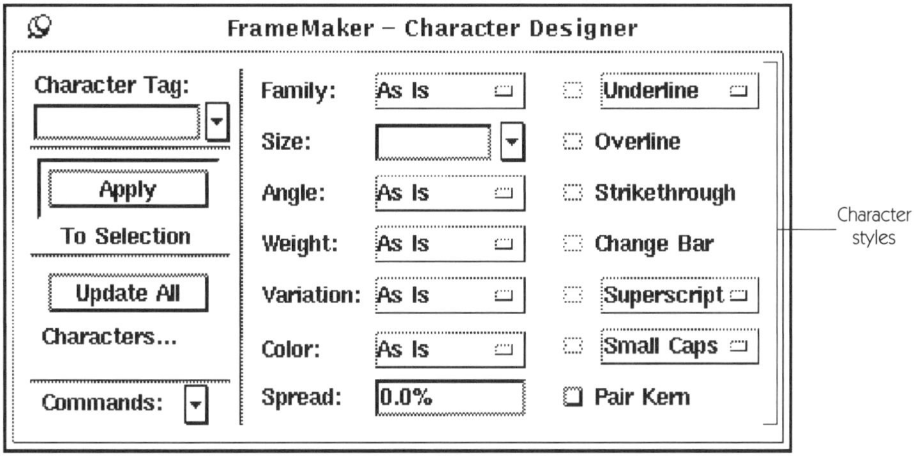

Figure 4.11   The Character Styles area of Character Designer.

<hr>

Steps

1.   Select a format from the **Tag** pop-up menu.
2.   Select the check boxes (see Figure 4.11) for the special character styles you want to use for the format.
3.   Click **Update All** to make the settings permanent to the tag.

What To Do If

• You can select as many characteristics as you want for a tag.

See Also

• Applying a Font Style, p. 69.

Specifying Special Capitalization | 68

You can specify whether a paragraph or text range should be uppercase, lowercase, or small caps. Generally you're more likely to apply special capitalization to a text range than to a whole paragraph, except in the case of heading paragraph tags.

Small caps are generally 80 percent of the size of the current font size. You can customize the size of small caps in the Document dialog box. Small caps are most frequently used for acronyms or names that are all uppercase. Using small caps helps the acronym or name blend with the text around it.

Assumptions

- The Paragraph Designer window is open in the Default Font Properties, or the Character Designer is open.
- The format is already created.

Exceptions

- You can use these steps for text that is not tagged, or if no tag exists, by clicking **Apply To Selection** instead of **Update All**.

Steps

1. Select a format from the **Tag** pop-up menu.
2. Select the check box by the capitalization pop-up menu.
3. Select the capitalization style you want from the pop-up menu.
4. Click **Update All** to make the settings permanent to the tag.

What To Do If

- If you want to define the size of Small Caps, select **Document** from the Format menu and specify the size in the **Size** text box.

  The size is based on a percentage of the point size of the text being formatted as small caps. For example, if the point size defined for a paragraph tag is 10 points, the small caps text will be 8 points for a size set at 80 percent.

TIP

If you want to make your text all uppercase within a paragraph, use small caps instead of all uppercase text. This makes your text more readable and does not make the uppercase text look disproportionate with respect to the rest of the paragraph.

- If you apply Small Caps to text typed in mixed uppercase and lowercase, the text turns to uppercase and small caps.

_____ **See Also**

- Applying a Font Style, p. 69.

Specifying Subscripts and Superscripts | 69

FrameMaker makes using subscripts and superscripts very easy by providing the option as a character style. Once you select subscript or superscript as a characteristic for text, FrameMaker places the text correctly with respect to the text around it.

Subscripts and superscripts are by default 65 percent of the size of the current text. However, you can control the size and placement of subscripts and superscripts in the Document dialog box.

_____ **Assumptions**

- The Paragraph Designer window is open in the Default Font Properties, or the Character Designer is open.

- The format is already created.

_____ **Exceptions**

- You can use these steps for text that is not tagged, or if no tag exists, by clicking **Apply To Selection** instead of **Update All**.

_____ **Steps**

1. Select a format from the **Paragraph Tag** pop-up menu.

2. Select the check box by the **Subscript/Superscript** pop-up menu.

TIP

Use a superscript to create a second reference to a footnote. For example, if you insert a footnote "_a_" on a page, and want to reference to it again later on in the page, insert a superscript "_a_" and cross-reference it to the actual footnote. For more information on footnotes, see "Creating Footnotes" in Chapter 5.

3. Select the script style you want from the pop-up menu.

4. Click **Update All** to make the settings permanent to the tag.

What To Do If

- If you want to define the size of subscripts and superscripts, select **Document** from the Format menu and specify the size in the **Size** text box.

    The size is based on a percentage of the point size of the text being formatted as a subscript or superscript. For example, if the point size defined for a paragraph tag is 10 points, the subscript or superscript text will be 6.5 points for a size set at 65 percent.

- If you want to define the offset of subscripts and superscripts, select **Document** from the Format menu and specify the offset in the **Offset** text box.

    The offset is based on a percentage of the point size of the text being formatted as a subscript or superscript. For example, if the point size defined for a paragraph tag is 10 points, the subscript or superscript offset will be 4 points up or down respectively, for a size set at 65 percent.

See Also

- Applying a Font Style, p. 69.
- Creating Footnotes, p. 152.

Defining Headings

Headings play a key role in your documents. They are the visual and content guide for a document. Different types of headings, when used consistently, provide a road map for readers. They use the visual cues to establish where they are in the document, and the content cues to establish how important the information in a section is to them.

There are a variety of ways in which you can format headings to differentiate the types or levels of sections they are heading and the kind of information that follows them.

Headings are used to generate tables of contents and to use as cross-references. As such, in FrameMaker each type of heading needs its own paragraph tag. FrameMaker provides you with the flexibility to create

- Normal headings, which you can format any way you want
- Side heads, which run right beside the text instead of before it
- Run-in heads, which are the first word or phrase within a paragraph

Each of these types of headings can have its own paragraph tag and can therefore be used to generate lists or as cross-references.

Defining Side Headings | 70

Side heads are frequently used to denote large sections within a document or to make it easy to scan a document for specific information. Format text as a side head has always been a painful process for writing and layout tools.

This version of FrameMaker introduces a powerful new function that enables you to create a side head and to establish its width and its positioning with minimum effort. You can specify these settings in the new Pagination Properties window (see Figure 4.12).

Assumptions

- The Paragraph Designer window is open in the Pagination Properties.
- The format is already created.

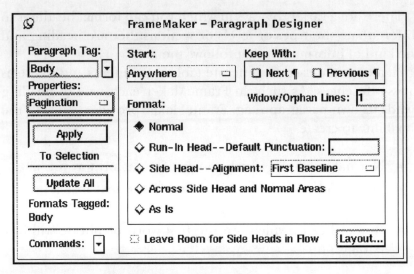

Figure 4.12   The Pagination Properties window.

Exceptions

- You can use these steps for text that is not tagged, or if no tag exists, by clicking **Apply To Selection** instead of **Update All**. However, all paragraphs are affected by a side head. Once the side head area is defined, all normal paragraphs in the text flow move to the normal-text area of the text column.

- Full-width heads do not move to the normal-text area; they remain the same.

- You do not need to create a separate text flow or column to define a side head. This is defined using the normal text column and flow.

- Indents and tabs set for other paragraphs are relative to the normal-text area. Do not change them to match the new width of the text column.

Steps

1. Click **Layout** to open the Side Head Layout dialog box, shown in Figure 4.13.

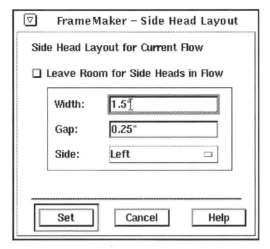

Figure 4.13 The Side-Head Layout dialog box.

2. Turn on **Leave Room for Side Heads in Flow**.

3. Specify the width of the side head.

4. Specify the gap between the side head and the normal-text column.

5. Select the side of the page the side heads will be placed on from the **Side** pop-up menu. You have the option to select the Left side, Right side, Inside, or Outside of a page. The Inside and Outside options refer to the sides in a double-sided document.

6. Click **Set**.

7. Select an option from the **Side Head Alignment** pop-up menu to align the side head with respect to the paragraph beside it.

8. Click **Update All** to make the settings permanent to the tag.

TIP

Table indents are not affected by using side heads. If you want your tables to align with the normal-text column, reset the indents to match the normal-text column width.

What To Do If

• If you want to turn off the side heads and return all text to a single area in the text column, turn off **Leave Room for Side Heads in Flow**.

- If you want to create a full-width paragraph when side heads are turned on, click on the paragraph you want to designate as full-width, go to the **Pagination** Properties, click **Across Side Head** and **Normal Areas**, and click **Apply to Selection**.

71 ▷ Defining Run-In Headings

Run-in headings are frequently used as lower-level headings or headings for short sections. FrameMaker enables you to create separate paragraph tags for run-in headings, even though they visually are part of a paragraph. This enables you to use different font settings for the run-in headings, yet make them consistent throughout. Most importantly, it enables you to use the headings to generate tables of contents and to cross-reference.

Assumptions

- The Paragraph Designer window is open in the Pagination Properties.
- The format is already created.

Exceptions

- You can use these steps for text that is not tagged, or if no tag exists, by clicking **Apply To Selection** instead of **Update All**.

Steps

1. Click **Run-in Head** and specify the punctuation and spacing after the head in the Default Punctuation text box.
2. Click **Update All** to make the settings permanent to the tag.
3. Go to the **Default Font** properties.

> **TIP**
>
> Run-in headings are separate paragraphs, even though they are in the same line as normal text. As separate paragraphs, you can include them in tables of contents, running headers, and footers, and you can cross-reference them.

4. Change the run-in head's font, if necessary, to make it stand out from its surrounding text.

5. Click **Update All** to make the settings permanent to the tag.

What To Do If

- If you want the paragraph that contains a run-in head to be set further apart from the preceding paragraph than a regular paragraph, set the Space Above of the run-in head to be larger than the Space Below of the body text.

Creating Reverse Color Headings   72

As a matter of style, you might want to create a format for reverse color headings. These headings are white on black, or whatever color combination suits your document. FrameMaker does not provide a heading style you can use for this purpose. However, there is a workaround using a one-cell table and its properties.

Assumptions

- You've created a one-cell table format and the insertion point is inside it.
- You've created a new paragraph tag for the reverse color text.
- The Paragraph Designer is open.
- The Table Designer is open.

Steps

1. Go to the **Default Font Properties** window.

2. Set the color of the paragraph to **White**.

3. Click **Update All**.

4. Apply the paragraph tag to the paragraph in the table cell.

5. Go to the Table Designer.
   The properties should match the format of your one-cell format.

6. Go to the **Shading** properties and select **100%** for the body fill of the table.

7. Click **Update All**.
   The table format should store the name of the paragraph tag in the cell.

8. Every time you need a reverse color title, insert the table format you created.
   All the properties, including the reverse color text and fill, should be present in the new table.

What To Do If

- None.

See Also

- Creating Tables, p. 196.

Adding Graphics to a Paragraph

Occasionally, you might want to use a rule or icon above or below a heading or a type of paragraph, such as an alert or a warning. For these occasions, FrameMaker enables you to create a rule or graphic using the graphics tool, and to add it to a paragraph tag as one of its properties. A paragraph tag that has a graphic assigned to it will always appear with it. Conversely, removing the graphic from the tag is as easy as just changing a setting, and the graphic will disappear from any paragraph tagged with it.

Creating the Graphics in the Reference Page   73

The first step to using a graphic with paragraph is creating it some-where where FrameMaker can find it. To do this, the Reference Pages are the appropriate place. FrameMaker looks for frames containing graphics to use with paragraphs in the Reference Pages.

When you create the frame and graphics to use for paragraphs, you also specify the spacing between the text and the graphic. FrameMaker uses the width and length of the frame, not of the graphic itself, when adding it to a paragraph tag.

Assumptions

- You are at the Reference Pages.
- You want to create a graphic to use above or below a specific type of paragraph, such as a heading.

Exceptions

- Although you can keep boilerplate graphics in the Reference Pages, you cannot attach them to a paragraph tag anywhere but above and below the paragraph. To place graphics somewhere other than above or below a paragraph, use an anchored frame.

Steps

1. Draw an unanchored frame.
   When you draw the frame, the Frame Name dialog box opens.
2. Specify a name for the frame.
3. Click **Set**.
4. Draw the graphic in the frame, or import a graphic file into the frame.

5. Type the frame's name above the frame to keep track of the frames, using the **Text Line** tool in the graphic tools palette.

6. Go back to **Body Pages**.

What To Do If

- If you want to adjust the distance between the graphic and the paragraph it is attached to, adjust the height of the reference frame. The height of the frame determines the position of the graphic relative to the paragraph.

- If you want to rename the reference frame, select the frame, click the frame's name on the status bar, to display the Frame Name dialog box, and change the name.

- If you rename the reference frame, be sure to update the related paragraph tags. Otherwise, the paragraphs will not have the graphic attached.

See Also

- Creating Graphics, p. 289.
- Importing a Graphic, p. 278.
- Adding Graphics Above or Below a Paragraph, below.

74 Adding Graphics Above or Below a Paragraph

Once you create the frame and graphic to use with paragraphs, FrameMaker can use it. You can see the list of frames available in the Frame Above and Frame Below pop-up menus in the Advanced Properties window. Every frame you create in the Reference Pages is listed in both lists, so you can use one for both above and below or different ones for above and below.

_____ **Assumptions**

- You have already created a reference frame with a graphic in the Reference Pages.

_____ **Exceptions**

- You cannot attach graphics to a paragraph tag anywhere but above and below the paragraph. To place graphics some-where other than above or below a paragraph, use an an-chored frame.

_____ **Steps**

1. Go to the **Reference Pages**.
2. Draw or import the graphic in a reference frame.
3. Go back to the **Body Pages**.
4. Click on the paragraph above which you want to insert a line.
5. Open the Paragraph Designer.
6. In the Advanced Properties, select the name of the refer-ence frame from the Frame Above or Frame Below pop-up menu.

_____ **What To Do If**

- If you want to change the graphic you are using, select the new reference frame from the Frame Above or Frame Below pop-up menu.

- If you want to have the same graphic above and below the paragraph, select the reference frame from both the Frame Above and Frame Below pop-up menus.

- If you want to have a graphic above and a different one below the paragraph, select the respective reference frames from the Frame Above and Frame Below pop-up menus.

TIP

If you want to place an icon or specific text beside para-graphs throughout your document, you can create a side head with a very small point size and add the graphic or text above or below the paragraph using the Advanced Prop-erties. Then all you need to do is add an extra paragraph before the text para-graph and apply the side head tag con-taining the graphic. The graphic, how-ever, will not be perfectly lined up with the paragraph; it will be slightly above or below the first line.

- If you want to create a box around a paragraph, create a single-cell table without heading or footing rows. Then adjust the size and format of the text in the table to look the way you want.

   If you want the cell text to be different from the cell body tag you already have, create a new tag for it. If you intend to use this box more than once, create a table format for it. You can also reverse the color or use other special effects in the table.

See Also

- Using Reference Pages, p. 379.
- Chapter 6, "Using Tables."

Chapter
5

Creating Footnotes

Creating Lists

Creating Cross-References

Using Variables

USING
WRITING
TOOLS

Creating Footnotes

FrameMaker footnotes are versatile and very easy to use. Once you set the properties you want for footnotes and their reference characters, FrameMaker automatically takes care of numbering, positioning, and deleting footnotes as necessary.

You can specify the look and position of footnotes and footnote references. Futhermore, if you move, add, or delete text that contains a footnote reference, FrameMaker adds or deletes the footnote and renumbers the others. You can specify more than one reference to a footnote by using cross-references. If this is the case, and the footnote has been deleted, you will have unresolved cross-references.

FrameMaker handles table footnotes similarly to regular footnotes. You follow the same steps to use or set up the properties for table footnotes. Table footnotes are displayed below a table, and, unlike regular footnotes, they can appear on a different page than the footnote reference. For example, in a multipage table, the footnotes appear below the end of the table, not at the bottom of each page that contains the table segments.

75   Inserting Footnotes

To insert a footnote, decide the position of the footnote reference and insert the footnote. FrameMaker numbers and formats the reference, renumbers any footnotes that follow, formats the footnote text, and inserts a separation above the first footnote in a page.

Assumptions

- You want to insert either a regular footnote or a table footnote.

- The cursor is positioned where you want to insert the reference to the footnote.

_____ **Exceptions**

- You can't edit the characters that denote the footnotes using these steps. For information on controlling these characters, see "Specifying Footnote Numbering Styles."

_____ **Steps**

1. Select **Footnote** from the Special menu (or press **Esc r s f**).
   FrameMaker inserts the footnote reference and places the cursor where the footnote will be. If you are using numbers for your footnotes, they will be renumbered accordingly.

2. Type the text of the footnote.

3. Click where you want to continue working on the main text.

> **TIP**
> To increase the amount of space allowed in each page or column for footnotes, adjust the maximum footnote space per column. For more information, see "Formatting Footnotes".

_____ **What To Do If**

- If you want to delete a footnote, select the footnote reference and press **Delete**. When you select the reference, you can see the footnote is selected as well.

- If you want to place two footnote references in a row, type a space or comma before you place the second one. Otherwise, FrameMaker will not create the second footnote.

- If you want to change the format of footnotes, modify the paragraph tag you are using for it.

_____ **See Also**

- Specifying Footnote Numbering Styles, p. 159.
- Formatting Footnotes, p. 157.

Inserting Multiple References to a Footnote

You can insert multiple references to a footnote by using cross-references. Insert the first reference to the footnote normally, then create cross-references to the existing footnote. To format the extra references properly, make sure they are superscripts. Use the format definition **<Superscript><$paranumonly>** to number and format references correctly.

Assumptions

- You want to insert an extra reference for either a regular footnote or for a table footnote.
- You created a cross-reference format for extra footnote references using the <Superscript>< $paranumonly> building blocks.
- The cursor is positioned where you want to insert the extra reference to the footnote.
- You saved the document.

Exceptions

- None.

> **TIP**
> The cross-reference format needs to display the footnote format as a superscript. Use the <Superscript> <$paranumonly> building blocks for the cross-reference formats to display the number as a superscript.

Steps

1. Select **Cross-Reference** from the Special menu.
2. Select the **Footnote** or **TableFootnote** paragraph tag from the Source Type list.
   If you are using another Paragraph tag for the footnote or table footnote, select that one instead.
3. Select the footnote to which you are cross-referencing from the **Reference Source** list.

4. Select the cross-reference format you created from the **Format** pop-up menu.

5. Click Insert (or press **Esc s c**).
   FrameMaker inserts a cross-reference to the footnote that should look exactly like the first footnote reference.

_____ **What To Do If**

- If you want to create more than one extra reference to a footnote, repeat these steps.

- If the document changes, make sure you check that the cross-references are still resolving correctly. If footnotes are moved, deleted, or renumbered, FrameMaker does not update the cross-references automatically.

_____ **See Also**

- Creating Cross-References, p. 172.

Inserting Endnotes | 77

FrameMaker does not create endnotes automatically in the same way it does footnotes. However, there is a work-around that enables you to create and maintain endnotes by using cross-references. In this respect, endnotes are more difficult to maintain, and you have to remember to check and update your cross-references as you update your document.

To format the endnote references properly, make sure they are superscripts. You can number and format references correctly by using the format definition <Superscript><$paranumonly>.

_____ **Assumptions**

- You want to insert an endnote either in regular text or in a cell.

- You created a paragraph tag for endnotes.

- You created a cross-reference format for endnote references using the <Superscript>< $paranumonly> building blocks.

- You saved the document.

Exceptions

- Inserting an endnote does not automatically place notes at the end of your document. You have to do this manually.

- The references to an endnote are cross-references, not footnote references.

Steps

TIP

The cross-reference format should make the endnote format stand out from the text around it. The <Superscript> <$paranumonly> building blocks for the cross-reference formats display the number as a superscript.

1. Type in the endnotes at the end of your document using the **endnote** paragraph tag.

2. Position your cursor where you want to insert a reference to an endnote.

3. Insert a cross-reference to the endnote (or press **Esc s c**).

What To Do If

- If you want to delete an endnote, make sure to delete all cross-references to it.

- If you move text that contains a cross-reference to an endnote, make sure that the order of the endnotes is still correct.

- If you want to change the format of the endnote, modify the paragraph tag you created for it.

See Also

- Creating Cross-References, p. 172.

Formatting Footnotes | 78

FrameMaker provides a default setting for footnotes. However, you may find that the default does not fit the design of your document. In this case, you can modify the settings to match your style. FrameMaker enables you to modify the style of the footnote references, the numbering format, and the paragraph format for the footnote text. You can also specify whether a separator should be used and if so, the distance between the separator and the first footnote or the text above it.

You can modify the settings for both regular and table footnotes using these steps. However, to modify the table footnote formats, you need to place the insertion point in a table. That way, the Table Footnote dialog box will be displayed instead of the regular Footnote dialog box.

Assumptions

- There are paragraph tags in the catalog that you want to use for footnotes or table footnotes.
- The cursor is positioned in regular text if you are changing the format of regular footnotes.
- The cursor is positioned in a table if you are changing the format of table footnotes.
- The footnotes are placed above the bottom margin.

Exceptions

- You cannot change the footnote numbering format using the paragraph tag numbering properties.
- You can assign a new paragraph format using the Footnote Properties after you have inserted footnotes only to footnotes inserted after you make the change. To apply the new paragraph tag to existing footnotes, apply the tag to them directly.

- For table footnotes, you cannot set a maximum space for footnotes, restart the numbering at each page, or set a starting footnote number.

Steps

1. Select Footnote Properties from the Format menu (or press **Esc o f**).

   If you are formatting regular footnotes, the Footnote Properties dialog box opens. If you are formatting table footnotes, the Table Footnote Properties dialog box opens. Both dialog boxes look exactly the same (see Figure 5.1).

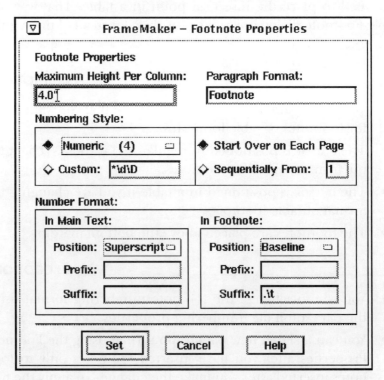

Figure 5.1   The format text boxes of the Footnote Properties dialog box.

2. Type the space you want to allow for footnotes in each column in the **Maximum Height Per Column** text box.

3. Type the paragraph format you want to use for footnotes in the **Paragraph Format** text box.

4. Click **Set**.

_____ **What To Do If**

- If you want to modify the format for footnotes without changing the paragraph tag assigned to them, use the Paragraph Designer to update the tag.

_____ **See Also**

- Specifying Footnote Numbering Styles, below.

Specifying Footnote Numbering Styles | 79

You can specify the numbering style for footnotes and the custom characters to use, and you can set regular footnotes to start at any number you want. If you set up custom characters, FrameMaker uses them in the order you specify them, and repeats the sequence after it uses all the characters available.

You can also specify the format of the reference characters in the main text and in the footnotes. These must be specified separately; therefore, you have the flexibility to specify superscripts for the reference characters in the main text, and normal in the footnote itself. Both numbers can be subscripts, superscripts, or baseline numbers. Also, they can both have a prefix or suffix. For example, you can number footnotes according to their chapter, and you can add punctuation after the reference character in the footnote.

Making changes to the numbering properties for footnotes affects all footnotes. Note that the font and size of the numbers are determined by the font and size of the text around them.

Assumptions

- The cursor is positioned in regular text if you are changing the format of regular footnotes.

- The cursor is positioned in a table if you are changing the format of table footnotes.

- The Footnote Properties dialog box is open (to open it, press **Esc o f**).

Exceptions

- For table footnotes, you cannot restart the numbering at each page or set a starting footnote number.

Steps

> **TIP**
>
> If you want to change the subscript or superscript settings for footnotes, use the superscript and subscript settings in the **Document Format** dialog box. Note that changes to these settings will affect all subscripts and superscripts in your document.

1. Select the numbering style and format from the **Numbering Style** and **Number Format** pop-up menu.

2. Select the position for the reference number in the **In Main Text: Position** pop-up menu.

3. Select the position of the reference number of the footnote in the **In Footnote: Position** pop-up menu.

4. Specify any prefix or suffix for the footnote number in the **Prefix** or **Suffix** dialog boxes.
   You have the flexibility to assign different prefixes and suffixes to the reference number and the footnote number.

5. Click **Set**.

What To Do If

- If you want to specify a character other than a number as the footnote character, use the **Custom** text box to specify the characters. If you want to specify a special character in the Custom dialog box, use the backslash equivalent for it.

- If you want to change the look of the subscript or superscript, go to the **Document Properties** window. For information, see "Specifying Subscripts and Superscripts."

_____ **See Also**

- Using Special Characters, p. 42.
- Specifying Subscripts and Superscripts, p. 139.

Modifying Footnote Separators   80

A footnote separator is the line, or other graphic element, that separates regular text from footnotes. FrameMaker places this separator automatically above the first footnote in a page.

Footnote separators are stored in a frame on the Reference Pages. You can control the distance between the text above or below the separator by adjusting the height of the frame. You can also change the content of the frame to specify a different graphic element as a separator.

_____ **Assumptions**

- You are in the Reference Pages.

_____ **Exceptions**

- The footnote separators are not specified in the Advanced properties of the paragraph tag assigned to a footnote.

_____ **Steps**

1. Look for the **Reference Page** that contains the footnote separator frame.
   The regular footnote separator is labeled "Footnote," and the table footnote separator is labeled "Table Footnote."

2. Modify the separator. You can modify either the frame or the graphic.
    You can make any modification or addition to the line inside the frame using the graphic tools.

3. Go back to the **Body Pages**.
    The changes made to the footnote separator should be reflected in the existing footnotes.

What To Do If

- If you want to place the first footnote closer to the text or table, reduce the height of the frame.

- If you want to place the first footnote closer to the separator, move the graphic down inside the frame.

- If you do not want to use a separator, go to the **Reference Pages** and delete the graphic inside the frame, but do not delete the frame.

- If you want to change the distance between footnotes and regular text, adjust the height of the frame. Whether there is a graphic element in the frame or not does not affect this setting.

See Also

- Using Reference Pages, p. 379.

Creating Lists

Aside from regular body text, the most frequently used editorial element is a list. Bulleted lists, numbered lists, check lists, and numbered paragraphs are used and updated constantly. Every time you make a change to any of these elements, you have to make sure everything else related to it is updated as well.

For example, whenever you reorganize a book, the chapter numbers have to be updated to match the changes. Chapter numbers may affect figure and table numbers, section numbers, and page numbers. Also, whenever you create a numbered list of any sort, any time you change or update it you have to make sure all the numbers are adjusted appropriately.

FrameMaker's autonumbering capabilities enable you to create lists or series of numbered paragraphs with minimal effort and without having to renumber items manually. You can create paragraph tags to suit every type of numbering your document requires.

Also, the same features that allow you to create autonumbered paragraphs enable you to create paragraphs with specific characters or words as part of their autonumber format. For example, you can create bulleted lists, figure captions that include text and autonumbering, or labels composed from plain text, such as the "To:" and "From:" labels of a memo.

Creating Numbered Lists | 81

Creating numbered lists and paragraphs means creating paragraph tags that contain a specific autonumber format for the numbering style you need. The characteristics of the numbering are determined by the building blocks, or counters, and character formats you choose for the autonumber format in the Numbering properties of the Paragraph Designer.

You can also use the autonumber format to create bulleted lists, check lists, and labels for a paragraph. You can use building blocks, text, or any combination thereof. Use the character formats to give the character or text a different look from the normal text. If you leave the Character Format text box empty, the character or text takes the default font of the paragraph tag.

Assumptions

- The Paragraph Designer is open in the Numbering properties window.

- The format is already created.
- You've decided on the building blocks to use for the type of autonumbering you need. You can use more than one building block, or counter, to define an autonumber format.

Exceptions

- FrameMaker always continues to increment from one autonumbered tag to the next unless a reset tag is used in between. Always use a tag to reset the numbering at the beginning of a new list.

Steps

1. Select the building blocks with the numbering style appropriate for your list from the **Building Blocks** list. The building blocks available to you are listed in Table 5.1.

Table 5.1   Autonumbering Building Blocks

Building Block (Counter)	Results in...
\b	Bullet symbol
\t	Tab
< n >	Arabic number (1, 2, 3,...) set to the same value as the number preceding it
< n+ >	Arabic number set to increment by 1
< n = 1 >	Arabic number set to 1, you can set this building block to any number

2. Select a character format for the numbers from the **Character Format** scroll list.
   The character formats listed in this list are formats in the Character Catalog.

3. Select a position for the number from the **Position** pop-up menu.

4. Click **Update All**.

5. Go to the **Basic** properties.

6. Set the tab positions and indents for the paragraph.
   If you insert a tab in the autonumber format (**/t**), define a tab stop. Move the left indent and the first tab stop to the same position in the ruler.

7. Click **Update All**.

TIP

For simple numbered lists, create a tag with the counter set to 1, such as < *n* = 1 >, to reset the lists; otherwise the numbers continue to increment. Use tags such as Item for resetting and "Item +" for incrementing.

Examples Autonumber Formats	Example Results
\b	• This is a bullet symbol
\b\t	• This is an item with a tab
Figure <n> . <n+ >	Figure 1.1 Figure 1.2
Chapter <n+ >	Chapter 1 Chapter 2
< n = 1 >< n+ > < n = 1 >< n+ >	1. First item in a list 2. Next item in the list 1. First item in another list 2. Next item in the new list

(continues)

Table 5.1 (cont)	
Building Block (Counter)	**Results in . . .**
< a >< A >	Alphabetic numbering style (a, b, c, . . . , or, A, B, C, . . .) set to the same value as the number preceding it
< a+ >< A+ >	Alphabetic numbering style set to increment by 1
< a = 1 >< A = 1 >	Alphabetic numbering style set to 1, you can set this building block to any letter
< r >< R >	Roman numeral (i, ii, iii, . . . , or I, II, III, . . .) set to the same value as the number preceding it
< r+ >< R+ >	Roman numeral set to increment by 1
< r = 1 >< R = 1 >	Roman numeral set to 1, you can set this building block to any numeral
< >	Autonumber set to the same value as the one preceding but that does not display
< = 0 >	Autonumber reset to zero that does not display (This building block is not in the list; it needs to be typed in.)

1. Indents are for illustration purposes only.

Examples Autonumber Formats	Example Results
Figure < A > . < a+ >	Figure B.a
	Figure B.b
	Figure B.c
Section < A+ >	Section A
	Section B
< a = 1 >< a+ >	a. First item in a list
< a = 1 >< a+ >	b. Next item in the list
	a. First item in another list
	b. Next item in the new list
Figure < R > − < r+ >	Figure III-i
	Figure III-ii
Subsection < r+ >	Subsection i
	Subsection ii
< R = 1 >< R+ >	I. First item in a list
< R = 1 >< R+ >	II. Next item in the list
	I. First item in another list
	II. Next item in the new list
< n+ >< = 0 >< = 0 >	1. Santa Clara[1]
<>< a+ ><>	a. Marketing
<>< a+ ><>	b. Info
<><>< r+ >	Development
<><>< r+ >	i Jennifer A.
< n+ >< = 0 >< = 0 >	ii Lee T.
<>< a+ ><>	2. Raleigh
<><>< r+ >	a. Marketing
	b. Info
	Development
	i Mary C.

What To Do If

- If you want to use autonumbering for a table, create auto-numbering tags specifically for that. Set the left indent and first tab stop to a value appropriate for the space of the table cells.

- If you want to create a bulleted list, select the bullet building block (**/b**) from the Building Blocks list, followed by a tab (**/t**) or by spaces.

- If you want to use another symbol for bullets, such as a check list, create a character tag that uses the font you want to use for the bullet, such as Zapf Dingbats.

  When you create the bullet paragraph tag, assign the character corresponding to the symbol you want to use instead of using **/b**. Select the character tag you created from the Character Format list.

- If you want to create a label, such as "To:" and "From:" in a memo, type the label in the **Autonumber Format** text box, followed by a tab or spaces.

- If you want to create a tag that places specific text in a line, such as "To: Lynn Rollins," type the text with any required tabs or spaces in the **Autonumber Format** text box.

  Note that you cannot use this feature for paragraphs that are more than one line long.

See Also

- Specifying Cell Numbering, p. 255.
- Defining Different Series of Lists, below.

82 Defining Different Series of Lists

Many documents require several types of autonumbered paragraphs. For example, your document may have numbers for chapters, sections, figure and table captions, and numbered lists. In cases like this, you need to use **series labels** to identify one numbering series from another.

Each series is numbered independently from every other series, and an autonumbered paragraph's number is determined by the previous paragraph with the same series label in the flow. Therefore, different sets of steps would not require a different series, and if you base the numbering of one paragraph on that of another, such as section numbers based on chapter numbers, they must belong to the same series.

Since the autonumber format can use multiple counters, you can create a variety of paragraphs based on others. Each counter basically increments according to the building block used in its format. If you think of it in terms of a table, you can visualize how to use the counters to create levels of numbers based on previous paragraphs within the same series. This technique works without affecting the counters of the previous level of number.

For example:

Format	Result	What the counter does

E:$< n+ >$. $< n = 0 >$
  $< = 0 >$
	2.0	$<$increments$>$.
		  $<$resets to zero$>$
		  $<$resets, not displayed$>$

E:$< n >$. $< n+ ><>$	2.1	$<$stays the same$>$.
		  $<$increments$>$
		  $<$stays, not displayed$>$

E:$< n >$. $< n >$.
  $< n+ >$
	2.1.1	$<$stays$>$.$<$stays$>$.
		  $<$increments
		  and displays$>$

If you follow the counters in this example vertically, you can see how the counters in the same series increment based on one another.

Assumptions

- You have more than one type of paragraph that requires autonumbering.
- You've decided on the building blocks to use for the type of autonumbered paragraphs you need.

Exceptions

- Do not use different series of labels for numbered paragraphs based on section numbers. For example, for Chapter 2 you want the figure and table numbering to be Figure 2.1, Figure 2.2, Table 2.1, Table 2.2, and so on. For more information, see "What To Do If" for this task.
- You don't need to use different series labels for outline style numbering.

Steps

> **TIP**
>
> Decide on a default series that you use for formats that do not need independent numbering, such as three levels of lists that get reset at the first item anyway. This will help you keep track of relatively few series and could prevent numbering problems in files in a book.

1. Make a list of the different types of autonumbering you need.
   For example, chapter numbers, section numbers, figure and table numbers, three levels of numbered lists, and two levels of procedural steps.
2. Select an alphabetic character as a label for each series.
   For example, C for chapters, S for sections, F for figures, and T for tables.
3. Create the tags for the different types of autonumbered paragraphs you need.
   Type the label and a colon in the Autonumber Format text box before you select the building blocks.

What To Do If

- If you want to create numbered paragraphs based on section numbers, they must be in the same series. You can use building blocks such as the following:

Building Blocks	Results in ...
S:Section< n+ >< = 0 >< = 0 >	Section 1

Because ...

The first counter is set to increment; the first instance of this tag starts the count. The second and third counter reset at 0. This resets the second and third counter at every instance of this tag.

Building Blocks	Results in ...
S:Figure< n > . < n+ ><>	Figure 1.1

Because ...

The Figure and Table tags keep the first counter the same to reflect the section number, then increment the second and third counter respectively. The Figure and Table each use a different counter and keep the other's counter to the same.

Building Blocks	Results in ...
S:Figure< n > . < n+ ><>	Figure 1.2
S:Table< n > . <>< n+ >	Table 1.1
S:Table< n > . <>< n+ >	Table 1.2
S:Section< n+ >< = 0 >< = 0 >	Section 2
S:Table< n > . <>< n+ >	Table 2.1
S:Figure< n > . < n+ ><>	Figure 2.1
S:Table< n > . <>< n+ >	Table 2.2
S:Figure< n > . < n+ ><>	Figure 2.2
S:Table< n > . <>< n+ >	Table 2.3
S:Section< n+ >< = 0 >< = 0 >	Section 3
S:Table< n > . <>< n+ >	Table 3.1
S:Figure< n > . < n+ ><>	Figure 3.1

- If you want to create outline-style lists, use the same technique just described. You can also use this technique when using alphabetic characters rather then numbers. For example:

Building Blocks	Results in ...

For numerical outlines:

H:	< n+ >< = 0 >< = 0 >	1
H:	< n > . < n+ ><>	1.1
H:	< n > . < n > . < n+ >	1.1.1
H:	< n+ >< = 0 >< = 0 >	2
H:	< n > . < n+ ><>	2.1
H:	< n > . < n > . < n+ >	2.2.1

For mixed outlines (indents are for illustration purposes only):

H:	< R+ >< = 0 >< = 0 >	I
H:	<>< n+ > . <>	1.
H:	<><>< a+ >)	a)
H:	<><>< a+ >)	b)
H:	<>< n+ > . <>	2.
H:	<><>< a+ >)	a)
H:	<><>< a+ >)	b)
H:	< R+ >< = 0 >< = 0 >	II
H:	<>< n+ > . <>	1.
H:	<><>< a+ >)	a)
H:	<><>< a+ >)	b)

See Also

- Creating Numbered Lists, p. 163.

Creating Cross-References

Cross-references are a simple concept, but both their manual and automatic implementation can be complex, time-consuming, and tedious. With FrameMaker you can handle cross-references in a relatively simple and quick manner. However, as materials get updated, or you start cross-referencing within documents and document sets, or you move or delete source cross-references, you're faced with unresolved cross-references.

The advantage of automating cross-references is in maintaining them more effectively, finding and pinpointing any problems with them quickly, and resolving those problems efficiently and painlessly. Also, since automatic cross-references are so flexible, you may find yourself using them for different purposes, such as endnotes or extra references to footnotes. However, you must remember to maintain and update cross-references and to check for unresolved instances frequently.

Inserting Cross-References ▽ 83

FrameMaker enables you to use two types of cross-references: to paragraphs and to spots. Paragraph cross-references are references to specific paragraphs, such as headings, table titles, or figure captions. Spot cross-references are references to specific words or sentences within a paragraph. When you insert a cross-reference to a paragraph, FrameMaker also inserts a marker on the paragraph to which you are referencing. If you insert a cross-reference to a spot, you need to insert a cross-reference marker and identifier at the spot first.

The cross-reference markers keep track of the paragraphs and spots which you reference. FrameMaker then knows that the source of a cross-reference was moved or deleted when you update cross-references.

Assumptions

- If you are cross-referencing another document, the document is open and saved.
- The insertion point is placed where you want the cross-reference.

Exceptions

- You cannot insert a cross-reference in text created with the graphics tool.

Steps

1. Select **Cross-Reference** from the Special Menu (or press **Esc s c**). The Cross-Reference dialog box opens (see Figure 5.2).

2. Select the document you are cross-referencing from the **Source Document** pop-up menu.
   If the information you are cross-referencing is not in another document, set the pop-up menu to **Current**, since the source is in the current or open document.

3. Select the paragraph type you are cross-referencing from the **Source Type** scroll list.

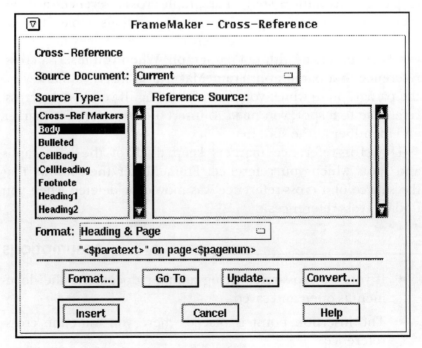

Figure 5.2   The Cross-Reference dialog box.

FrameMaker displays all the paragraph tags available in the document that you are cross-referencing in the Source Type scroll list. Once you select the paragraph tag, all the paragraphs in the document with that tag are displayed.

4. Select the specific paragraph you want to cross-reference from the **Reference Source** scroll list.

5. Select the format of the cross-reference from the **Format** pop-up menu.
   The format of the cross-reference determines how the text appears where you insert the cross-reference. For example, assuming that you selected a heading in the previous steps, if you choose the format Heading and Page, the text would show the text of the heading and the page number where the heading is located; for example, " 'Creating Footnotes' on page 109."

6. Click **Insert**.

What To Do If

- If you want to insert a spot cross-reference, first insert a cross-reference marker on the spot to which you want to cross-reference. When you insert a cross-reference to a spot, select **Cross-Ref Markers** from the Source Type scroll list.

- If you want to display the text you are cross-referencing, double-click the cross-reference and click **Go To** in the Cross-Reference dialog box.

- If you want to generate a list of external cross-references, select **Generate** from the File menu. You can select **List of References** from the List pop-up menu, and specify **External Cross-Refs** in the Set Up File dialog box.

- If you want to convert your cross-references to text, you can convert all the cross-references in a document, all the cross-references with a specific format, or all the cross-references in selected text. To convert to text, open the **Cross-Reference** dialog box and click **Convert**. Indicate which cross-reference to convert, and click **Convert**. Once they are converted, you can edit them like regular text. However, FrameMaker does not recognize converted cross references as cross-references; therefore, you must maintain and update them manually.

See Also

- Creating Spots to Cross-Reference, below.

84 Creating Spots to Cross-Reference

You have to mark a spot to reference before you can insert a spot cross-reference. A spot cross-reference points to a word or sentence within a paragraph, as opposed to the full paragraph. Unlike a paragraph, a word or sentence does not have a handle that Frame-Maker can point to, such as a tag, so you have to create it.

Mark a spot to reference by placing a cross-reference marker in that spot. Give the marker a name or identifier so you can track it later. You can keep track of the markers by generating a list.

Assumptions

- You want to insert a spot cross-reference.
- The insertion point is placed where you want to mark the spot.

Exceptions

- None.

Steps

1. Select **Marker** from the Special Menu (or press **Esc s m**). Figure 5.3 shows the Markers dialog box.

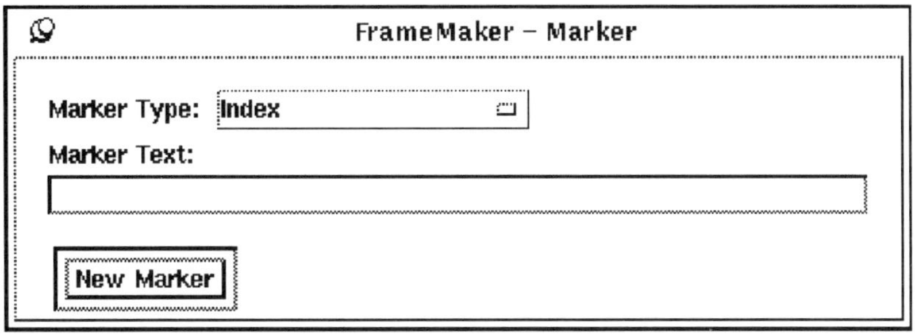

```
 ⊙                    FrameMaker – Marker

  Marker Type:  Index                    ⌑
  Marker Text:
  ┌─────────────────────────────────────────┐
  └─────────────────────────────────────────┘

    ┌──────────────┐
    │  New Marker  │
    └──────────────┘
```

Figure 5.3   The Markers dialog box.

2. Select **Cross-Ref** from the Marker Type pop-up menu.

3. Type the name of your marker in the **Marker Text** text box. When you insert a cross-reference to this spot, the name is listed in the Reference Source scroll list when you select Cross-Ref Markers from the Source Type scroll list.

4. Click **New Marker**.

What To Do If

- If you want to generate a list of cross-reference markers, select **Generate** from the File menu. You can select **List of Markers** from the List pop-up menu, and specify **Cross References** in the Set Up File dialog box.

- If you delete a paragraph that contains a cross-reference marker, any cross-references to that spot will be unresolved. For information on dealing with unresolved cross-references, see "Resolving Missing Cross-References."

See Also

- Creating Generated Lists, p. 424.
- Resolving Missing Cross-References, p. 184.

> **TIP**
>
> The marker text shows up in the Cross-Reference dialog box in the Reference Source list, so you can pick a spot to cross-reference. A descriptive identifier for spot cross-references helps you pick the right spot to reference.

Creating and Modifying Cross-Reference Formats

You determine the content of a cross-reference by specifying its format. A cross-reference will pick out the information it needs from its source depending on its format.

For example, if the format includes the following words and building blocks:

> See <Emphasis>< $paratext>
>   <Default Font> on page < $pagenum>

the cross-reference's content could be: "See **Opening your Bank Account** on page 22." On the other hand, if the format extracted the page number only, such as in

> See page < $pagenum>

the cross-reference would read "See page 22."

FrameMaker provides a few default formats that you can modify, or you can create your own. You can use a combination of text and building blocks, and you can combine as many building blocks as you need to use cross-references effectively.

Formats also enable you to maintain consistency in the style of your cross-references. For example, you can establish a style for referencing other documents that is different from the style you use to reference sections of the same document. You can also be consistent in the way you reference figures, tables, or examples, across all your documents.

Assumptions

- The Cross-Reference dialog box is open (you can press **Esc s c** to open it).
- You do not want to use an existing cross-reference format.

Exceptions

- None.

_____ **Steps**

1. Click **Format**.

   The Edit Cross-Reference Format dialog box (see Figure 5.4) opens.

2. Type a name for a new cross-reference format in the **Name** text box, or click on the name of the cross-reference format you want to modify in the **Formats** scroll list.

   Note that format names are case-sensitive. For example, you can define a format named "Cautions" and another named "cautions."

   Place or modify the format definition in the **Definition** text box. The definition can consist of text and building blocks. For example, the definition for Heading and Page is

   $$< \$paratext > onpage < \$pagenum > .$$

   The building blocks available to you are listed in Table 5.2.

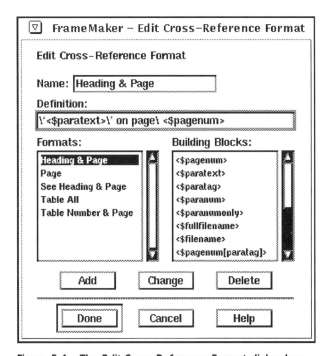

Figure 5.4   The Edit Cross-Reference Format dialog box.

Table 5.2 Cross-Reference Formats Building Blocks

Building Block	Results in . . .
< $pagenum >	The page number of the referenced text or spot
< $paratext >	The text of the referenced paragraph
< $paratag >	The tag of the referenced paragraph
< $paranum >	The autonumber of the referenced paragraph, including the text in the autonumber format
< $paranumonly >	The autonumber of the referenced paragraph, excluding the text in the autonumber format
< $fullfilename >	The path to the referenced document
< $filename >	The name of the referenced document
< $pagenum[paratag] >	The page number of the paragraph formatted with the specified tag, preceding the referenced text or spot
< $paratext[paratag] >	The text of a paragraph formatted with the specified tag, preceding the referenced text or spot
< $paratag[paratag] >	The tag of a paragraph formatted with the specified tag, preceding the referenced text or spot
< $paranum[paratag] >	The autonumber of a paragraph formatted with the specified tag, preceding the referenced text or spot; this format includes the text in the autonumber format
< paranumonly[paratag] >	The autonumber of a paragraph formatted with the specified tag, preceding the referenced text or spot; this excludes the text in the autonumber format
Character Format	The text following the character format building block changes to the format you specify; use the Default Font building block if you want to end the special formatting before the end of the cross-reference text

Example Cross-Reference Format Definitions	Example Results
\ '< $paratext > \ ' on page < $pagenum>	"Importing Formats" on page 68
reference all tags named < $paratag>	reference all tags named Heading
< $paranum> on page < $pagenum>	Figure 5.5 on page 120
see Screen < $paranumonly> —< $paratext> on page < $pagenum>	see Screen 5.5—The Cross-Reference dialog box on page 120
to find < $filename>, go to < $fullfilename>	to find chap05.doc, go to c:\ books\ fm-unix\ work\ chap5\ chap05.doc
see \ '< $paratext >\ ' in \ '< $paratext[Heading] \ ' on page \ ' < $pagenum[Heading] \ '	see "Inserting Endnotes" in "Creating Footnotes" on page 111
reference all < $paratag[Heading3]> tags that precede a < $paratext>	reference all Heading3 tags that precede a TIP
see \ '< $paratext >\ ' in < $paranum[paratag]>	see "For numerical outlines:" in Table 5.6.
see \ '< $paratext >\ ' in table number < $paranumonly[paratag]>	see "For numerical outlines:" in table number 5.6
<Emphasis> \ '< $paratext >\ ' <Default Font> on page < $pagenum>	**"Importing Formats"** on page 68

3. Click **Add** if the format definition is new, or **Change** if you're modifying an existing format definition.

4. Click **Done**.

What To Do If

• If you want to specify quotes or special characters as part of a format definition use a backslash equivalent. For more information, see "Using Special Characters."

See Also

• Using Special Characters, p. 42.

86 ▾ Updating Cross-References

Whenever you update a document, you run a risk of moving or deleting cross-reference sources. You can resolve any problems with your cross-references by updating them routinely when you modify a document.

If you move a cross-reference source, you can specify the source's new location when you update cross-references. If you delete a source, you can find all references to it and delete them.

Assumptions

• The Cross-Reference dialog box is open (you can press **Esc s c** to open it).

Exceptions

• If you are using conditional text, hidden cross-references are not updated. Make sure the cross-references you want to update are displayed.

Steps

1. Click **Update**.
   The Update Cross-References dialog box (see Figure 5.5) will be displayed.
2. Click the button in the Update Cross-References dialog box that indicates which cross-references you want to update. You can choose to update the cross-references to text in the current document, to all open documents, or to all documents.
3. Click **OK**.

What To Do If

- If unresolved cross-references exist, the Update Unresolved Cross-References dialog box opens. For more information, see "Resolving Missing Cross-References."
- If you update a cross-reference format definition, Frame-Maker also displays the Update Cross-References dialog box. Decide which cross-references to update and click **OK**.

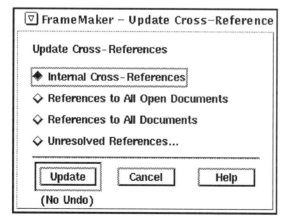

Figure 5.5 The Update Cross-References dialog box.

See Also _____

- Resolving Missing Cross-References, below.

| 87 | **Resolving Missing Cross-References** |

When you update cross-references, FrameMaker tells you if you have unresolved cross-references. FrameMaker does not resolve them for you, but, since it places a marker on every cross-reference source, it can tell you whether the reference is still there.

If a cross-reference source is deleted, you can use the Find/Change feature to find the unresolved cross-references and delete them as well. If a cross-reference source is moved, you can show FrameMaker where to find it by using the Update Unresolved Cross-references dialog box.

You can also generate a list of unresolved cross-references to keep track of whether the unresolved cross-references are internal or external. This list also displays the paragraph tag, text, and page number of the unresolved cross-reference.

Assumptions _____

- The Cross-Reference dialog box is open (you can press **Esc s c** to open it).
- Text to which cross-references exist has either been moved or deleted.

Exceptions _____

- None.

Steps _____

1. Click **Update**.
   The Update Cross-References dialog box will open.

2. Click **Unresolved References**.

3. Click **Update**.

   The Update Unresolved Cross-References dialog box (see Figure 5.6) will be displayed.

4. Select a file listed in the **Unresolved References to Files Named** scroll list.

   These files contained text that was referenced, but these references have now been moved or deleted.

5. Select a file listed in the **For Cross-References to Selected File**, Look In scroll list.

   These files contain the text that was referenced. If you know where the text is, select the file.

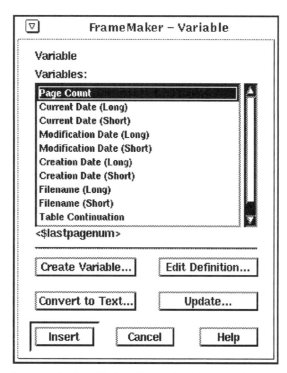

Figure 5.6 The Update Unresolved Cross-References
dialog box.

6. Click **Update**.

7. Click **Done**.

What To Do If

- If you deleted a cross-reference marker but still need it, search for the referenced text and insert a new marker.

- If you delete referenced text, delete any cross-reference markers inserted in it.

- If you want to generate a list of unresolved cross-reference, select **Generate from the File** menu. You can select **List of References** from the **List** pop-up menu, and specify **Unresolved Cross-Refs** in the **Set Up File** dialog box.

See Also

- Updating Cross-References, p. 182.

Using Variables

FrameMaker enables you to work with two distinct types of variables: system variables and user variables. System variables are variables supplied by the system for information such as page numbering, page count, dates, and filenames. User variables are variables you create for wording that may change throughout your documentation, such as product names or legal verbiage.

System variables are composed of building blocks that you can use in any combination along with normal text. You can modify system variables, but you cannot add your own.

User variables are composed of text and character formats. You can use a variable in place of a word or phrase throughout your documents. When the word or phrase changes, you don't have to find it in your document. Just change the definition of your user variable, and it is changed everywhere you used it.

Inserting Variables | 88

You can insert user and system variables by picking the variable you want from the scroll list in the Variable dialog box.

When you insert a variable, FrameMaker displays the text that a variable specifies, not the variable format. For example, if you insert a variable for the file name of the current file, FrameMaker displays the name, not the building block that specifies the file name in the variable format.

Assumptions

• The insertion point is placed where you want the variable.

Exceptions

• You cannot insert a variable in text created with the graphics tool.

• When you insert a variable for the page number in a Master Page, you will see a pound sign (#) instead of the number. However, when you go to the Body Pages, you will the current page number.

Steps

1. Select **Variable** from the Special menu (or press **Esc s v**). Figure 5.7 shows the Variable dialog box.
2. Select the variable from the **Variable** scroll list. The list contains system variables and any user variables you create. To insert a variable by typing its name, press **Esc q v Control + 0**.
3. Click **Insert**.

What To Do If

• If the list does not have a variable with the definition you need, you can create one that does.

> **TIP**
>
> Use variables for any type of text, date, or counter that changes throughout the life of a document. Replacing the value or content of a variable globally is then reduced to modifying the variable definition.

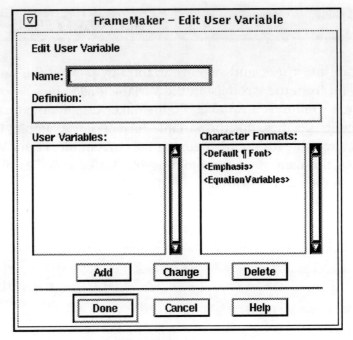

Figure 5.7 The Variable dialog box.

- If a system variable has a definition close to what you need, you can modify its definition to match what you need.

- If you want to edit a variable, double-click it to open the Variable dialog box. Click **Edit Definition** to edit the format of the variable.

- If you want to move a variable, select the variable by clicking it once, then cut and paste it into its new position.

- If you want to replace a variable, double-click it to open the Variable dialog box, select a new variable, and click **Replace**.

- To delete a variable, select it and press **Delete**. You cannot delete a variable using the backspace key.

- If you want to convert your variables to text, you can convert all variables in a document, all variables with a specific format, or all variables in selected text.

To convert to text, open the **Variable** dialog box and click **Convert to Text**. Indicate which variables to convert, and click **Convert**. Once they are converted, you can edit them like regular text. However, FrameMaker does not recognize them as variables, and you have to maintain and update them manually.

See Also

- Creating User Variables, below.
- Modifying System Variables, p. 190.

Creating User Variables | 89

Create user variables for text that changes often, such as code and product names, or for text that is used frequently but can be mistyped easily, such as the a part number or name of a book. You can specify special character formats for user variables if you want the variables to stand out from the surrounding text. For example, you might want a book title to be all italics, or a part number to be displayed in bold text.

Assumptions

- The insertion point is placed where you want the variable.
- The Variable dialog box is open (you can press **Esc s v** to open it).
- You have already decided on the name of the variable, the text it will contain, and its character format.

Exceptions

- You cannot create variables that contain the building blocks used by system variables.

Steps

1. Click **Create Variable**, or press **Esc q v Control + 0**. FrameMaker displays the Edit User Variable dialog box.

2. Type the name of the new variable in the **Name** text box.

3. Place the variable definition in the **Definition** text box. The variable definition can contain text and character formats.

4. Click **Done**.

What To Do If

- If you want to change the variable definition, select the Variable in the **Variable** text box and click **Edit Definition**.

See Also

- Modifying System Variables, below.

90   Modifying System Variables

You can modify system variables to display the information you want. Since the building blocks used by system variables are not available to create user variables, this is the only way for you to use them.

Assumptions

- The insertion point is placed where you want the variable.
- The Variable dialog box is open (you can press **Esc s v** to open it).

Steps

1. Select the system variable you want to modify (or press **Esc q v Control + 0**).

2. Click **Edit Definition.**
   Figure 5.8 shows the Edit System Variable dialog box.

3. Change the variable definition.
   Building blocks appropriate for the type of variable are listed in the Building Blocks scroll list. For example, for a date variable, the date, time, and time building blocks are listed.

4. Click **Edit** in the Edit System Variable dialog box.

5. Click **Replace** in the Variables dialog box.
   All variables in your document that used the previous definition change to the new one.

> **TIP**
>
> If you have the chance, experiment with the building blocks. This will give you a much better idea of how you can use system variables effectively.

What To Do If

• If you want to modify the variable definition for page numbering variables, go to the Master Pages. The complete list of variables for page numbering is displayed only there. For example, the Page Count variable is not available when you open the Variables dialog box from the Body Pages.

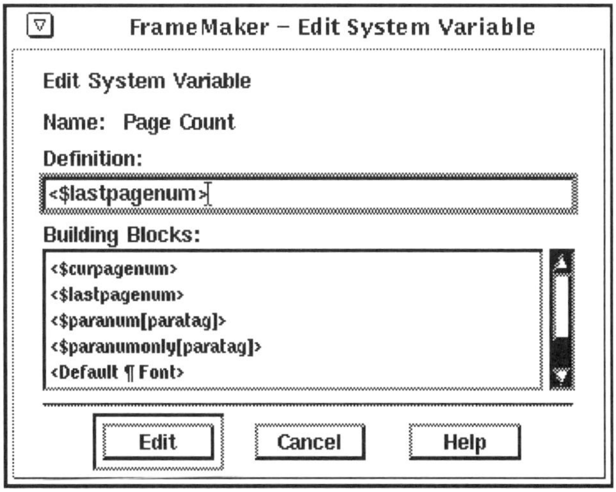

Figure 5.8   The Edit System Variable dialog box.

See Also

- Creating User Variables, p. 189.

91 ▼ Using System Variables

System variables are generally used for headers and footers, inserted in the Master Pages. System variables include definitions for page numbers, page count, dates, and running headers and footers that you can modify for your specific needs.

FrameMaker automatically updates system variables inserted in Master Pages, such as variables for the current time, which change every time you open the document. For variables that are inserted in the Body Pages, however, you have to explicitly tell FrameMaker to update them.

Most system variables are available at all times. However, if you look at the scroll list in the Variable dialog box, you will find that some system variables can be used or are available only for specific functions. For example, you can use the Current Page # and Running H/F variables only in the Master Pages. If you open the Variable dialog box while you are in the Body Pages, these variables are not available.

Assumptions

- You want to create headers, footers, or use text found somewhere other than the variable definition itself.

- The insertion point is placed where you want the variable.

- The Variable dialog box is open. (You can press **Esc s v** to open it).

Exceptions

- None.

Steps

1. Edit the variable to include the building blocks that pick up the information you want to use.

2. Insert the variable. You can press **Esc q v Control + 0** to insert variable by typing its name. These variables are generally used for headers and footers.

What To Do If

- If you want to display these variables in the header or footer of a document, go to the Master Pages and insert the variable in the header and footer areas. If you have more than one Master Page, do this for every one.

- If you are displaying a condition tag, replace **hitag** and **lotag** with condition tags you want to find, and **nomatch** with the text that should appear if there is no match. For example, pages that match hitag display the content of hitag where the variable is placed, and pages that do not match either hitag or lotag display the content of nomatch.

- If you want to display dictionary-style headers or footers in a document, insert different variables on the right and left master pages and modify the variable definition. The right and left master pages should use Running H/F 1 and Running H/F 2 respectively with the following building blocks:

      Left page   <$paratext[paratag]>
      Right page   <paratext[+, paratag]>

  Replace paratag with the tag you use for definition terms. FrameMaker looks for the first occurrence of the tag on the left page and the last occurrence on the right page, as indicated by the plus (+) sign.

- If you want to display the content of any one of several tags, replace paratag with a list of the tags, separated by commas.

For example, if you want to display either the title or first level heading as a header, use the building block

<$paratext[Title, Heading1]>

FrameMaker displays the first one it finds.

See Also

- Inserting Variables, p. 187.

Chapter
6

Creating Tables

Modifying Tables

Creating and Updating Table Formats

USING
TABLES

Creating Tables

The first step in creating a table of information in FrameMaker is to insert an empty table into the document. Each table has a format, which determines how the table will look. The table formats are kept in a Table Catalog, similar to the Paragraph Catalog. Like the other formats and catalogs in FrameMaker, you can add new table formats to the catalog or update existing formats. You can also apply any of the formats to new or existing tables in the document.

Normally, you would enter information directly into the cells after creating an empty table. However, if you have already entered the information in a document, FrameMaker enables you to save time by converting this text into a table. After you've completely entered the content, FrameMaker gives you maximum flexibility in rearranging your information or adding and deleting rows and columns in the table.

92 ▽ Inserting Tables

Before you can enter information in a table, you must insert an empty table into the document. While inserting a table, you can also select its format, which controls important characteristics of the appearance and layout of the table.

If you already have other tables elsewhere in the document, you don't always need to create a new one. One alternative is to select an existing table and copy it to the new location. You can then replace the existing content with new information as appropriate.

The formats available in the Table Catalog may vary depending on the template you use to create the document. For example, the blank document includes two table formats, known as Format A and Format B.

_____ **Assumptions**

- None.

_____ **Exceptions**

- You can't insert a table in a footnote.

_____ **Steps**

1. Position the cursor on the line to which you want to anchor the table, and click.

2. Select **Insert Table** in the Table menu.
   The Insert Table dialog box will appear (see Figure 6.1). This dialog box enables you to select the Table Tag from the list of formats in the Table Catalog. It also enables you to set the number of columns, body rows, heading rows, and footing rows for the table.

3. Select a table format by clicking in the list.
   The name of the format you selected will be displayed in the Table Tag field.

> **TIP**
>
> As with character and paragraph formats, you should insert a table format in the Table Catalog if you plan to create several tables using the same style.

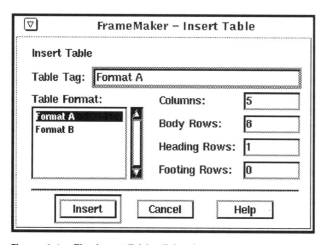

Figure 6.1   The Insert Table dialog box.

4. Modify the number of rows or columns in the new table, if necessary.

    You can change these values later, so use a best guess to set the number of rows and columns for now.

5. Click the **Insert** button.

    The table is inserted and anchored on the line where the cursor was positioned.

What To Do If

- If you made a mistake, you can modify nearly all aspects of the table at a later time. If you change your mind about the need for a new table, you can remove the entire table by selecting it and deleting it.

See Also

- Deleting or Moving a Table, p. 200.
- Inserting Text in a Table, p. 206.
- Converting Text to Tables, p. 214.

93   Manipulating a Table

Since many of the operations you'll normally perform on tables require you to select some or all of it, it's important to know how to manipulate the cells of a table. FrameMaker enables you to select any range of cells from a single cell to the entire table. You can also easily select entire rows or columns.

Assumptions

- You want to select part of a table.

Exceptions

- None.

Steps

- Select several cells in the table by dragging through the cells.

  You can also select a single cell using this dragging method. To do this, click inside the cell, drag the cursor through the cell border, and then drag the cursor back into the cell without lifting the mouse button.

  When you select a cell, row, or column in a table, a small selection handle appears on the side of the selected object. This indicates that you have selected the cell (or rows and columns) and not the contents of the cell. This selection handle is illustrated in Figure 6.2.

- Select an entire row or column in a table by dragging across the cells.

- Select the entire table by dragging across the heading row and then down through the first cell in the body rows.

  Another method to select the entire table is to select any cell in the table and choose **Select All of Table** in the Edit menu. This option appears only when you have one or more cells already selected in the table.

> **TIP**
>
> You can select an entire column by dragging from a column header into the first cell of a body row.

Table 18: San Jose/San Francisco CalTrain Schedule

Destination	Train 41	Train 43	Train 45	Train 47
San Jose	7:10	7:31	8:00	9:00
Santa Clara	7:15	7:36	8:05	9:05
Sunnyvale	7:23	7:44	8:13	9:13
Palo Alto	7:37	7:58	8:27	9:26
Belmont	7:53	8:15	8:43	9:42
San Mateo	8:02	-	8:51	9:50
Bayshore	8:23	-	9:12	10:11
San Francisco	8:40	8:45	9:26	10:25
Destination	Train 41	Train 43	Train 45	Train 47

Figure 6.2 A selected column with its handles.

What To Do If

- If you want to extend or reduce a selection in a table, click on the last cell you want included while pressing the **Shift** key.
- You can duplicate a table by using the regular copy and paste operations. Select the table in the document and choose **Copy** from the Edit menu. Position the cursor where you would like to insert the table and select **Paste** from the Edit menu.

See Also

- Inserting Text in a Table, p. 206.
- Splitting and Combining Tables, p. 221.
- Resizing Columns, p. 227.
- Resizing Rows, p. 229.

94 Deleting or Moving a Table

There are several occasions when you may need to remove a table in FrameMaker. For example, you may want to delete a newly created table whose format is not the type of table you need. You may also want to move a table from one location to another or to another document. Finally, you may simply want to remove a table and all the information because it is no longer needed.

Assumptions

- None.

Exceptions

- None.

Steps

1. Select the table you want to move or delete.
   A fast way to select the table is to select any cell in the table and choose **Select All of Table** in the Edit menu. If the option doesn't appear in the menu, you probably haven't selected a cell in the table.

2. To delete the table, select **Clear** in the Edit menu.
   Click on the option to **Remove Cells from Table** and click **Clear**. This removes the entire table from the document, instead of simply deleting the cell contents.

3. To place the table on the clipboard for later pasting, select **Cut** in the Edit menu.
   As with the clear operation in the preceding step, click **Remove Cells from Table** and click **Cut.**

4. To paste the table, click in the line where you want to insert the table.

5. Select **Paste** in the Edit menu.

> **TIP**
>
> Press the right mouse button and select **Cut** or **Clear** in the pop-up menu to remove the selected table.

What To Do If

- If you unintentionally cut or delete a table, you can undo the operation by selecting **Undo** from the Edit menu right away.

- If you want to copy a table to the clipboard to duplicate it elsewhere without removing the original, select the table and choose **Copy** in the Edit menu.

See Also

- Manipulating a Table, p. 198.
- Converting a Table to Text, p. 219.
- Deleting Rows and Columns, p. 225.

95 ◢ Rotating a Table

Sometimes a table looks better when it's rotated on a page. For example, if the table has a large number of columns and relatively few rows, you may want to place all the information on one page by rotating the table to Landscape orientation, putting the top of the table along the left-hand or right-hand edge of the page.

FrameMaker enables you to place a rotated table on a page by itself or between paragraphs of unrotated, normal text.

Assumptions

- You want to rotate a table that is on a page by itself or a table that is on a page with text.

Exceptions

- None.

Steps

To rotate a table on a page by itself, you need to create a rotated Master Page and then apply this to the Body Page containing the table.

1. Select **Master Pages** in the View menu.
   FrameMaker displays the Master Pages in the document.
2. Select **Add Master Page** in the Special menu.
   The Add Master Page dialog box appears. You can specify the initial layout of the master page using this dialog box.
3. Click on the option to **Copy from Master Page,** and select **Right** from the pop-up menu to specify that the new Master Page will be based on the standard FrameMaker Master Page.

4. Enter a name for the Master Page in the **Name** text box, and click **Add.**
   FrameMaker creates the new Master Page in the document.

5. Select **Pages:Layout Commands** in the Format menu.

6. Select **Clockwise** or **Counter Clockwise** from the Rotate Page pop-up menu in the Layout Commands window, and then close the Layout window.
   You have now specified a rotated Master Page in the document. To rotate the table, you will now have to apply this Master Page to the Body Page containing the table.

7. Select **Body Pages** in the View menu.

8. Display the page with the table and select **Pages:Master Page Usage** in the Format menu.
   FrameMaker displays the Master Page Usage dialog box (Figure 6.3). You can assign a Master Page to the Body Page using this dialog box.

9. Select **Custom Master Page** from the pop-up menu in the **Use** area, and then choose the Custom Master Page that you created earlier.

10. Select **Current Page** in the On area of the dialog box, and then click **Set**.
    This selects the Body Page on which you want to apply the Master Page. FrameMaker rotates the table on the page.

To rotate a table in a page with unrotated text, you will need to create an anchored frame and place a text column in it. You can then place the table in this text column and rotate the column.

1. Click in the text where you want to anchor the frame that will contain the table, and then select **Anchored Frame** in the Special menu.
   FrameMaker displays the Anchored Frame dialog box.

TIP
You can select a text column by **Control-**clicking in it.

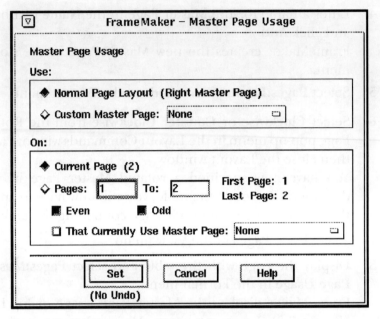

Figure 6.3 **The Master Page Usage dialog box.**

2. Select **Below Current Line** in the Anchoring Position area of the dialog box.

3. Specify the width and the height of the frame in the **Size** area, and then click **New Frame**.
FrameMaker creates a new anchored frame. You will now need to add a text column in the anchored frame.

4. Select the **Text Column** tool in the Tools palette (see Figure 6.4).

5. Drag diagonally in the anchored frame to draw the text column, and release the mouse button when the text column is the right size.

6. Double-click in the text column to set the insertion point.

7. Insert a new table in the new text column.

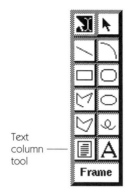

Text
column —————
tool

**Figure 6.4   The Text Column
Tool.**

You can also cut or copy a table from somewhere else and paste it into the text column.

8.   Select the text column by **Control**-clicking in it.

9.   Hold down the **Control** key and drag a handle of the text column using the right mouse button.

This will rotate the text column. When you have rotated the text column 90 degrees, you're done. See Figure 6.5.

What To Do If

•   If you apply a rotated Master Page to a Body Page and the table on the page moves to a different location because of formatting changes, you'll have to apply the Master Page to the new page containing the table.

See Also

•   Rotating Cells, p. 232.

The following table contains a few of the popular morning commuter trains running between San Jose and San Francisco, California. Train service is provided through the joint efforts of Caltrans, the California Department of Transportation, and the Santa Clara, San Mateo, and San Francisco county transit districts.

Table 20: San Jose/San Francisco CalTrain Schedule

Destination	Train 41	Train 43	Train 45	Train 47
San Jose	7:10	7:31	8:00	9:00
Santa Clara	7:15	7:36	8:05	9:05
Sunnyvale	7:23	7:44	8:13	9:13
Palo Alto	7:37	7:58	8:27	9:26
Belmont	7:53	8:15	8:43	9:42
San Mateo	8:02	-	8:51	9:50
Bayshore	8:23	-	9:12	10:11
San Francisco	8:40	8:45	9:26	10:25
Destination	Train 41	Train 43	Train 45	Train 47

Figure 6.5   An example of a rotated table with unrotated text.

96   Inserting Text in a Table

Text is probably the most common type of information that you'll use in a table. FrameMaker treats each cell in the table as a text column, enabling you to type, format, and cut and paste in the same way you would anywhere else in the document. For example, you can apply either a character or paragraph format to text in a table cell.

_____ **Assumptions**

- You want to insert variables, cross-references, footnotes, and markers in a table cell.

_____ **Exceptions**

- If you insert a footnote in a cell, the footnote text will appear directly beneath the table.

_____ **Steps**

1. Click in the cell you want to enter text.
2. Enter the text in the cell.
   The text you enter uses the default paragraph format for the table. You can change the format for any paragraph in a cell, or apply a different format to a paragraph in a cell.

_____ **What To Do If**

- Since the tab has a special meaning in a table, enter **Esc Tab** to insert a tab in the cell.

_____ **See Also**

- Inserting Graphics in a Table, p. 210.
- Inserting Tables in a Table, p. 212.
- Converting Text to Tables, p. 214.

Creating Multipage Tables | 97

Sometimes you need to include more information in a table than will fit on a single page. When this happens, FrameMaker automatically extends the table over two or more pages, making sure to display the title of the table, along with the heading and footing rows, on each page. This is helpful, because the information in the table is kept in context and the reader does not have to flip pages to understand the meaning.

FrameMaker also helps you make the information more usable by enabling you to include special text in the title and heading rows of the tables. For example, you may want to use the word "(Continued)" on the second and following pages of a multipage table to indicate that all the information belongs together. Another option is to include the Table Sheet count on the page. For example, each page of the table could be marked as "Sheet 1 of 4," "Sheet 2 of 4," and so forth.

You can use two system variables with multipage tables: Table Continuation and Table Sheet. The Table Continuation variable displays the text that indicates that the table is being continued; and the Table Sheet variable displays the sheet count information.

Assumptions

- You have a multipage table. FrameMaker takes care of splitting the table over multiple pages. All you have to do is add the special text using the system variable, if required.

Exceptions

- None.

Steps

1. Click in the title or heading where you want to place the special text.
    To enable FrameMaker to use the special text across the entire multipage table, you must click in the title or heading on the first page of the table. This line will mark the spot where you want to insert the system variable to display the special continuation or sheet count information.
2. Select **Variable** in the Special menu to open the Variable dialog box, which lists the system variables you can insert into your document.

3. Select either **Table Continuation** or **Table Sheet** from the list of variables.

   By default, the Table Continuation variable inserts the text "(Continued)," which FrameMaker displays starting on page two of the table. The variable includes a space, so you don't have to insert one.

   The Table Sheet variable displays "(Sheet xx of yy)," which also starts on the second page. If the table contains only a single page, the text will not be displayed.

4. Click **Insert** to place the variable in the table.

   Figure 6.6 shows the second page of a multipage table.

_____ **What To Do If**

- If you want to use text different from the defaults supplied with these variables, you can edit the variable definitions and include your preferences. For example, you may want to use the text "And on and on . . . " instead of the standard "(Continued)." For more information, refer to the See Also section below.

_____ **See Also**

- Modifying System Variables, p. 190.

- Splitting and Combining Tables, p. 221.

Table 19: San Jose/San Francisco CalTrain Schedule (Continued)

Destination	Train 41	Train 43	Train 45	Train 47
Belmont	7:53	8:15	8:43	9:42
San Mateo	8:02	-	8:51	9:50
Bayshore	8:23	-	9:12	10:11
San Francisco	8:40	8:45	9:26	10:25

Figure 6.6   Page two of a multipage table using table Continuation.

98 Inserting Graphics in a Table

Many tables require you to add information that is richer than plain text. For example, in a factory you may need to create an inventory of parts that includes line drawings to help differentiate similar components. Or the human resources department may insist on including scanned photos of personnel for security reasons. Either way, FrameMaker helps you by giving you the flexibility to include drawings or imported graphics inside any cell in a table.

Assumptions

- You want to center the graphic within the table cell. If required, you can modify the Paragraph format of the cell to change the positioning of the graphic.

Exceptions

- None.

Steps

1. Click in the cell where you want to include the graphic, and then select **Paragraphs:Designer** in the Format menu (or press **Esc o p d**).

2. Select **Center** as the alignment in the Basic Properties.
   By selecting Center, you are requesting FrameMaker to center the paragraph horizontally within the table cell.

3. Turn off **Fixed** in the Line Spacing section in the Basic Properties, and then click **Apply to Selection**.
   This enables you to affect the height of the cell when you specify the size of the anchored frame that will contain the graphic or drawing.

4. Select **Middle** as the vertical alignment in the Table Cell Properties, and then click **Apply to Selection** and close the Paragraph Designer.
   This positions the paragraph in the vertical middle of the table cell.

5. Select **Anchored Frame** in the Special menu.
   You will use this dialog box to specify the properties of the anchored frame that will contain your graphic.

6. Select the **At Insertion Point** check box.

7. Specify the size of the anchored frame by entering the width and height, and then click **New Frame**.
   FrameMaker inserts an anchored frame in the table cell.

8. Insert the graphic in the frame.
   You can cut and paste a graphic into the cell, or you can use the drawing tools in the Tools palette to create an illustration. You may need to align the graphic within the frame or resize the frame to display the graphic better. Figure 6.7 shows an example of the results.

See Also

- Resizing Columns, p. 227.
- Straddling (Combining) Cells, p. 231.

Table 1: Fancy-Smancy Software Inc. Personnel Table

Photo	Name	Address	City	State
	David Heintz	2180 Fortune Drive	San Jose	California

Figure 6.7 A table with a graphic in a cell.

Inserting Tables in a Table

Sometimes even relatively simple information needs to be structured in such a way that certain sections contain greater detail than others. This is especially true when the information is hierarchical in nature, such as an organization chart or a factory part that is made up of even smaller components.

One way to present this type of information is to include a reference within a cell to another table which contains this extra information. However, if the extra information is not overly complex, you may consider including a table within a cell. FrameMaker enables you to present tables within tables and control how they appear on the page.

Assumptions

- None.

Exceptions

- None.

Steps

> **TIP**
>
> Specify the width and height of the anchored frame to be slightly larger than expected size of the table. You can always fine-tune your settings later.

1. Click in the cell where you want to insert the table.

2. Select **Anchored Frame** in the Special menu.
   FrameMaker displays the Anchored Frame dialog box. Using the dialog box, select **Below Current Line**, set the alignment as **Center**, and specify the width and the height of the frame. See Figure 6.8.

3. Click **New Frame**.
   FrameMaker creates an anchored frame in the cell.

4. Resize the columns of the table if the frame is wider than the cell.

5. Use the **Tools Palette** to add a text column.

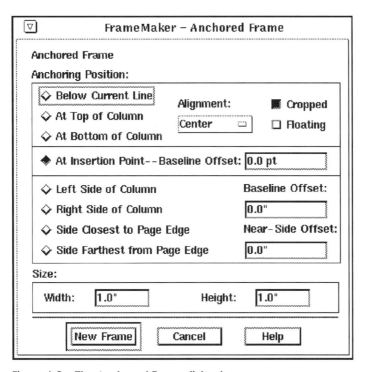

Figure 6.8   The Anchored Frame dialog box.

The text column tool is illustrated in Figure 6.4. If the Tools Palette is not visible, select **Tools** from the Graphics menu to display it.

6. Click in the new text column and insert the table.
    Use the same steps described earlier under Inserting Tables to create the table within the text column.

What To Do If

• None.

See Also

• Adding Text Columns, p. 304.
• Inserting Tables, p. 196.

100 ⌄ Converting Text to Tables

It's not always convenient to create a table and enter information from scratch. Many times the information is already available in a form that FrameMaker can understand. For example, you may have already entered the content as text, or you may be moving the information from another application to FrameMaker. You can convert the text into a table using only a few mouse clicks.

When converting text to tables, you need to specify whether each paragraph of text should be treated as a row of information or as a separate cell. If you specify that a paragraph should become a row in the new table, you need to inform FrameMaker how to divide up the row into multiple cells.

For example, FrameMaker permits you to specify whether cells are delimited by a tab, a certain number of spaces, or some other character such as a comma. Indeed, if you are importing data from a personal computer, many programs have the capability to output their data separated by commas (comma-delimited format).

Assumptions

- You have text in FrameMaker that you want to convert to tables.

Exceptions

- None.

TIP

When moving data from another application to FrameMaker, use a consistent way to separate the data.

Steps

1. Select the text you want to convert to a table.

2. Select **Convert to Table** in the Table menu.
   FrameMaker displays the Convert to Table dialog box (see Figure 6.9) to collect the instructions for converting the information into a table.

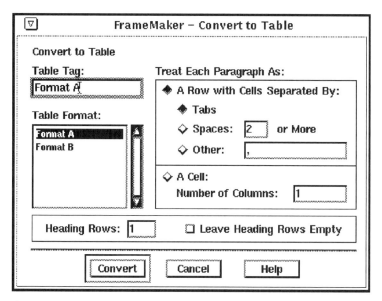

Figure 6.9   The Convert to Table dialog box.

3. Choose a table format from the list.
   The table format controls the appearance and properties of the new table.

4. Select the method FrameMaker uses to determine cell and row boundaries.
   If the text is formatted using tabs, select **Tabs** in the dialog box. If the information is delimited using spaces, click **Spaces** and enter the number of spaces FrameMaker should find before creating a new cell. Normally, this number is two or more.

5. If your text uses some other character to separate the information, click **Other** and enter the characters used to delimit the text.
   As mentioned, this character is often a comma; however, your text may use another character.

6. If you want to place each paragraph in its own cell, click on **Cells** and enter the number of columns you want the new table to have.

7. Enter the number of paragraphs in the text that are headings in the **Heading Rows** field.
This enables you to convert some of the paragraphs in the text to form the heading of the new table. If your text does not contain any headings, click **Leave Heading Rows Empty**.

8. Click **Convert** to change the text to a table.
You may need to resize the rows and columns of the table to make the information more readable. Figure 6.10 shows an example of the results.

See Also

- Converting an Imported File to a Table, p. 217.

- Converting a Table to Text, p. 219.

Name, University, City, State
Bob Marx, San Jose State University, San Jose, California
Art Makosinski, University of Victoria, Victoria, British Columbia
Philip Chibante, Rice University, Houston, Texas
Guy Groen, McGill University, Montreal, Quebec
Rocky Bitton, San Jose State University, San Jose, California

Table 1:

Name	University	City	State
Bob Marx	San Jose State University	San Jose	California
Art Makosinski	University of Victoria	Victoria	British Columbia
Philip Chibante	Rice University	Houston	Texas
Guy Groen	McGill University	Montreal	Quebec
Rocky Bitton	San Jose State University	San Jose	California

Figure 6.10   Before and after converting text to a table.

Converting an Imported File to a Table | 101

Some of the information you need to incorporate into a document may already exist in other files. You can always import this information into FrameMaker and later create a table. For example, you may need to incorporate the financial projections for your department into a report to present to your supervisor. Since this information is stored in a spreadsheet, you decide that a table is a logical way to present the data in your FrameMaker document. FrameMaker makes it easy for you to perform this conversion.

Assumptions

- None.

Exceptions

- You can't place a table created from an imported file in a footnote or into another table.
- You can only convert text files into FrameMaker tables.
- You must convert the entire file. You cannot convert only a portion of a file into a table using the steps in this section.

Steps

1. Click where you want to create the new table.
   FrameMaker will insert the table of imported text directly below the line where you clicked.

2. Select **Import > File** in the File menu.
   FrameMaker displays the Import File dialog box (see Figure 6.11), which contains the directories and files from which you can select the file you want to import.

3. Click **Copy into Document**.
   By selecting this option, you create a copy of the information which is stored directly in the FrameMaker document.

> **TIP**
> Importing the file by reference reduces the size of your document.

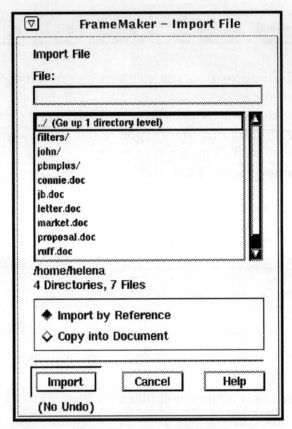

Figure 6.11   The Import File dialog box.

If you later remove the original document, the information you copied will remain intact.

4. Click **Import**.

FrameMaker displays the Reading Text File dialog box. This dialog enables you to control the way FrameMaker treats the text when importing the file.

5. Click the **Convert to Table** option.

The Convert to Table dialog box is displayed, enabling you to select a format for the new table.

6. Select a format from the list and click **Convert**.
    FrameMaker imports the file into the document, and the
    information is converted into a table using the format you
    specified.

What To Do If

*   If you want to insert information from a text file into an
    existing table, first import the file into the document as
    a table, using the steps in this task, and then merge the
    information with the existing table.
*   If the imported file contains extra tabs or carriage returns,
    you can edit the table after importing by using regular Copy
    and Paste operations on the cell contents.

See Also

*   Converting Text to Tables, p. 214.
*   Converting a Table to Text, below.
*   Splitting and Combining Tables, p. 221.

Converting a Table to Text 102

FrameMaker enables you to convert tables into text by changing
each table cell into a separate paragraph. Since a table is a two-
dimensional structure, there are two ways FrameMaker can order
the newly created paragraphs: by moving across each row before
moving down to the next row, or by moving down each column
before moving to the next column in the table. You select which
order FrameMaker performs the conversion.

Assumptions

*   None.

Exceptions

- None.

Steps

1. Click in the table you want to convert to text paragraphs.

2. Select **Convert to Paragraphs** in the Table menu.
   FrameMaker displays the Convert to Paragraphs dialog box
   (see Figure 6.12), enabling you to select whether you want
   the table converted by rows or by columns.

3. Select **Row by Row** or **Column by Column** and click **Convert**.
   FrameMaker converts the table into separate paragraphs,
   following the order you selected in the dialog box.

What To Do If

- If you want to merge the paragraphs, use the standard Cut
  and Paste operations.

See Also

- Converting Text to Tables, p. 214.
- Converting an Imported File to a Table, p. 217.

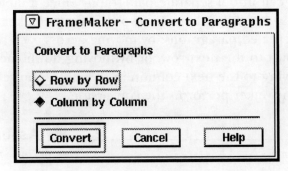

Figure 6.12   The Convert to Paragraphs dialog box.

Splitting and Combining Tables | 103

Many people create a FrameMaker document by first entering most of the information and then going back to shape and form the content into a presentable form. Sometimes this can mean massive changes and restructuring. Information contained in tables is not immune to these changes. Therefore, FrameMaker allows you to reorganize your content by splitting a table into two or more tables or by combining the content of two or more tables into a single one.

Assumptions

- You have two tables to combine and they match in either the number of rows or the number of columns. For example, if you combine rows of cells, the destination table must have the same number of columns. Likewise, if you combine columns of cells, the destination table must contain the same number of rows.

Exceptions

- None.

Steps

1. To split a table, select the rows or columns you want to remove, and select **Cut** in the Edit menu.

2. Click in a text column, and select **Paste** in the Edit menu. FrameMaker creates a new table in the text column and anchors it at the location that you clicked. The format of the new table is the same as that of the table from which you cut the rows or columns.

3. To combine two tables, select the rows or columns from one table, and select **Cut** from the Edit menu.

4. Click in the second table, and select **Paste** from the Edit menu.
   FrameMaker displays either the Paste Rows (see Figure 6.13) or Paste Columns (see Figure 6.14) dialog box, depending on the object you are pasting.

5. Select where you want to paste the rows or columns.
   You can paste rows above or below the current rows in the destination table. You can also replace the selected rows in the destination. Your options for pasting columns are very similar; you can insert the columns to the left or to the right, or you can replace the currently selected columns.

What To Do If

- If you want to combine the information of two tables, while still keeping the original table intact, select **Copy** instead of **Cut** in the Edit menu when performing the steps.

See Also

- Straddling (Combining) Cells, p. 231.

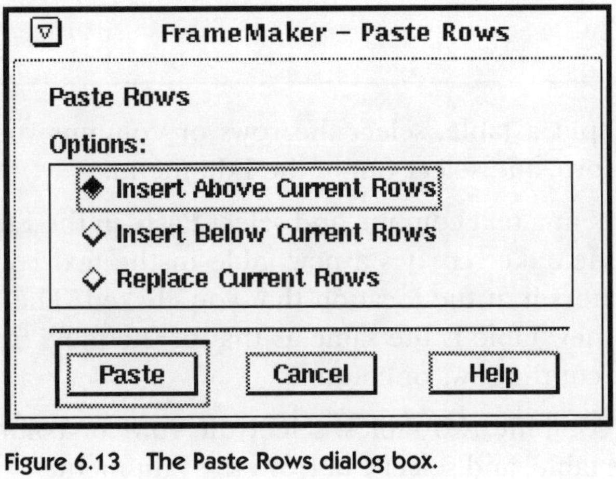

Figure 6.13   The Paste Rows dialog box.

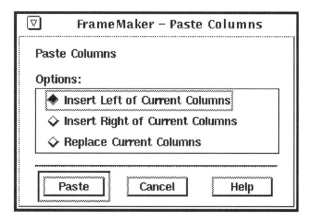

Figure 6.14   The Paste Columns dialog box.

Modifying Tables

It's practically impossible to foresee exactly how a table is going to look before you start adding the information to the cells. Even then you may need to modify the table to accommodate new information or to remove unneeded content. FrameMaker provides several options for you to modify the layout of a table after you've created it.

For example, FrameMaker enables you to add new rows and columns to an existing table. You can also squeeze more information into each cell by resizing the rows and columns. Depending on the content of the cells, you may find that certain information is easier to read if the cell is rotated on its side. In other cases, it may make sense to combine several cells together into one.

FrameMaker also gives you the ability to highlight important information that you feel should stand out in the table. By applying eye-catching characteristics to the cells, such as special borders or shaded cells, you can call attention to the information stored there.

104 ⟩ Adding Rows and Columns

When you add rows or columns, you can specify how many to add, along with where you want to insert them in the table, in a single step. While the most common operation is to insert blank new rows or columns to hold new information, FrameMaker also enables you to duplicate existing rows or columns within a table.

Assumptions

- When you click in a table to insert new rows or columns, the new cells will adopt the paragraph format of the cell in which you clicked.

Exceptions

- None.

Steps

TIP

You can add a new row to a table by pressing **Control+Return** in the previous row.

1. Click in a cell next to where you want to insert the new cells.
2. Select **Add Rows** or **Columns** in the Table menu.
   FrameMaker displays the Add Rows or Columns dialog box (see Figure 6.15).
3. Fill in the number of either rows or columns you want to insert.
4. Select where you want the new rows or columns to be added.
   You can insert rows above the selection point, below the selection, or to the header and footer. When adding columns, you can insert the new cells to the left or right of the selection point.
5. Click **Add** to insert the new cells.

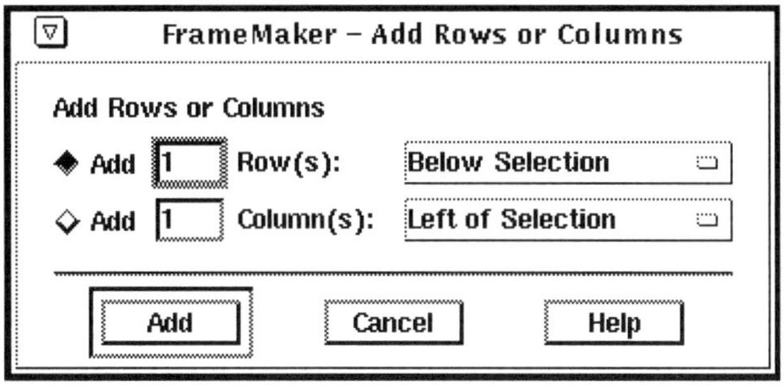

Figure 6.15   The Add Rows or Columns dialog box.

What To Do If

- None.

See Also

- Deleting Rows and Columns, below.

Deleting Rows and Columns | 105

By nature of the way information is organized in tables, people insert entire rows or columns to a table when new content needs to be added. Likewise, when information needs to be removed from a table, it usually means deleting one or more rows or columns from the table. FrameMaker makes both of these operations easy.

Assumptions

- FrameMaker asks for confirmation only before deleting the contents or the actual cells of an *entire* row or column in a table. If only a few cells are selected, FrameMaker will delete them without double-checking with you.

Exceptions

- None.

Steps

1. Select the rows or columns you want to delete, and then press the **Del** key.

   Remember, you can select an entire column by dragging from a column header into the first cell that is part of the body rows. Otherwise, drag across the entire row or column to select it.

   The Clear Table Cells dialog box (see Figure 6.16) appears, asking whether you want to leave the cells empty (remove the contents while leaving the empty cells in place) or remove the cells and the content completely from the table.

2. Select **Remove Cells from Table** and click **Clear**.

What To Do If

- If you want to delete only the content from the rows or columns and leave the empty cells intact, select **Leave Cells Empty** in the Clear Table Cells dialog box.

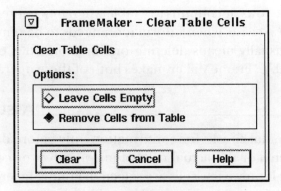

Figure 6.16   The Clear Table Cells dialog box.

_____ **See Also**

- Adding Rows and Columns, p. 224.

| Resizing Columns | 106 |

You can increase or decrease the width of each column individually in a table. In addition, you can specify that all columns within a table are to be assigned the same width. A quick way to change the width of a column is by using the mouse. By selecting and dragging the handle of a column, you can change its width without upsetting the size of the other columns. However, this change does affect the overall width of the table, so you should make changes with care.

_____ **Assumptions**

- You want to change the width of a column.

_____ **Exceptions**

- None.

_____ **Steps**

1. Select the column and drag its handle to change the width of a single column.
   This changes the selected column and leaves all other columns unmodified. However, the overall width of the table will increase or decrease depending on the changes you make.

2. Select a cell to the left of a column border and **Meta**-drag the handle to move a border between two columns.
   When you Meta-drag, you hold down the Meta key while dragging the selection handle with the mouse. This changes

TIP

You can snap the columns to a grid by selecting **Snap** in the Graphics menu before changing the width.

the size of the two columns on either side of the selected cell, but it does not change the overall width of the table.

3. To make all columns the same width, select the entire table and choose **Resize Columns** from the Table menu. FrameMaker displays the Resize Selected Columns dialog box (see Figure 6.17). Click by the option **To Equal Widths Totalling** and leave the value beside it unchanged. This will make all columns fit into the size of the current table.

What To Do If

*   If you want to change the width of several columns at a time, select the columns and drag the handle to match the new width. As you drag, FrameMaker changes the width of each column in proportion to their original size, thereby increasing or decreasing each the proper amount.

*   If you want to specifically set the widths of a column, select the cells and choose **Resize Columns** in the Table menu.

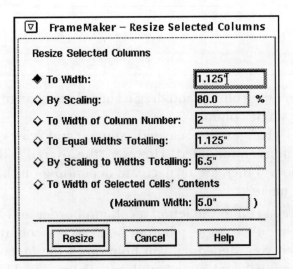

Figure 6.17 The Resize Selected Columns dialog box.

You can then modify the width in several different ways, including setting the specific width in inches and other measures.

_____ **See Also**

- Manipulating a Table, p. 198.
- Resizing Rows, below.
- Straddling (Combining) Cells, p. 231.

Resizing Rows | 107

When you enter text in a cell, FrameMaker does its best to adjust the height of the row automatically to match the height of the largest cell. Sometimes you need extra control over the appearance of the table, FrameMaker enables you to control the height of a row. This lets you include some white space around the contents of the cell and make the information more readable. However, you can also streamline a table by making all the rows the same size.

_____ **Assumptions**

- You want to change the size of a row.

_____ **Exceptions**

- None.

_____ **Steps**

1. Click in the row you want to modify.
2. Select **Row Format** in the Table menu.
   FrameMaker displays a dialog box (see Figure 6.18) where you can specify the maximum and minimum height for the row.

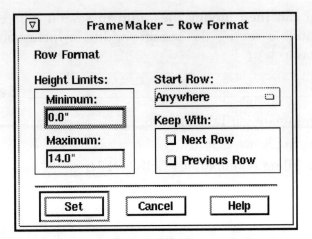

Figure 6.18 The Row Format dialog box.

3. Enter the row height in the **Minimum** text box and click **Set**.
   FrameMaker changes the height of the row to this new value.

What To Do If

- If you want to make all rows the same height, hold down **Shift + Control** and draw a selection border around the row. FrameMaker displays the height of the tallest row in the status bar. Click in the row and insert this height in the **Minimum** text box in the Row Format dialog box (as described in the Steps).

See Also

- Resizing Columns, p. 227.
- Straddling (Combining) Cells, p. 231.

Straddling (Combining) Cells | 108

Tables are a wonderful way to organize information, especially highly structured content. However, this can sometimes get in the way of making information presentable and understandable by imposing a rigid structure made up of fixed rows and columns. FrameMaker gives you a way to bypass this rigidity without losing any of the advantages of the table's structure.

You can do this by combining or straddling two or more cells in rows and columns. The text and graphics in these cells are also straddled together as if the content were in an ordinary cell. However, the previous contents of the cells are placed in their own paragraphs.

Just as you can straddle cells, FrameMaker also enables you to unstraddle them.

Assumptions

- You want to combine row cells.

Exceptions

- You can only straddle row cells of the same type. This means that you can't straddle heading and body rows together, but you can straddle any or all of the body rows in the table.

Steps

1. Select the cells you want to straddle.

2. Select **Straddle** in the Table menu.
   FrameMaker straddles the selected rows and columns in the table, placing the contents of each of the former cells in separate paragraphs. See Figure 6.19.

TIP

You can unstraddle several cells at a time by selecting them and choosing **Unstraddle** in the Table menu.

Table 1: Fancy-Smancy Software Inc. Personnel Table

Photo	Name	Address	City	State
 David Heintz		2180 Fortune Drive	San Jose	California

Figure 6.19   Straddling cells in a table.

What To Do If

- If you want to unstraddle a cell, select the cell and choose **Unstraddle** in the Table menu. FrameMaker puts all the content in the upper leftmost cell. You must redistribute the content among the original cells.

See Also

- Manipulating a Table, p. 198.
- Resizing Columns, p. 227.
- Resizing Rows, p. 229.

109   Rotating Cells

If you need to squeeze a lot of information into a single cell or several adjacent cells, things can get crowded very quickly. One way to get around this content squeeze is to rotate some of the cells. While FrameMaker enables you to rotate any cell in the table, one of the best uses of this feature is to rotate the heading cells in the table.

Assumptions

- You want to rotate a cell in a table.

_____ **Exceptions**

- None.

_____ **Steps**

1. Select the cells you want to rotate.
2. Select **Rotate** in the Graphics menu.
   FrameMaker displays the Rotate Table Cells dialog box (see Figure 6.20), which enables you to specify the orientation of the cells.
3. Select the orientation for the cell and click **Rotate**.
   The cells you selected will be rotated in the proper orientation. See Figure 6.21.

_____ **What To Do If**

- When you type in rotated cells, the cell height increases to match the content, as you would expect. If you want the text to wrap in the cell, you must limit the height of the rotated cell. When the typed text reaches this maximum height, the text will automatically wrap.

_____ **See Also**

- Rotating a Table, p. 202.

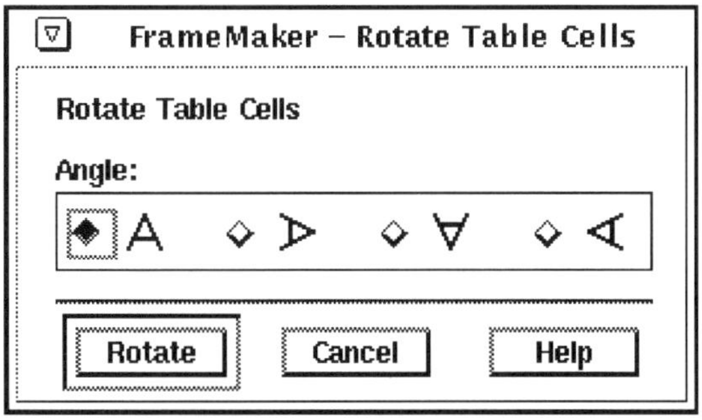

Figure 6.20   The rotate table cells dialog box.

Table 1: San Jose/San Francisco CalTrain Schedule

Destination	San Jose	Santa Clara	Sunnyvale	Palo Alto	Belmont	San Mateo	Bayshore	San Francisco
Train 41	7:10	7:15	7:23	7:37	7:53	8:02	8:23	8:40

Figure 6.21   A table using rotated cells.

110   Using Interesting Rulings and Shadings

Some information in the table may be more important than other information. FrameMaker enables you to highlight these cells using custom rulings and cell shadings. The ruling options enable you to add special cell borders that emphasize certain entries in the table. Likewise, shading can be a very effective way to attract attention to the contents of one or more cells.

Assumptions

- The custom ruling and shading settings are not stored as part of the format in the Table Catalog. When you apply a format from the Catalog to a table in your document, the custom rulings and shadings are retained.

Exceptions

- None.

TIP
Select **From Table** in the Custom Ruling and Shading pop-up menus to make the selected cells look like other cells in the table.

Steps

1. Select the cells, rows, or columns you want to customize.
2. Select **Custom Ruling and Shading** in the Table menu. FrameMaker displays the Custom Ruling and Shading dialog box (see Figure 6.22).

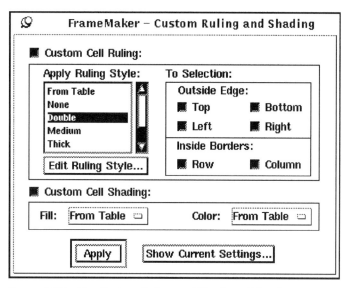

Figure 6.22   The Custom Ruling and Shading dialog box.

3. Turn on **Custom Cell Ruling**.
   If you want to modify only the cell shading, keep this option off and proceed to step 6.

4. Select the ruling style you want to apply to the selected cells.
   You can select one of several styles from a scrolling list.

5. In the To Selection area, choose the edges and borders you want to apply the ruling style.

6. Turn on **Custom Cell Shading**.
   If you do not want to change the cell shading, turn this option off and proceed to the last step.

7. Select a fill percentage using the **Fill** pop-up menu, then select a color using the pop-up menu, and then click **Apply**.

FrameMaker applies your custom ruling and shadings to the cells you selected. See Figure 6.23.

Table 2: San Jose/San Francisco CalTrain Schedule

Destination	Train 41	Train 43	Train 45	Train 47
San Jose	7:10	7:31	8:00	9:00
Santa Clara	7:15	7:36	8:05	9:05
Sunnyvale	7:23	7:44	8:13	9:13
Palo Alto	7:37	7:58	8:27	9:26
Belmont	7:53	8:15	8:43	9:42
San Mateo	8:02	-	8:51	9:50
Bayshore	8:23	-	9:12	10:11
San Francisco	8:40	8:45	9:26	10:25
Destination	Train 41	Train 43	Train 45	Train 47

Figure 6.23   An example of using custom ruling and shading

What To Do If

- If you want to use reverse color in a cell, set the Fill in the Custom Cell Shading area to 100%, change the Color to black, and apply the setting. Using the Character Designer, set the Color of the text to white and apply to the selection. You may consider creating either a character or paragraph tag for reverse color if you plan to use this throughout your document.

See Also

- Defining Ruling Properties, p. 262.
- Defining Shading Properties, p. 264.

Creating and Updating Table Formats

FrameMaker uses a table format to control the appearance of tables in the document. Whenever you insert a new table, you are asked to specify a format to which the table will conform. This format defines many aspects of how the table is displayed in the document, including the alignment, margins, title positioning, ruling, and shading.

Like Paragraph formats, FrameMaker stores Table formats in a catalog, each with a particular name called a tag. You select from these tags to create a new table and to apply a format to an existing table. You can change the format of a table using the Table Designer. You can also create formats and add them to the catalog.

Creating a New Table Format | 111

When you create a new document, FrameMaker supplies one or more table formats, which you can use right away. However, these formats are quite basic and will probably not be adequate when you start fine-tuning the overall appearance of your documents. Fortunately, FrameMaker makes it easy to create new table formats to suit just about any need.

To create a new format, select an existing format and make modifications to its properties. You can then give the new format a name (tag) and add it to the Table Catalog for future use.

Assumptions

- You may want to create a table that does not exactly match the format of any existing table.

Exceptions

- None.

Steps

1. Click in a table whose format resembles the one you want to create.

TIP

Name table tags to reflect their use, and not the appearance of the table format.

You can select any table to create a new format; however, you can save some time by selecting either the table you want to change, or a table that has a format close to the new format you want to add.

2.   Make any modifications to the number of rows and columns in the table.

Your new table may require a different layout from the existing format. Add or remove and heading and footing rows, and adjust the number of rows and columns that appear in the table. You should also change the widths of the columns at this time, if necessary.

3.   Select **Table Designer** in the Table menu.

FrameMaker displays the Table Designer (see Figure 6.24), where you can modify many of the table's properties. The Table Designer has more properties than FrameMaker can display in a single dialog box. Therefore, as with the paragraph formats, the table properties are divided into groups, with each group containing several related properties. The

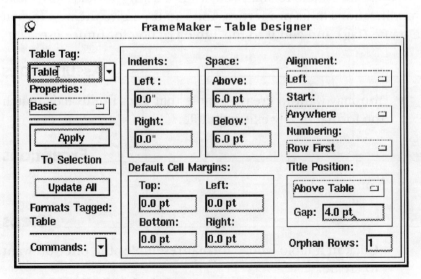

Figure 6.24   The Table Designer.

three table groups have the following names: Basic, Ruling, and Shading. You select the group you want to modify under the heading Properties in the upper left-hand corner of the Table Designer.

4. Change the **Basic, Ruling**, and **Shading** properties of the table as required, then click **Apply** to apply the changes. to the selected table.

5. Create paragraph formats for the text in the table.
   You can use the Paragraph Designer to format the title, headings, footing, and body cells within the table.

6. When done, select **New Format** from the Commands pop-up menu.
   This menu is located in the lower left-hand corner of the Table Designer window. FrameMaker displays the New Format dialog box (see Figure 6.25), requesting you to name the new format by assigning it a tag.

7. Enter the name (tag) for the new format.
   You should make this name descriptive for both you and others who will use the tag. It's a good idea to create and use tags consistently across all your documents.

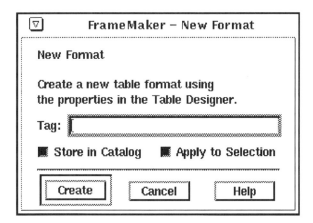

Figure 6.25   The New Format dialog box.

8. Select the **Store in Catalog** checkbox.
   This instructs FrameMaker to add the new format to the Table Catalog and enables you to use it to format other tables in your document.

9. Select the **Apply to Selection** option if you want the changes to be applied to the current table, and then click on **Create**. You should select this checkbox if you've made changes to the table format since you last applied the format to check the appearance of the table.

What To Do If

- If you want to see the current properties of a table, select the table when the Table Designer window is visible. The settings reflect the current table, which may or may not be the same as the properties of the tag stored in the Table catalog.

See Also

- Applying a New Table Format, below.
- Deleting a Table Format, p. 246.

112   Applying a New Table Format

When you create a table, you assign a format describing its properties and appearance in the document. However, this format does not have to be permanent. You can apply a new format to any table in the document. You may want to do this to make several tables assume a consistent format, thereby making related information easier to read and understand. Similarly, you may want to jazz up your document by applying special shadings and rulings, giving your work a professional appearance.

Assumptions

- You want to apply the new format only to the current table, not to the Table Catalog or other tables in the document. To update those, see "What To Do If" in this task.

Exceptions

- When you apply a new format to a table, FrameMaker doesn't override the default properties such as the number of heading, footing, and body rows or the number of columns. In addition, your custom settings are preserved.

Steps

1. Click in the table to which you want to apply the new format.
2. Select **Table Designer** in the Table menu.
   Use the Table Designer window to apply new formats to a table.
3. Select the new format from the **Table Tag** pop-up menu. You can display this menu by clicking on the arrow underneath the Table Tag heading in the upper left-hand corner of the Table Designer.
4. Click **Apply to Selection**.
   This applies the new format to the current table. It doesn't change the Table Catalog or modify any other table in the document.

What To Do If

- To update the Table Catalog along with all the tables in the document that are formatted using this particular tag, click **Update All** instead of **Apply to Selection**.
- If you want to update several tables at once, click in any table and choose **Global Update Options** in the Commands pop-up menu, located in the lower left-hand corner of the

Table Designer. FrameMaker displays a dialog box for you to change all tables and catalog entries, all matching tags in selection, or all tables tagged with a particular format.

See Also

- Creating a New Table Format, p. 237.
- Updating a Table Format, below.

113 ▶ Updating a Table Format

It's common to make several changes to a table format before finally arriving at a design that matches the document and presents the information clearly. When you complete this design process, the final format for the table probably bears little resemblance to any of the formats in the Table Catalog.

If you plan to use this format with other tables in the document, you may want to update the format in the Table Catalog. When you update a format, the properties are applied to existing tables elsewhere in the document that use the same tag.

Assumptions

- You want to change a table format.

Exceptions

- The changes you make in a table format will not take effect until you apply the changes or update the properties for the format. You can do this by clicking Apply to Selection or Update All in the Table Designer.

Steps

1. Click in the table that has the format you want to change, and then select **Table Designer** in the Table menu. FrameMaker displays the Table Designer window.

2. Select the tag of the format you want to update in the **Table Tag** pop-up menu. The Table Tag pop-up menu is located in the upper left-hand corner of the Table Designer window.

3. Modify the properties of the table.
    Experiment with the design of the table until you find a format that matches the requirements of the document. With each modification, you can see the effects by clicking **Apply To Selection**.

4. Click **Update All** when you are satisfied with the table format.
    If some tables have format overrides, FrameMaker displays an Alert dialog box to request whether it should retain these overrides or remove them when applying the new format.

5. Click to either retain or remove overrides in other tables. FrameMaker updates the format in the Table Catalog, enabling you to use this format with new tables you create using this tag. It also updates the other tables in the document that use the current tag, either retaining or removing the specific format overrides depending on the option you selected.

What To Do If

-   If you want to reset the properties in the Table Designer after you've made some unwanted changes, select **Reset Window from Selection** in the Commands pop-up menu. You can reset changes only if you haven't applied the changes to the table or updated the catalog. The properties are reset according to the settings of the current table.

See Also

-   Creating a New Table Format, p. 237.
-   Updating Specific Properties Globally, p. 244.
-   Deleting a Table Format, p. 246.

Updating Specific Properties Globally

There are some characteristics that you may want to use in all the table formats in your document. For example, you may prefer to have the title displayed below each table. FrameMaker enables you to modify specific properties for one or more table formats without affecting the other properties in the format. This ensures that all the table formats contain the properties you want without having to go through and set each one individually.

Assumptions

- You want to change one or more properties in more than one table format at once.

Exceptions

- None.

Steps

1. Click in a table.
   You can also select several consecutive tables in the document. When you click in a single table, you can update all the table formats in the document. If you select consecutive tables, you can update the formats of these tables, but not all the table formats. To select more than one table, you need to select the anchor symbols of the tables. The anchor symbols are the inverted T's that position the table in the text.

2. Select **Table Designer** in the Table menu.
   FrameMaker displays the Table Designer window.

3. Choose the **Properties** group from which you'll select the properties you want to update globally. You can select the properties group using the Properties pop-up menu in the upper, left-hand region of the Table Designer.

4. Select **Set Window to As Is** in the Commands pop-up menu. This changes all the properties to As Is, which means that FrameMaker will not change these properties when you update all the other table formats.

5. Set the properties you want to update across the other formats.
    Only set the properties that you want to change globally; leave the others with the As Is setting.

6. Select **Global Update Options** in the Commands pop-up menu.
    FrameMaker displays the Global Update Options dialog box (see Figure 6.26) You can specify which property groups to use for the update and identify which table formats FrameMaker should update.

7. Select the current property group in the **Use Properties** section.
    The current property group will be displayed as either Basic Properties Only, Ruling Properties Only, or Shading

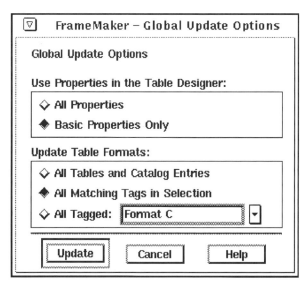

Figure 6.26   The Global Update Options dialog box.

Properties Only to match the current properties you were modifying in the Table Designer window.

8. Select **All Tables and Catalog Entries** in the Update Table Formats area, and then click **Update.**

What To Do If

*   None.

See Also

*   Updating a Table Format, p. 242.

115   Deleting a Table Format

When you no longer need a table format, FrameMaker offers you the option to delete it from the catalog. For example, you may have added several table formats when experimenting with the design of your document, and you no longer need a couple of them. Likewise, if you copied a table catalog from another document, it may contain a few formats that you never intend to use.

Assumptions

*   You have table formats in the catalog that you will not use and wish to remove.

Exceptions

*   If you have tables in the document that use a particular tag, you can still remove the tag from the Table Catalog. This will have no effect on the tables; however, you will now have tables that don't have a corresponding tag in the catalog.

_____ **Steps**

1. Select **Table Designer** in the Table menu.
    FrameMaker displays the Table Designer window.

2. Select **Delete Format** in the Commands pop-up menu.
    The Commands pop-up menu is accessible in the bottom
    left-hand corner of the Table Designer window. Frame-
    Maker displays the Delete Formats from Catalog dialog box
    (see Figure 6.27).

3. Select the table format in the list and click **Delete**.
    You can repeat this process and delete several formats in a
    row.

4. Click **Done**.
    FrameMaker removes the formats from the catalog only
    after you click Done.

> **TIP**
>
> Cleaning up the
> Table Catalog makes
> it easier for you and
> others to maintain
> your documents.

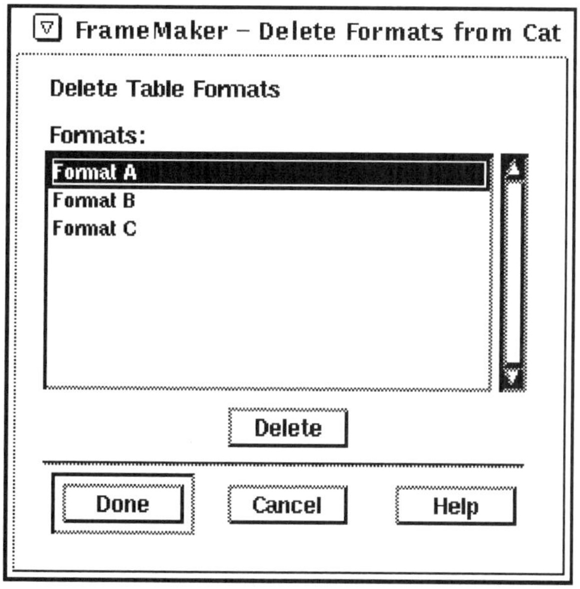

Figure 6.27   The Delete Formats from Catalog dialog
box.

What To Do If

- If you change your mind or unintentionally click Delete to remove a table format, you can reverse your action by clicking **Cancel**. Even though the format disappears from the list after you click Delete, FrameMaker doesn't remove it from the catalog until you click Done.

See Also

- Creating a New Table Format, p. 237.

116 ▼ Specifying the Alignment of a Table

The reasons for aligning a table are similar to those for aligning text in a text column. The way you place information on the page has a great effect on how it is read and understood. Therefore, FrameMaker gives you flexibility in controlling the alignment of the table in the text column. For example, you can specify the table to be flush with the left margin, flush with the right margin, or centered between the two.

Note that the final horizontal placement of the table depends not only on the alignment, but also on the indents that you specify for the table.

Assumptions

- You wish to change the alignment of a table.

Exceptions

- None.

Steps

1. Click in the table.
2. Select **Table Designer** in the Table menu.

FrameMaker displays the Table Designer window. The table alignment is part of the Basic Properties.

3. Choose **Left, Right**, or **Center** from the Alignment pop-up menu.
    The Alignment pop-up menu is located in the upper right-hand corner of the Table Designer window.

4. Click **Apply to Selection**.
    FrameMaker applies the selected alignment to the table.

What To Do If

*   None.

See Also

*   Indenting Tables, below.
*   Defining Cell Margins, p. 252.

Indenting Tables | 117

One of the ways you can control the appearance of a table in the document is to specify how the table is indented in the text column. You can specify both the left and right indent for a table. These indents, together with the table's alignment, determine where the table will appear.

For example, if you left-align a table, its edge will be positioned at the left indent in the text column. Likewise, a right-aligned table will have its edge at the right indent. In the case of a center-aligned table, the table will be centered between the left and right indents.

Assumptions

*   You wish to set the left and right indents in order to determine the distances of the edges of the table from the borders of the text column.

Exceptions

- None.

Steps

1. Click in the table you want to indent.

2. Select **Table Designer** in the Table menu.
    FrameMaker displays the Table Designer window. The left and right indent of the table are part of the Basic Properties (see Figure 6.28).

3. Enter values for the left and right indent in the Table Designer.
    These values specify the indent of the table with respect to the text column and not the edge of the page.

4. Click **Apply to Selection**.
    FrameMaker applies the indent changes to the table.

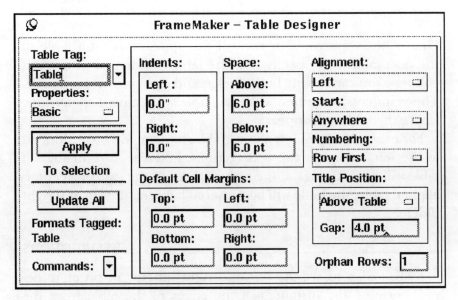

Figure 6.28   The Basic Properties in the Table Designer.

_____ **What To Do If**

- None.

_____ **See Also**

- Defining Cell Margins, p. 252.

Defining the Space Above and Below a Table

118

Setting appropriate values for the spacing above and below a table is as important as setting the proper spacing for paragraphs. If you specify too little space, your document can appear cluttered and difficult to read. Likewise, too much space makes the document look less professional. With FrameMaker you can control the spacing between tables and objects around them.

FrameMaker uses special rules to determine the spacing between a paragraph of text and a table. When the table is below the paragraph, FrameMaker takes the spacing below the paragraph and the spacing above the table and uses the larger value. Similarly, when the table is above a paragraph, FrameMaker consults the spacing above the paragraph and the spacing below the table and, again, takes the larger value.

_____ **Assumptions**

- You wish to set the spacing above or below a table.

_____ **Exceptions**

- When the table appears at the top of a column, FrameMaker does not use the setting for spacing above the table. Likewise, FrameMaker ignores the setting for spacing below the table when the table is at the bottom of a column.

Steps

1. Click in the table.

2. Select **Table Designer** in the Table menu.
   FrameMaker displays the Table Designer window. The spacing values for the table are part of the Basic Properties.

3. Enter values for the spacing **above** and **below** the table.

4. Click **Apply to Selection**.
   FrameMaker applies the Above and Below spacing changes to the table.

What To Do If

- None.

See Also

- Specifying the Alignment of a Table, p. 248.

119   Defining Cell Margins

FrameMaker gives you the ability to specify how text columns should be positioned within a table cell. The primary way you can do this is by defining the cell margins. A cell margin is the space from the edge of the cell to the text column in the cell. Note that paragraph indents in a table cell are measured from the cell margins.

Cell margins are measured in units called points. FrameMaker enables you to specify the number of points from the top, bottom, left, and right. For example, you can have a cell margin that is 10 points from the top and 5 points from the bottom. In most cases, you will probably want to use the same margins for all the cells in a table. However, FrameMaker gives you the option to customize individual cells, if required.

Assumptions

- You wish to set the cell margins in a table.

Exceptions

- Custom cell margins take precedence over regular, default cell margins. If you specify new default cell margins for a table, the custom margins will be retained.

Steps

1. Click in the table whose cell margins you would like to modify.

2. Select **Table Designer** in the Table menu.
   The Table Designer window appears. The Default Cell Margins for the table are part of the Basic Properties.

3. Enter values for the top, bottom, left and right cell margins, as appropriate.

4. Click **Apply to Selection**.
   FrameMaker applies the default cell margin changes to the table.

> **TIP**
> Making the top margin slightly larger than the bottom will make the text look vertically centered in the cell.

What To Do If

- If you want to change the margins for a single cell, click in the first paragraph of the cell and select **Paragraphs: Designer** in the Format menu. You can then specify the top, bottom, left, and right margins as part of the Table Cells properties in the Paragraph Designer.

See Also

- Resizing Columns, p. 227.

120 Specifying Where to Start a Table

Most tables in a document will likely appear directly under their anchor symbols in lines of text. However, in certain cases, you may want to have a table start at another location, such as the top of a page or the top of a text column. For example, you may want an important table to start at the top of the page for increased visibility. FrameMaker enables you to make these specifications and more.

You can also specify the table to float. When a table is floating, FrameMaker can move the table to the next text column in the document without moving the line of text that holds the anchor symbol for the table. If the table is moved, FrameMaker fills the space below the line containing the anchor symbol with text, instead of leaving it blank.

Assumptions

- You wish to set the specification that FrameMaker will use in deciding where to place a table.

Exceptions

- None.

Steps

TIP

Use Top of Page and Top of Column carefully, because they can add an excessive amount of blank space to your document.

1. Click in the table.
2. Select **Table Designer** in the Table menu.
   FrameMaker displays the Table Designer window. The setting that controls where the table starts is part of the Basic Properties.
3. Choose the placement from the **Start** pop-up menu.
   The Start pop-up menu is located near the upper right-hand corner of the Table Designer window. The following table placement options are offered: As Is, Anywhere, Top

of Column, Top of Page, Top of Left Page, Top of Right Page, and Float.

4. Click **Apply to Selection**.
    FrameMaker applies the new placement to the table.

_____ **What To Do If**

*   If you want FrameMaker to decide where to place the table based on the current formatting and other table properties, select **Anywhere** in the Start pop-up menu.

_____ **See Also**

*   Defining the Space Above and Below a Table, p. 251.
*   Defining the Table Title Position, p. 257.

| Specifying Cell Numbering | **121** |

FrameMaker includes several features for numbering sections of text, for times when you need to convey a certain sense of order to your information. For example, the Steps in this task are numbered to indicate that they must be carried out in the sequence described.

Since the information found in tables is also frequently order-dependent, you can specify a numbering for the cells. Using the Table Designer, you can instruct FrameMaker to number the cells in sequence across the rows or down the length of the columns.

_____ **Assumptions**

*   None.

_____ **Exceptions**

*   None.

Steps

1. Click in the table for which you want to set the numbering.

2. Apply an autonumber paragraph tag to the table cells.
    If you don't have a paragraph format in the Catalog, you'll need to create one. For more information, see the section on Creating Numbered Lists.

3. Select **Table Designer** in the Table menu.
    FrameMaker displays the Table Designer window. The cell numbering for the table is part of the Basic Properties.

4. Select **Row First** or **Column First** in the Numbering pop-up menu.
    The Numbering pop-up menu is located in the middle, right-hand side of the Table Designer window. Selecting Row First will number the cells across the rows, whereas Column First numbers down the columns.

5. Click **Apply to Selection**.
    FrameMaker applies the cell numbering changes to the table. Figure 6.29 shows examples of results.

Table 2: Volunteer List

Finance	Engineering	Marketing
1 Ross	2 Dave	3 John
4 Lisa	5 Anand	6 Richard S.
7 Uday	8 Jennifer	9 Carey

Table 3: Volunteer List

Finance	Engineering	Marketing
1 Ross	4 Dave	7 John
2 Lisa	5 Anand	8 Richard S.
3 Uday	6 Jennifer	9 Carey

Figure 6.29 Tables using row first and column first numbering.

What To Do If

- None.

See Also

- Creating Numbered Lists, p. 163.

Defining the Table Title Position | 122

The title of the table is an important part of the information you are trying to convey. In some cases, you may want to draw extra attention to the title by controlling its placement and how close it appears to the table. With FrameMaker you can position the title either above or below the table and specify the size of the gap between the title and the table.

Assumptions

- None.

Exceptions

- None.

Steps

> **TIP**
> Position the title consistently throughout the document.

1. Click in the table.
2. Select **Table Designer** in the Table menu.
   The Table Designer appears in a window. The title positioning for the table is part of the Basic Properties.
3. Select **Above Table**, **Below Table**, or **No Title** from the Title Position pop-up menu.
   The Title Position pop-up menu is located near the lower, right-hand side of the Table Designer window. Selecting Above Table places the title directly above the title, whereas Below Table positions the title below the table.

4. Enter the amount of space between the table and the title in the **Gap** text box.

5. Click **Apply to Selection.**
   FrameMaker applies the title positioning to the table. See Figure 6.30 for examples.

What To Do If

- If you want to display the title only on the first page, you need to create a separate title paragraph directly above the table. Since this paragraph serves as the title, make sure to specify that the table itself is untitled. Finally, to ensure that the title and the table are always kept together, turn on the **Keep With Next** setting in the Pagination properties in the Paragraph Designer.

- If you don't want to include a title with the table, or you want to remove an existing title, click in the table and choose **No Title** in the Title Position pop-up menu. After selecting this option, remember to apply the changes to the table.

Table 3: CalTrain Schedule - Departing San Jose

Destination	Train 41	Train 43	Train 45	Train 47
San Jose	7:10	7:31	8:00	9:00

Destination	Train 41	Train 43	Train 45	Train 47
San Jose	7:10	7:31	8:00	9:00

Table 4: CalTrain Schedule - Departing San Jose

Destination	Train 41	Train 43	Train 45	Train 47
San Jose	7:10	7:31	8:00	9:00

Figure 6.30   Tables with title above, below, and no title.

See Also

• Specifying Where to Start a Table, p. 254.

Keeping Rows Together | 123

Sometimes when a table is broken across two pages, certain information may get orphaned and lose its context. This is especially true if the information in one row is closely related to either the preceding or following row. Instead of formatting objects around the table to coax FrameMaker to display the information together, you can specify rows in a table that should always be kept together.

For example, you can instruct FrameMaker that a particular row should always be displayed with either the previous or next row in the table.

Assumptions

• The Next Row and Previous Row options are custom settings for the table. This means that if you apply a new format to the table, these settings will not be affected. Likewise, if you use this table to insert a new format in the Table Catalog, this setting will not be saved as part of the format.

Exceptions

• None.

Steps

1. Select the row that should be kept with the previous or next row.

2. Select **Row Format** in the Table menu.
   FrameMaker displays the Row Format dialog box (see Figure 6.31).

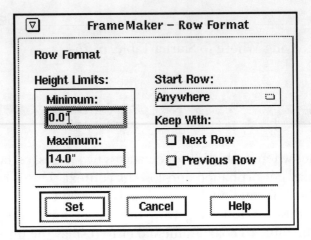

Figure 6.31   The Row Format dialog box.

3. Turn on **Next Row** or **Previous Row** in the Keep With area of the dialog box.
    You can click on either or both settings, depending on which rows you want to keep together.

4. Click **Set**.

What To Do If

• If, instead of keeping rows together, you want to force FrameMaker to break a table at a specific location, you can specify the row which you want to appear at the top of the next column or page. Select **Row Format** in the Table menu, choose either **Top of Column**, **Top of Page**, **Top of Left Page**, or **Top of Right Page** in the Start Row pop-up menu, and click **Set**.

See Also

• Defining the Number of Orphan Rows, p. 261.

Defining the Number of Orphan Rows 124

When a table is too large to fit in the current column or page, FrameMaker breaks the table and positions each segment automatically. However, if there isn't enough room on the first page, FrameMaker may only be able to display a very small part of the table, perhaps only one or two rows. In some cases, this may be acceptable; however, it usually makes the table confusing and the document appear poorly designed.

Fortunately, FrameMaker lets you specify where it should break a table. You must indicate the minimum number of body rows in a table that should be displayed on a page or column. This number is called the table's orphan rows. Unless FrameMaker can display this minimum number of rows, it will move the whole table to the next page or column.

Assumptions

- You can instruct FrameMaker never to break a table across pages or columns.

Exceptions

- None.

Steps

1. Click in the table.
2. Select **Table Designer** in the Table menu.
   FrameMaker displays the Table Designer in a window. The orphan rows option is part of the Basic Properties.
3. Enter the number of rows in the **Orphan Rows** text box. This number specifies the minimum number of rows that must appear on a page or column before FrameMaker moves the whole table to the next page.
4. Click **Apply to Selection**.

> **TIP**
>
> Setting the orphan rows to 3 works well for most tables.

What To Do If

- If you want to instruct FrameMaker never to break the table across columns or pages, enter a very large setting in the Orphan Rows text box. For this purpose, 99 would be a sufficiently large value.

See Also

- Keeping Rows Together, p. 259.

125 Defining Ruling Properties

One of the best ways to improve the appearance of the tables in a document is to experiment with different rulings. You can use rulings to separate rows or to place a border around a table. Using rulings imaginatively can greatly enhance the reader's ability to understand the information in the tables.

When you set up the rulings for a table, you can specify regular rulings and custom rulings. Regular rulings affect the entire rows and columns in a table and are part of the table format that is stored in the Table Catalog. Custom rulings gives you more freedom by not being restricted to complete rows and columns. They are also not part of the format stored in the Table Catalog. FrameMaker includes six styles of ruling, ranging from very thin lines to thick and double ruling.

Assumptions

- You want to set rulings for body rows, heading and footing rows, columns, and the edge of tables.

Exceptions

- None.

_____ **Steps**

1. Click in the table in which you want to change the rulings.

2. Select **Table Designer** in the Table menu.
   FrameMaker displays the Table Designer window.

3. Select **Ruling** in the Properties pop-up menu.
   The Properties pop-up menu is located in the upper, left-hand region of the Table Designer (see Figure 6.32).

4. Specify the column rulings for the table.
   There are three pop-up menus with which you can specify the column rulings. The first two pop-up menus enable you to set the ruling style for a particular column, ranging from the 1st column to the 12th. The third pop-up menu enables you to specify the ruling style for all other columns (other than the one you selected in the first pop-up menu). If you want all the column rulings to be the same, make sure that you select the same ruling style from the second and third pop-up menus.

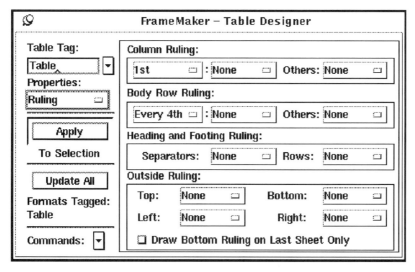

Figure 6.32   The Ruling Properties in the table designer.

5. Specify the body row rulings.
   The pop-up menus in the Body Row Ruling area function in the same way as the Column Ruling. Again, if you want all the body row rulings to be the same, select the same style from the second and third pop-up menus.

6. Select the heading and footing row ruling styles.
   You can select the ruling styles that separate the heading and footing rows from the table body rows. If you have more than one row in either the heading or footing, you can also specify the ruling styles between these rows.

7. Choose the ruling styles for the outside edge of the table.

8. Click **Apply to Selection**.

What To Do If

- If you want to customize the ruling of an individual cell, row, or column, select the cells you want to modify and choose **Custom Ruling and Shading** in the Table menu. Using the Apply Ruling Style dialog box, you can apply ruling styles to any part of a table.

See Also

- Using Interesting Rulings and Shadings, p. 234.
- Defining Shading Properties, below.

126 ▽ Defining Shading Properties

Effective use of shading can make your tables look professional and help highlight important information. You can specify shading percentages for the heading, footing, and body rows of the table. You can also specify two percentages for the body rows and columns, giving you the ability to create some very interesting effects.

For example, you can specify alternate body rows in the table to have a light shading and no shading. This creates a pleasant appearance that also helps the reader to follow related information across a row.

Assumptions

- None.

Exceptions

- None.

Steps

1. Click in the table for which you want to specify the shading.
2. Select **Table Designer** in the Table menu.
   FrameMaker will display the Table Designer window.
3. Select **Shading** in the Properties pop-up menu.
   The Properties pop-up menu is located in the upper, left-hand region of the Table Designer (see Figure 6.33).

> **TIP**
>
> You can help readers to scan across a row or down a column by shading it.

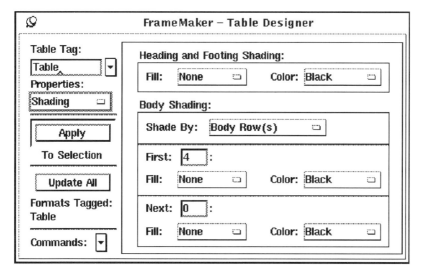

Figure 6.33   The Shading Properties in the table designer.

4. Select a **Fill** percentage for the heading and footing rows, along with a color.
   You can specify these settings in the Heading and Footing Shading area of the Table Designer. If you don't want the heading and footing rows to have a shading, select **None** from the Fill pop-up menu.

5. Select shading by rows or by columns in the **Shade By** pop-up menu.
   The shading options for the body rows and columns are located in the Body Shading area of the Table Designer.

6. Enter the number of rows or columns for the first shading pattern in the **First** edit box.

7. Select the **Fill** percentage and **Color** of the first shading pattern for the table body.
   FrameMaker applies this shading to the first number of rows or columns you specified in step 6. As with the heading and footing shading, you can use the option **None** to specify no shading.

8. Enter the number of rows or columns for the second shading pattern in the **Next** edit box.

9. Select a **Fill** percentage and **Color** for the second shading pattern.

10. Click **Apply to Selection**.
    See Figure 6.34 for an example.

What To Do If

- If you want to shade both rows and columns in a table, you have to customize the shading for the individual rows, columns, or cells. To do this, select the rows, columns, or cells that you want to shade and choose **Custom Ruling and Shading** in the Table menu. Select the fill percentage and the color of the shading and apply the settings.

Table 1: San Jose/San Francisco CalTrain Schedule

Destination	Train 41	Train 43	Train 45	Train 47
San Jose	7:10	7:31	8:00	9:00
Santa Clara	7:15	7:36	8:05	9:05
Sunnyvale	7:23	7:44	8:13	9:13
Palo Alto	7:37	7:58	8:27	9:26
Belmont	7:53	8:15	8:43	9:42
San Mateo	8:02	-	8:51	9:50
Bayshore	8:23	-	9:12	10:11
San Francisco	8:40	8:45	9:26	10:25
Destination	Train 41	Train 43	Train 45	Train 47

Figure 6.34   An example of using shadow in a table.

_____   **See Also**

- Using Interesting Rulings and Shadings, p. 234.
- Defining Ruling Properties, p. 262.

Chapter
7

WORKING
WITH GRAPHICS

Anchoring Objects

Most documents contain a mixture of text and graphics to convey information to the reader. While text and graphics are often handled separately when the document is being created, they are usually closely related when finally placed on the printed page. FrameMaker enables you to capture this association by creating and positioning anchored frames in the document.

Anchoring an object to text has definite advantages. For example, if you are producing a report describing the quarter's sales figures for each department, and you decide to highlight the information using charts, you can place each of the diagrams in a frame anchored to the text. When you edit or reformat the document, FrameMaker keeps each object anchored to the text as you intended.

127 | Creating an Anchored Frame

An anchored frame is a container for objects such as illustrations, drawings, clip art, and imported graphics. When you position an anchored frame, FrameMaker takes care of making sure that the frame remains anchored to the text. You are still free to edit and reformat the text around it. This can be very useful when you need to associate an illustration with a piece of text, for example.

Note that FrameMaker creates an anchored frame automatically whenever you import or paste a graphic at the insertion point.

After creating an anchored frame, you can edit any of its properties, including its positions relative to the text column or to the lines of text in the column.

Assumptions

- You wish to create a frame anchored to a particular point in the current text.

_____ **Exceptions**

- None.

_____ **Steps**

1. Click in the text at the point where you want to anchor the frame.

2. Select **Anchored Frame** in the Special menu. FrameMaker displays the Anchored Frame dialog box (see Figure 7.1). You can use this dialog box to specify several properties of the new frame, including its position and size.

3. Select the frame's position in the **Anchoring Position** area. FrameMaker gives you great flexibility in positioning the

> **TIP**
>
> Use an anchored frame when you want to associate the object with some text in the document.

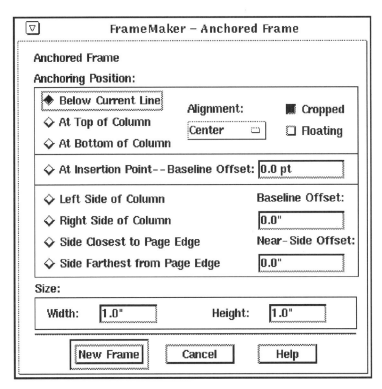

Figure 7.1   The Anchored Frame dialog box.

frame. However, if you are unsure about the options, specify the frame to be anchored either below the current line or at the top or bottom of the column.

4. Select the alignment of the frame using the **Alignment** pop-up menu.
    You can specify the frame to be left-, right-, or center-aligned in the text column.

5. Enter the width and the height of the frame in the **Size** area.

6. Click **New Frame**.
    FrameMaker creates a new anchored frame and places the anchor symbol at the insertion point.

What To Do If

*   If you don't want the frame to move when the surrounding text is reformatted, you should use an unanchored frame instead of an anchored frame. Another option is to create the drawing (or import the graphic) directly on the page itself. You may want to do this if you are designing stationery and want the logo to always appear in the same location on the page.

See Also

*   Positioning an Anchored Frame, below.
*   Placing Objects in an Anchored Frame, p. 276.
*   Creating Unanchored Frames, p. 300.

128 ▽ Positioning an Anchored Frame

FrameMaker gives you many options for positioning objects in relation to the associated text or to the text column containing the anchor. FrameMaker enables you to highlight information in a frame by positioning the frame to appear in the margin of a page. For small graphics and symbols, you can do the opposite and position the frame to appear directly in line with the text. In fact, FrameMaker is even able to treat the frame as another word and move it to become part of its regular formatting.

When you place a space on either side of the anchor symbol, FrameMaker treats the frame like a word and moves it to the next line when necessary during formatting.

Assumptions

- You wish to change the positioning of an anchored frame.

Exceptions

- None.

Steps

1. Select the anchored frame.
   You can do this either by selecting the frame's anchor symbol in the text column or by clicking on the frame's border (if you have borders visible).

2. Select **Anchored Frame** in the Special menu.
   You can edit the properties of the frame using the Anchored Frame dialog box.

3. Select the **Anchoring Position** for the frame.
   You can position the frame to appear either below the current line of text or at the top or bottom of the column.

4. Choose the alignment of the frame from the **Alignment** pop-up menu.
   You can select the alignment of the frame to be either left, right, or center in the text column.

5. Turn on **Cropped** if you want to prevent the frame from extending beyond the edge of the text column.

6. Turn on **Floating** to enable a frame to move to the next column.

TIP

When you are using a single-column page, you may want to turn off the Cropped option, enabling you to display a frame that extends into the margins of the page. However, if you are positioning a frame on a two-column page, you probably do not want the figure to obscure the second column, and thus you should turn on the Cropped feature.

TIP

You can place small frames containing graphics in line with the rest of your text.

By turning Floating on, you permit FrameMaker to move the frame to the next column that will hold it in case there isn't enough room to hold the frame exactly where you anchored it (see Figure 7.2). If you turn the Floating option off, FrameMaker will move the frame to the next column and leave white space under the text line where the frame is anchored.

What To Do If

- If you want to shrink a frame to match the size of the contents and place it in line with the text, use the **Shrinkwrap** keyboard shortcut (**Esc m p**). If you want to enlarge a frame and position it below the line with the anchor symbol, use the **Unwrap** keyboard shortcut (**Esc m e**).

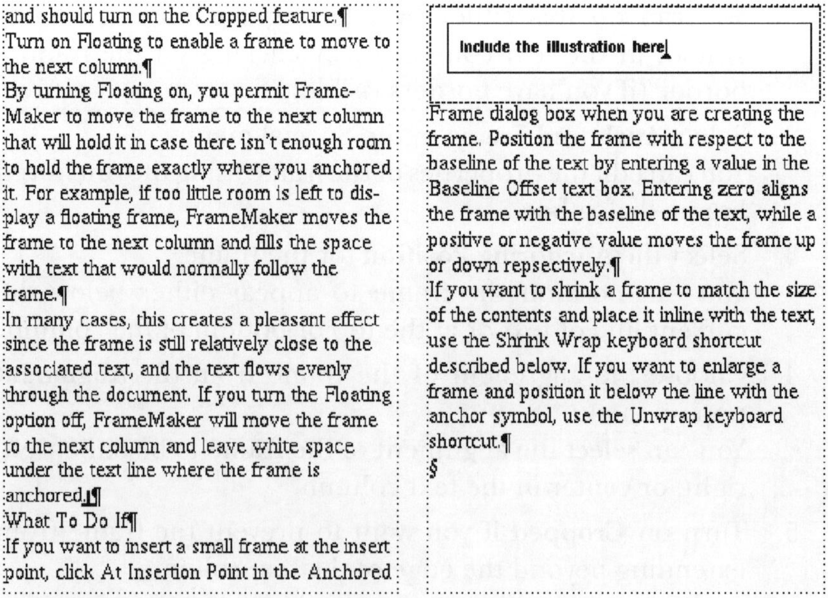

and should turn on the Cropped feature.¶
Turn on Floating to enable a frame to move to the next column.¶
By turning Floating on, you permit Frame-Maker to move the frame to the next column that will hold it in case there isn't enough room to hold the frame exactly where you anchored it. For example, if too little room is left to display a floating frame, FrameMaker moves the frame to the next column and fills the space with text that would normally follow the frame.¶
In many cases, this creates a pleasant effect since the frame is still relatively close to the associated text, and the text flows evenly through the document. If you turn the Floating option off, FrameMaker will move the frame to the next column and leave white space under the text line where the frame is anchored.¶¶
What To Do If¶
If you want to insert a small frame at the insert point, click At Insertion Point in the Anchored

Include the illustration here

Frame dialog box when you are creating the frame. Position the frame with respect to the baseline of the text by entering a value in the Baseline Offset text box. Entering zero aligns the frame with the baseline of the text, while a positive or negative value moves the frame up or down repsectively.¶
If you want to shrink a frame to match the size of the contents and place it inline with the text, use the Shrink Wrap keyboard shortcut described below. If you want to enlarge a frame and position it below the line with the anchor symbol, use the Unwrap keyboard shortcut.¶
§

Figure 7.2   A floating anchored frame.

- If you want to position the anchored frame in the margin, select one of the positions in the **Anchored Frame** dialog box.

_____ **See Also**

- Creating an Anchored Frame, p. 270.
- Placing Objects in an Anchored Frame, p. 276.

Modifying an Anchored Frame | 129

After creating an anchored frame, you can change many of its settings and properties and duplicate, delete, or resize a frame. These features are useful, because often it's faster to modify an existing frame than it is to create a new one.

_____ **Assumptions**

- You have an anchored frame; you can change its fill pattern, or the pen pattern of the border, and also modify the width and style of the line used to draw the frame's border.

_____ **Exceptions**

- None.

_____ **Steps**

1. Select the frame you want to modify.
2. Select **Anchored Frame** in the Special menu.
3. Modify any of the position settings of the frame.
   For more information about positioning the anchored frame, see "Positioning an Anchored Frame."
4. Enter the new width and height of the frame in the **Size** area.

TIP
You can quickly move a frame horizontally or vertically by **Shift**-dragging it.

TIP

If you want to re-size an anchored frame quickly, select the frame and drag one of the handles. If you need more control over the re-sizing, select **Object Properties** in the Graphics menu and modify the settings.

5. Click **Edit Frame.**
   FrameMaker applies the changes to the frame.

What To Do If

- If you want to move the frame slightly in the document, select the frame and drag it to the new location. This moves the frame while maintaining the location of the anchor symbol.
- If you want to change the frame's visible properties, such as its fill pattern or the pattern of its border, select the frame and modify the properties using the **Tools** palette.

See Also

- Positioning an Anchored Frame, p. 272.
- Placing Objects in an Anchored Frame, below.

130 Placing Objects in an Anchored Frame

Frames exist for the sole purpose of holding information that you want to convey to the reader. FrameMaker enables you to place several objects in a frame, including text lines, paragraphs of text in a text column, drawings, and imported graphics.

Assumptions

- You have an anchored frame.

Exceptions

- If the frame border isn't visible, choose **Borders** in the View menu.
- Any object that you draw outside of a frame will not be anchored to the text and will appear on the page instead.

_____ **Steps**

- Select the frame by clicking on the frame's border.
- To place a drawing in the frame, use the drawing tools in the **Tools** palette.
- To paste an object into an anchored frame, select the frame and choose **Paste** in the Edit menu.
FrameMaker pastes this object from the clipboard.
- To import a graphic into an anchored frame, select the frame and choose **Import>File** in the File menu.
- To insert text into an anchored frame, use the **Text Line** tool in the Tools palette.
The Text Line tool enables you to add single lines of text in the frame. You can use these lines for callouts or titles within the graphic.
- To insert a text column into an anchored frame, use the **Text Column** tool in the Tools palette.
Text columns are more flexible than text lines, because they enable you to add paragraphs of text, which are wrapped automatically. Another advantage is that you can insert cross-references, markers, or variables into a text column (see Figure 7.3).

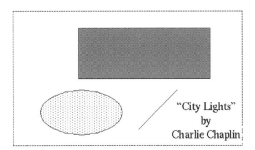

Figure 7.3 Example of Objects in an anchored frame.

What To Do If

- If a graphic doesn't move when you move the frame, the graphic has probably been drawn or inserted on the page instead of in the frame. You can move it into the frame by moving it away from the frame and then moving it back into the frame.

See Also

- Importing a Graphic, below.
- Drawing Lines, Arcs, and Curves, p. 292.
- Drawing Enclosed Objects, p. 294.

Importing Graphics

FrameMaker enables you to import graphics into the document and manipulate them like any other drawing. You can import graphics stored in these popular formats: bitmaps, Encapsulated PostScript (EPS), Desktop Color Separation (DCS), and insets. You can import a graphic into either an anchored or unanchored frame in the document, into a regular rectangle, or directly onto the page itself.

131   Importing a Graphic

When you import a graphic by copying, it becomes an integral part of the document. When you import a graphic by reference, you are not copying the graphic into the document but instead are importing the path and file name leading to the external file that contains the graphic. When you copy a graphic into a document, it's easier to move the text and the graphics around as a unit. This is because all the information is stored in one document. However, this also has the side effect of increasing the size of the file. In contrast, when you import a graphic by reference, FrameMaker inserts only the path and file name of the graphic. This obviously requires a very small amount of space; however, when you move a document to another workstation, you have to remember to copy all the graphic files as well.

Assumptions

- You have a graphic, and you have a destination location in mind.

Exceptions

- None.

Steps

1. Click in the place where you want to insert the graphic.
   You have several choices of where you can place imported graphics. If you want FrameMaker to create an anchored frame in a text column, click in the text column. Otherwise, if you want to place the graphic in an existing frame, select the frame. You can also position the graphic directly on a page by clicking in the page margin without clicking on any object or text column.

2. Select **Import>File** in the File menu.
   FrameMaker displays the Import File dialog box. You can specify the file name of the graphic, along with the method you want to use to import the file.

3. Select the graphic file to import.
   Use the list box to navigate the directory system until you find the document you want to import.

4. Choose the method you want to use to import the graphic.
   You can either copy the graphic into the document or import it by reference.

TIP

Importing a graphic by reference enables FrameMaker to always take the most recent version of the external graphic if it is modified.

TIP

If you want the imported graphics to output well to a printer, select a dpi resolution that divides evenly into your printer's resolution. In the case of a 300-dpi printer, which is the most common, you can select import resolutions of 75, 100, 150, or 300 dpi.

5. Click **Import**.

   If the graphic file you are importing is any type other than bitmap, you are done and the graphic will be displayed in the document. Otherwise, FrameMaker will display the Imported Graphic Scaling dialog box, requesting you to specify the bitmap's scale.

6. Select a scaling option and click **Set**.

   You can select one of the preset resolution scales in dots per inch (dpi), or you can enter a custom setting of your choice. The rule is that the larger the number of dpi, the smaller the actual graphic image in the document. If you want FrameMaker to scale the graphic to fit inside a selected rectangle, select this option in the dialog box.

What To Do If

- If you want to replace an imported graphic, select the graphic in the document that you want to replace, and perform the steps described in this task to import a new graphic. FrameMaker will select the same resolution for the new graphic as the one you're replacing. Of course, you can modify this choice, if desired.

- If you want to change the scale of a bitmap, select the graphic and choose **Scale** in the Graphics menu. You can then insert a scaling factor in the Scale dialog box.

See Also

- Creating an Anchored Frame, p. 270.
- Importing PostScript, below.
- Drawing Lines, Arcs, and Curves, p. 292.

132 Importing PostScript

To import PostScript into a document, you must first create a text column to contain the code. When you print the document,

FrameMaker uses this code to instruct the printer to construct the final printed output.

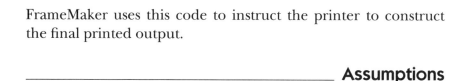

Assumptions

- You have a graphic, stored as a PostScript file, that you wish to import.

Exceptions

- Unless your workstation uses Display PostScript to draw images on the screen, you won't see the PostScript representation until you print the document.

Steps

1. Select the **Text Column** tool in the Tools palette.
   FrameMaker changes the cursor to the cross-hairs, which you can use to draw the text column on the page.

2. Drag the mouse diagonally to draw the text column.
   Release the mouse when the text column is the size you want.

3. Select **Import>File** in the File menu.
   FrameMaker displays the Import File dialog box.

4. Select the name of the PostScript file to import.
   Use the list box to navigate the directory system until you find the file you want to import.

5. Select **Copy into Document** in the dialog box.
   This causes the PostScript code to be included into the document.

6. Click **Import**.
   You can also use the paste operation to insert PostScript code into a text column. In a few cases, you may even want to type the PostScript code into the frame directly. However, you'll need to understand the PostScript page description language in order to do this.

TIP

If FrameMaker encounters an error in the PostScript code column, it will not print the rest of the document.

7. Select **Flow** in the Format menu.
   FrameMaker displays the Flow Properties dialog box (see Figure 7.4).

8. Turn off **Autoconnect** in the Flow Properties dialog box.

9. Turn on **Postscript Code** in the dialog box.

10. Click **Set**.
    After inserting PostScript code in a text column, FrameMaker enables you to select the text column as an object, but it prevents you from placing the insertion point in the column.

What To Do If

- If you want to include PostScript code from an external file into a PostScript column, edit the column as just described

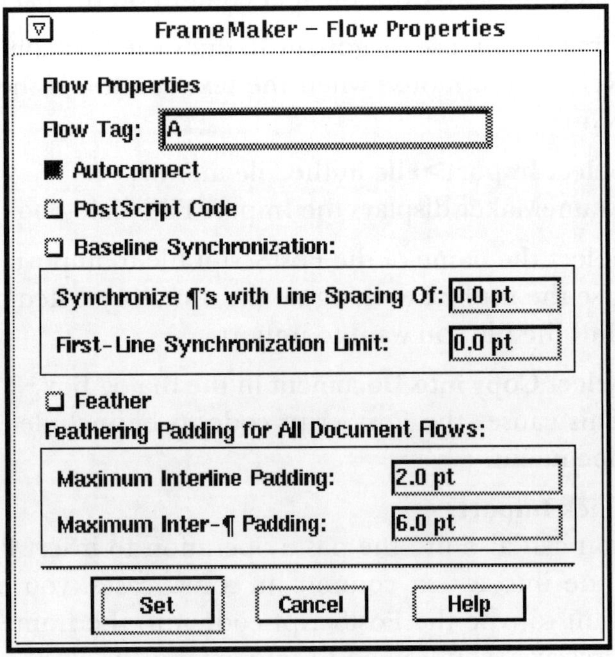

Figure 7.4   The Flow Properties dialog box.

and insert the following line in the PostScript code:

#include file_name

where "file_name" is the full path and name of the PostScript file. For example, the following line inserts the code stored in the file "diagram1.ps":

#include /usr/janos/grafs/diagram1.ps

See Also

- Creating an Anchored Frame, p. 270.
- Importing a Graphic, p. 278.

Locating Graphics Imported by Reference
133

When you import a graphic file by reference, the drawings and images are stored in their own files and are not stored as part of the FrameMaker document, which means that FrameMaker may not be able to find an imported file when opening the document if you moved or deleted the file.

Assumptions

- None.

Exceptions

- None.

Steps

1. When FrameMaker can't locate a graphic file, it displays a dialog box to inform you (see Figure 7.5). If you don't

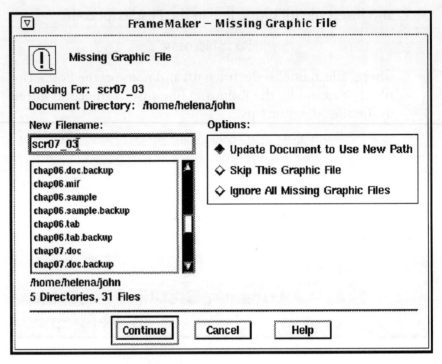

Figure 7.5   The Missing Graphic File dialog box.

want to locate this file, you can tell FrameMaker to skip this file and continue opening the document.

2. Navigate the directory system using the scroll list, and select the file for the missing graphic.

3. Click **Update Document to Use New Path.** FrameMaker will update the path and file name of the imported graphic in the document to point to the new file name.

4. Click **Continue.**

What To Do If

*   If you plan to move graphic files between different computer platforms, such as UNIX workstations, IBM PC compatibles, and Macintosh computers, use file names that are acceptable

by all the systems. For example, the Macintosh will not allow file names that include colons, while spaces may cause difficulties on some UNIX workstations.

PC-compatible computers running DOS and Windows have the most restrictive naming conventions; they disallow spaces and case-sensitive names and are limited to eight characters with a three-character extension. If you plan to move files around a lot, use the DOS conventions as the lowest common denominator.

See Also

- Creating an Anchored Frame, p. 270.
- Importing a Graphic, p. 278.

Creating an Inset | 134

FrameMaker enables you to start a special type of application, called an inset editor, from within your document; create a graphic; and insert it directly into your document. These graphics are called insets, and after you import them, you can quickly modify them by switching to the inset editor and pasting a new version of the graphic into the document.

Assumptions

- You can cut, copy, and paste insets in the same way you would any other graphic imported into FrameMaker.

Exceptions

- None.

Steps

1. Select **Inset** in the Special menu.

TIP

You can paste an inset directly into a text column and have FrameMaker create a frame automatically.

FrameMaker displays the Inset Editors dialog box. You can use this dialog box to select an inset editor to start within FrameMaker.

2. Select an editor in the scroll list.

The list contains all the inset editors that FrameMaker knows.

3. Click **Start**.

If the editor isn't already running, FrameMaker asks you to click **OK** to start the inset editor. If the editor is already running, the application's window will move to the front of the other windows.

4. Create the inset using the application.

Refer to the inset editor's documentation for more information about using this application.

5. Select a frame, rectangle, or page where you want to place the inset.

You can select a frame by clicking on its border. If you want FrameMaker to create a frame for you, place the insertion point in a text column where you want the new frame to be positioned.

To place the inset in a rectangle, select it by clicking. If you want to place the inset directly on a page, click in the margin of the page. Make sure not to click on any object such as a text column or graphic.

6. Select the paste command in the inset editor.

You will have to read the documentation of the particular inset editor to determine the command that performs this operation.

What To Do If

- If you want to edit the inset, double-click on it. FrameMaker will either start the editor or bring an already running copy in front of other windows on the screen. Use the inset editor to modify the graphic, and use the command in the editor that pastes the result back into the FrameMaker document.

_____ **See Also**

- Importing a Graphic, p. 278.

Capturing Screens | 135

If you are writing a manual about a software product, you will probably want to illustrate your descriptions using graphics of the program in operation. In this book, we often use screen captures as guide posts to help you make sure that you're performing the steps correctly. FrameMaker enables you to perform screen captures of any area on the workstation screen and store the images in the X11 **xwd** (X Window Dump) format.

Depending on your monitor, you can capture either color or monochrome images. If you capture a color image and later need to convert it to monochrome, FrameMaker provides a separate utility program called **xwd8to1** to perform this conversion.

_____ **Assumptions**

- You have a screen image you wish to capture.

_____ **Exceptions**

- None.

_____ **Steps**

1. Prepare the screen so that the image you want to capture is visible.
   Depending on the type of image you want to capture, you may want to position the target of the screen capture in such a way that other objects around it don't interfere.

> **TIP**
> Always assign meaningful names that describe the contents of the screen capture file so that you can easily identify it.

2. Select **Utilities>Capture** in the File menu (or press **Esc f t p**).

    FrameMaker displays the Capture dialog box (see Figure 7.6).

3. Enter the name of the file and the directory for the xwd image in the dialog box.

4. Click **Capture**.

    The pointer changes to cross-hairs, enabling you to select the region to capture on the screen.

5. Position the cross-hairs at one corner of the image.

6. Drag the capture border until it surrounds the region and release the mouse.

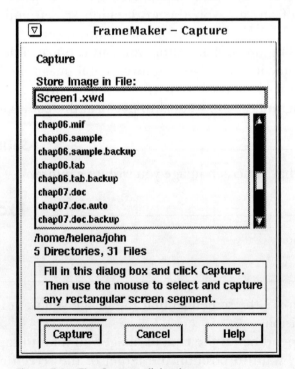

Figure 7.6   The Capture dialog box.

After you release the mouse button, FrameMaker informs you that it has captured the screen image.

7. Click **OK**.

What To Do If

*   If you make a mistake and capture the wrong image, simply repeat the steps and capture a new image.

*   If you have some extra bits around the edges of your image that you would like to crop, create a new FrameMaker document and import the screen capture into this document, using the resolution of your workstation monitor. Turn off the borders around the imported object, and crop the image by drawing objects with white fill and no pen. When you've removed all the unwanted bits, capture this image with the zoom setting at 100% so that the final image will look the same size as the original.

*   If you want to convert color xwd images to monochrome, use the FrameMaker **xwd8to1** command in a UNIX Xterm window. The utility creates a new file containing the converted monochrome image and leaves the original color image intact and unmodified.

See Also

*   Importing a Graphic, p. 278.

Creating Graphics

FrameMaker has several features that can help you create professional-looking figures and illustrations. For example, using the Tools palette you can draw lines, arcs, and freehand curves. You can also create closed objects such as rectangles, ovals, and polygons. You can label these objects by inserting lines of text and text columns.

Setting Up a Grid

FrameMaker supplies a pair of grids to help you control the placement and size of objects with precision. When selected, FrameMaker overlays the first grid on the screen and you can visually line objects up and size them with accuracy.

The second grid is called a snap grid and is not visible on the screen. When the snap grid is turned on, objects on the screen are attracted to this invisible grid and snap to it when drawn, moved, or reshaped. This grid makes it easy to quickly draw objects that are the same size and are lined up along the grid.

FrameMaker also enables you to select the spacing sizes for each of the grids to match the types of figures you are drawing.

Assumptions

- Even though the visible grid is displayed on the screen when you are working, it will not be printed as part of the document.

Exceptions

- None.

Steps

TIP

When setting the grid-spacing options, make the visible grid spacing a multiple of the snap grid spacing.

1. Select **Grid Lines** in the View menu to control the visible grid.

   The visible grid is a set of lines displayed on the screen to help you draw. Selecting this menu option toggles the current setting; it will hide or show the grid depending on whether it is already displayed or not.

2. Select **Snap** in the Graphics menu to turn the snap grid on or off.

   The snap grid is the invisible grid that acts like a magnet pulling objects in line with the spacing on the grid.

The Snap option in the menu toggles the current setting between on and off.

What To Do If

- If you want to set the spacing of the visible grid and the invisible snap grid, select **Options** in the View menu. Figure 7.7 shows the View Options dialog box.

  You can set the spacing for the visible grid by choosing a value in the Grid Lines pop-up menu. You can also specify the spacing for the snap grid by turning on the **Snap** option and entering a value in the **Grid Spacing** text box. When you are done, click **Set** to save the new settings.

See Also

- Drawing Enclosed Objects, p. 294.
- Resizing Objects, p. 309.
- Reshaping Objects, p. 311.

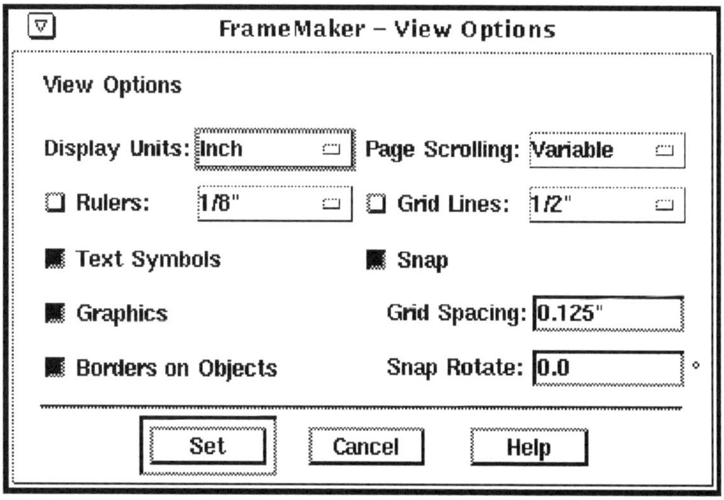

Figure 7.7   The View Options dialog box.

Drawing Lines, Arcs, and Curves

By using the Tools palette, you can draw lines, arcs, and freehand curves. Arcs are curved objects that look like sections of an oval or circle. A freehand curve, on the other hand, can take any curved shape and gives you maximum creative freedom.

Assumptions

- The Tools palette is displayed (press **Esc g T** to display it).

Exceptions

- None.

Steps

To draw a line:

- Click on the **Line** tool in the Tools palette (see Figure 7.8).
- Click on the starting spot of the line.

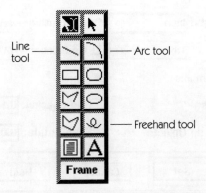

Figure 7.8   The Line, Arc, and Freehand tools in the Tools palette.

- Click on the spot where you want the line to end.
  If you are used to other graphics programs that let you drag the mouse from the beginning to end point, Frame-Maker also enables you to draw a line in that manner.

To draw an arc:

- Click on the **Arc** tool in the Tools palette.
- Position the cross-hairs at the starting point of the arc.
- Drag the mouse to form the arc. Don't release the mouse until you are satisfied with the shape of the arc.
  You can continue to drag the mouse along until the arc matches your intentions.
- Release the mouse button at the end point of the arc.

To draw a freehand curve:

- Click on the **Freehand** tool in the Tools palette.
- Position the pointer at the start of the curve.
- Drag the mouse along the path of the curve you want to draw.

Figure 7.9 shows examples of a line, arc, and freehand curve.

What To Do If

- If you want to draw lines that are connected, you can use the Line tool to connect them manually. However, it is probably easier to use the Polyline tool and draw all the lines automatically connected.

See Also

- Drawing Enclosed Objects, p. 294.
- Drawing Polylines and Polygons, p. 296.

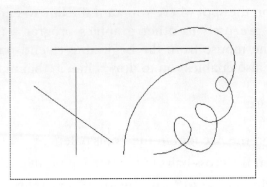

Figure 7.9   A line, arc, and freehand curve.

138   Drawing Enclosed Objects

FrameMaker helps you to draw the most common types of enclosed objects: rectangles and ovals.

Assumptions _____

- The Tools palette is displayed (press **Esc g T** to display it).

Exceptions _____

- None.

Steps _____

> **TIP**
> To drag a perfect square or circle, select the **Rectangle** or **Oval** tool and **Shift** + drag.

1.   In the Tools palette, click on the **Rectangle** tool to draw a rectangle, click on the **Oval** tool to draw an oval, or click on the **Rounded Rectangle** tool to draw this object. These tools are shown in Figure 7.10.

2.   Drag the mouse diagonally to draw the object.

3.   Release the mouse button to complete the object. Figure 7.11 shows examples.

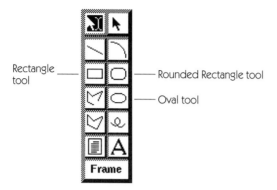

Rectangle tool — — Rounded Rectangle tool

— Oval tool

Figure 7.10 **The Rectangle, Oval, and Rounded Rectangle tools.**

What To Do If

- If you want to surround a graphic with a border, select the rectangle tool and draw the border. In the properties for the rectangle, make sure that the Fill pattern is set to None.

See Also

- Drawing Polylines and Polygons, p. 296.
- Drawing Regular Polygons, p. 298.

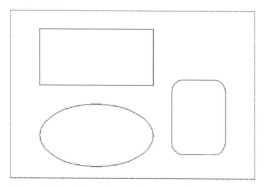

Figure 7.11 **Examples of rectangles, ovals, and rounded rectangles.**

Drawing Polylines and Polygons

FrameMaker provides two tools, known as polylines and polygons, to help you create types of odd shapes. A polyline is a series of line segments that are connected. You could create a polyline using the regular line tool; however, you would be responsible for making sure that the ends connect properly. Using the polyline tool, FrameMaker takes care of connecting the line segments automatically.

A polygon is a multisided closed object. A rectangle is an example of a four-sided polygon; however, polygons can have more than four sides. You can use the polygon tool to create objects with as many sides as you want; FrameMaker takes care of neatly drawing the objects on the page.

Assumptions

- The Tools palette is displayed (press **Esc g T** to display it).

Exceptions

- None.

Steps

1. In the Tools palette, click on the **Polyline** tool to draw this object, or click on the **Polygon** tool to draw a closed polygon.
   See Figure 7.12 for these tools.

2. Click at the starting point of the polyline or polygon.

3. Click at each corner (vertex) of the object.
   As you add each vertex, FrameMaker draws the object as it stands at the time. This gives you an idea of whether you are drawing the object as you intended.

> **TIP**
>
> **Shift +** click instead of click to drag a horizontal, vertical, or 45-degree segment of the polyline or polygon.

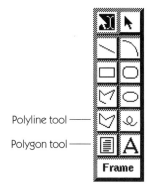

Polyline tool ——

Polygon tool ——

Figure 7.12   The Polyline and Polygon tools in the Palette.

4.   Double-click on the last vertex of the polyline or polygon. The final object is displayed with each of the vertices highlighted with a handle (see Figure 7.13).

_____ **What To Do If**

•   If you want to move the polyline or polygon immediately after drawing it, select any of the handles on the vertices and drag the vertex to a new position.

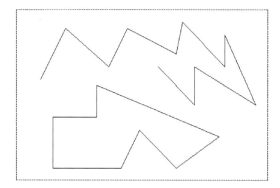

Figure 7.13   Examples of polylines and polygons.

- If you want to delete the object after you have completed drawing it, make sure it is selected and press the **Delete** key.

See Also

- Drawing Lines, Arcs, and Curves, p. 292.
- Drawing Regular Polygons, below.

140   Drawing Regular Polygons

A regular polygon has sides of equal length and equal angles. For example, an equilateral triangle has three sides with the same size and equal angles. Likewise, a pentagon has five equal sides with equal angles.

Assumptions

- The Tools palette is displayed (press **Esc g T** to display it).

Exceptions

- None.

Steps

> **TIP**
>
> You can draw a square or a circle by holding down **Shift** while drawing a rectangle or oval.

1. Draw a circle or square that is a bit larger than the regular polygon you want to create.
   It's important that the object be a circle or a square. If you draw a rectangle or oval instead, you will not create a regular polygon.

2. Select this object and choose **Set # Sides** in the Graphics menu.
   FrameMaker displays the Set Number of Sides dialog box (see Figure 7.14).

3. Enter the number of sides and the start angle of the regular polygon.

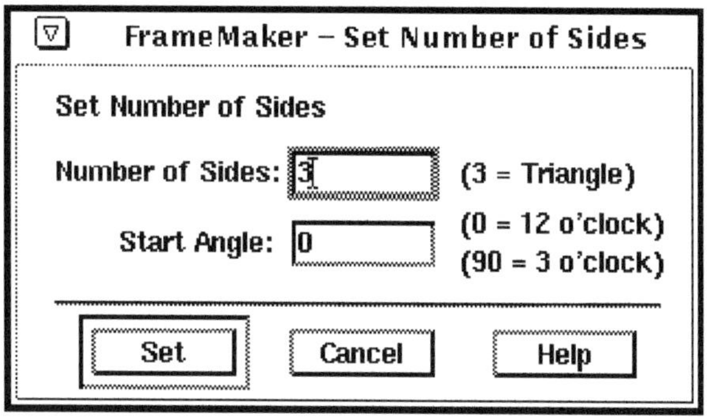

▽ FrameMaker – Set Number of Sides

Set Number of Sides

Number of Sides: 3̄   (3 = Triangle)

Start Angle: 0   (0 = 12 o'clock)
                  (90 = 3 o'clock)

Set   Cancel   Help

Figure 7.14 The Set Number of Sides dialog box.

The number of sides determines the shape of the polygon, and the start angle specifies the orientation of the object, with zero degrees pointing to the top of the page (see Figure 7.15).

4. Click **Set**.

_____ **What To Do If**

• None.

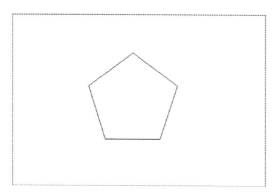

Figure 7.15 An example of a regular polygon.

See Also

- Drawing Polylines and Polygons, p. 296.

141 ### Creating Unanchored Frames

Certain graphics are closely tied to the text around them and should always be kept nearby to maintain the context of the illustration. However, other graphic objects should be placed in a particular location and never moved. For example, the logo of a company appearing on a letterhead should remain stationary, independent of the text on the page.

FrameMaker enables you to create a frame to hold these types of graphics. Instead of creating a frame that is anchored to surrounding text, you can create an unanchored frame. An unanchored frame remains at the same location on the page, even as you edit and format text in the document.

Assumptions

- You wish to place a graphic in a fixed location, not to be moved when the text changes.
- The Tools palette is displayed (press **Esc g T** to display it).

Exceptions

- None.

Steps

1. Click the **Frame** tool in the Tools palette (see Figure 7.16). FrameMaker changes the cursor to a cross-hairs, enabling you to draw the unanchored frame on the page.
2. Position the pointer at the start of the unanchored frame.
3. Drag diagonally to draw the frame on the page.

TIP

You can use unanchored frames to hold graphics on a reference page. Reference pages are useful for storing graphics that you plan to use frequently throughout the document. When you need a graphic, you can copy and paste it to a body page.

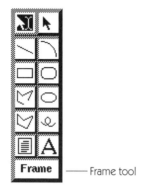
—— Frame tool

Figure 7.16 The Frame tool in the Tools palette.

4. Release the mouse button when done.
    FrameMaker creates an unanchored frame on the page.

_____ **What To Do If**

- If you want to associate the object with the surrounding text in the document, and have the object move with the text when you edit and format the document, use an anchored frame instead of an unanchored frame.

> **TIP**
> **Shift**-dragging will constrain the frame you draw to a square.

_____ **See Also**

- Creating an Anchored Frame, p. 270.
- Cropping Objects, p. 314.

Adding Text Lines   142

Many drawings or illustrations can get quite complex and may require special callouts to highlight important elements. You can enter single lines of text anywhere in a graphic or on the page. These lines of text are separate from any text column that you normally use to enter the bulk of your text. Also, when you enter the text, FrameMaker doesn't perform any of the word wrapping that you would expect with a text column.

When you enter lines of text, FrameMaker uses the character format of the text you last entered in the document. You can change this format anytime.

You can use FrameMaker's spell checker with lines of text you enter using the Text Line tool.

Assumptions

- You wish to install a text line.
- The Tools palette is displayed (press **Esc g T** to display it).

Exceptions

- You can't assign paragraph formats to lines of text. Similarly, lines of text cannot contain anchored frames, variables, markers, conditional text, or cross-references.

Steps

1. Select the **Text Line** tool in the Tools palette (see Figure 7.17).

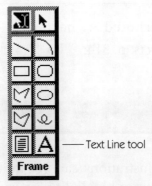

Text Line tool

Figure 7.17   The Text Line tool in the Tools palette.

FrameMaker changes the pointer to an I-beam, which indicates that you can insert text after positioning the cursor. You'll notice a small horizontal line close to the bottom of the I-beam. This is the position of the baseline for any characters you enter.

2. Click where you want to enter the text line.

3. Enter the line of text (see Figure 7.18).

_____ **What To Do If**

• If you want the text to appear in a different format, you can change it by using the Character Designer. To do this, select the text and choose **Characters:Designer** in the Format menu.

_____ **See Also**

• Adding Text Columns, p. 304.
• Creating Reverse Text, p. 320.

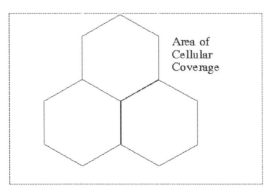

Figure 7.18   An example of a line of text in a graphic.

143 ▼ Adding Text Columns

Adding text to a graphic can be very useful in helping the reader understand the finer points of an illustration. Sometimes what you need is a full column of text with regular word wrap and formatting capabilities. FrameMaker enables you to add text columns to a graphic for these occasions. A text column permits you to enter several lines of text, which you can organize into paragraphs.

Use a text column instead of a line of text if you want to include the text in a generated list. You are free to insert variables, markers, conditional text, and cross-references in a text column.

Assumptions

- You wish to add text to a graphic and you need one or more of the text column features just described.

Exceptions

- None.

Steps

TIP
The bottom border of a text column changes to a solid line when you overflow the column with too much text.

1. Select the **Text Column** tool in the Tools palette (see Figure 7.19).
   FrameMaker changes the cursor to the cross-hairs, which you can use to draw the text column on the page.

2. Drag the mouse diagonally to draw the text column.
   Release the mouse when the text column appears as you intend.

3. Double-click in the new text column.
   This positions the insertion point inside the text column, enabling you to enter text as usual.

4. Enter the text.

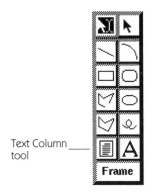

Text Column
tool

Figure 7.19   The Text Column tool in
the Tools palette.

_____ **What To Do If**

- If you need to enter more text than will fit in the text column, **Control +** click in the text column to select it and drag a handle to enlarge the column.

_____ **See Also**

- Adding Text Lines, p. 301.
- Chapter 10, "Creating Generated Files."

Changing the Look
of Objects

FrameMaker provides an extensive set of tools that enable you to change the appearance and layout of objects. You can flip objects to create mirror images, in addition to rotating them to any angle. You can also have FrameMaker smooth out an object that contains sharp corners.

144 ▼ Selecting Objects

After drawing or importing graphics into a document, you'll probably need to manipulate them several times before arriving at a polished look for the document. FrameMaker has two tools for selecting objects in the document: the Smart Selection tool and the Object Selection tool. You can select either tool by clicking in the Tools palette. When you finish drawing an object, Frame-Maker automatically selects that object and activates the Smart Selection tool.

Assumptions _____

- You wish to select one or more objects to modify them.

  The Smart Selection tool is usually more versatile than the Object Selection tool. This tool changes the pointer's shape depending on the type of object it is currently over. FrameMaker keeps the Smart Selection tool active by default. However, you can force FrameMaker to keep the Object Selection tool by **Shift**-clicking on it in the Tools palette.

  The Object Selection tool is less flexible, because you can select only objects with it. However, using this tool, you can select the entire text line or text column by clicking in it instead of positioning the insertion point in the text as you would with the Smart Selection tool. This is useful when you want to select a text column or text object and you do not want to position the insertion point in the text. See Figure 7.20.

Exceptions _____

- When a frame is selected, FrameMaker doesn't permit you to extend the selection to include any other objects.

- When you select several objects, they must all appear on the same page or be in the same frame.

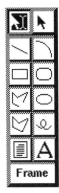

Figure 7.20 The Object Selection tools.

_____ **Steps**

1. Click on the object to select it.
   If the object has a fill pattern other than None, you can click anywhere in the object to select it. However, unfilled objects require you to click on the border to select them. When you click on an object, all other objects currently selected are deselected.

2. When the Smart Selection tool is active, **Control +** click on a text line or column to select the object.
   If you simply click on the object, you need to position the insertion point in the text instead of selecting the entire object.

3. Drag diagonally outside several objects to select them (see Figure 7.21).
   It's important to start dragging the mouse outside the first object and then extend the selection border to include the objects you want to select.

4. To select all the objects in a frame, select the frame and choose **Select All in Frame** in the Edit menu.

> **TIP**
>
> Use the Object Selection tool when you want to resize or move a text column as a single object.

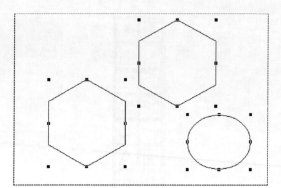

Figure 7.21   Several objects selected.

5. To select all the objects on a page, click outside any objects on the page and choose **Select All on Page** in the Edit menu.

    Make sure to click outside all objects on the page, including the text column. Clicking in the page margin works, as long as you don't have any objects positioned there.

6. **Shift + **click an object to add it to the current selection.

    You can use this Shift+clicking method to individually select several objects that may not be next to each other and would be difficult to include by dragging the selection border around them.

What To Do If

- If you inadvertently move an object when you are trying to draw a selection border around several objects, release the mouse button and select **Undo** in the Edit menu immediately.

- If you want to deselect all the objects selected, click outside all objects.

- If you want to deselect only one of several objects in the current selection, **Shift + **click the object.

- If you want to deselect several objects that are currently selected, **Shift +** drag diagonally over the objects you want to deselect. This will cause all the objects in the selection border to change their current selection state; any selected objects will be deselected, and objects that were unselected at the time will now be selected.

See Also

- Resizing Objects, below.
- Reshaping Objects, p. 311.
- Changing the Properties of an Enclosed Object, p. 315.

Resizing Objects   145

When drawing objects, you rarely get it right the first time. With FrameMaker you can change the size of the objects you create, either by using the mouse, when you need to perform quick modifications, or by using a dialog box, if you need to be more precise.

Assumptions

- You wish to resize an object.

Exceptions

- FrameMaker doesn't permit you to resize text lines.

Steps

1. Select the object you want to resize.
2. Drag one of the object's handles until it's the size you want. Drag the handle closest to the direction that you want to expand or contract the object. For example, if you want to extend the left side of the object, select the handle closest

> **TIP**
> **Shift +** drag the object when you resize to change the dimensions in proportion to its existing size.

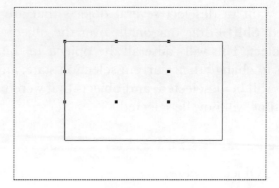

Figure 7.22   Resizing a rectangle using the handles.

to this side. If you want to contract the bottom right corner of the object, select this handle and drag the mouse toward the center of the object. See Figure 7.22.

What To Do If

- If you want to have precise control over resizing the object, select the object and choose **Scale** in the Graphics menu. The Scale dialog box appears (see Figure 7.23). Enter the new dimensions of the object in the dialog box and click

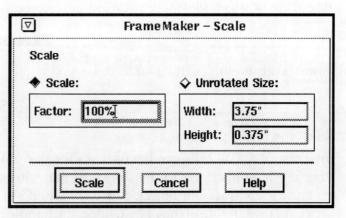

Figure 7.23   The Scale dialog box.

Scale. If you don't know the exact dimensions, you can also resize the object by specifying the factor FrameMaker should use in scaling the object. FrameMaker changes the width and the height of the object proportionally to the object's current size. A setting of 100% specifies the current size and will not change the object.

- If you want to maintain the proportions while resizing, **Shift +** drag a corner handle.

_____ **See Also**

- Selecting Objects, p. 306.
- Reshaping Objects, below.

| Reshaping Objects | 146 |

FrameMaker lets you change the shape of an object any time after you've drawn it. This means that you can add new corners to a polyline or polygon, change the location of the existing corners, modify the shape of an arc, and more.

_____ **Steps**

1. Select the object.
2. Choose **Reshape** in the Graphics menu (or press **Esc g r**). FrameMaker replaces the selection handles of the object with reshape handles. In the case of a polygon, the reshape handles will appear at the object's vertices. When reshaping a curve, FrameMaker displays a set of control points. You can reshape a curve using both the handles and the control points (see Figure 7.24).

   - To reshape a polygon, drag its reshape handles.
   - To reshape a curve, drag its handles or rotate using a control point.

TIP

Shift + drag the reshape handle to reshape an object in a horizontal or vertical direction.

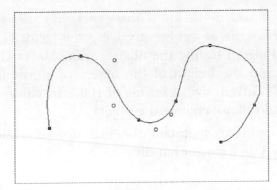

Figure 7.24 The reshape handles and control
points of a curve.

The reshape handles control the position of the curve.
FrameMaker displays two control points for each handle except for the one located at the end of the curve.
The control points determine the curvature of the
curve. When you reshape the curve by dragging the
handle, the control points are repositioned. You can
prevent the control points from moving by **Control**-
dragging the handle.

When you rotate the control points, FrameMaker displays a lever to indicate how the curvature is being
affected. As you rotate the lever, you modify the curvature on both sides of the reshape handle. You can have
FrameMaker change the curvature only of the nearest
side of the reshape handle by **Control**-dragging the
control point (see Figure 7.25).

- To reshape an arc, drag the reshape handle.
  FrameMaker displays the start and end angles of the
  arc and the percentage of a full circle that the arc
  represents. The start and end angle is measured from
  0 to 359 degrees, where 0 degrees points to the top of
  the page and progresses in a clockwise direction. The
  percentage of the arc is the area that the arc would

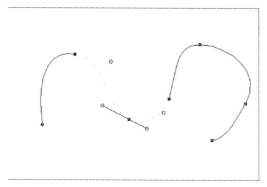

Figure 7.25 Changing the curvature using the
control lever.

occupy if it were drawn out to a full circle. For example,
an arc with 33 percent of a circle would be one-third of
the full circle in area.

What To Do If

- If you want to display the control points around another
  reshape handle on a curve, click on the new handle.

- If you want to specify the exact start and end angles for an
  arc, select it and choose **Object Properties** in the Graphics
  menu. Enter the values in the **Start Angle** and **End Angle**
  text boxes, and click **Set**.

- If you want to add or remove a corner from a line, polyline,
  polygon, or curve, select the object and choose **Reshape**
  in the Graphics menu. Click the middle mouse button on
  the object's border where you want to add the new corner.
  Likewise, to remove a corner, middle-click on an existing
  reshape handle.

See Also

- Selecting Objects, p. 306.
- Resizing Objects, p. 309.

147 ⟍ Cropping Objects

When you import graphics or images into a FrameMaker document, you may need to remove, or crop, some parts that are unneeded or unsuitable for the document. FrameMaker offers two ways of accomplishing this: with an anchored frame or with an unanchored frame. Your choice of whether to use an anchored or unanchored frame to hold a cropped image depends on whether or not you want the object to move with the surrounding text when it is edited and reformatted. Remember that an anchored frame is associated with the text where its anchor symbol appears. In contrast, an unanchored frame stays in the same place on the page regardless of the surrounding text.

Assumptions

- You have an image that you want to crop.

Exceptions

- None.

Steps

1. Create a new frame.
   You can create either an anchored or unanchored frame to hold the new, cropped image. Remember, to create an anchored frame, select **Anchored Frame** in the Special menu; to create an unanchored frame, click on the **Frame** button in the Tools palette.

2. Select the graphic and move it into the frame.

3. Click on the border of the frame to select it.

4. Resize the frame to display the cropped image.
   You can resize the frame by dragging any of its handles. FrameMaker displays only the area of the new resized frame (see Figure 7.26).

Figure 7.26 An example of a cropped image.

_____ **What To Do If**

- If you want to crop a section of an image that does not lend itself to the method described in the steps, you can use the following work-around. Using the Tools palette, create graphic objects, such as rectangles or ovals, that match the area that you want to crop from the image. Make sure that these objects use both a white Fill and white Pen pattern. After creating the objects, position them over the areas of the image that you want to crop.

_____ **See Also**

- Creating an Anchored Frame, p. 270.
- Creating Unanchored Frames, p. 300.

Changing the Properties of an Enclosed Object | 148

Objects such as circles and rectangles have several properties that you can modify to suit your document. You can modify the color of the object, its fill pattern, the line style of its border, and the pattern of its border.

Assumptions

- You want to change the properties of an enclosed object.

Exceptions

- None.

> **TIP**
> Holding down **Shift + Control** while selecting a color in the Tools palette will assign that color to all objects.

Steps

1. Select the object whose properties you want to change.
2. Click a pattern in the Fill area of the Tools palette (see Figure 7.27) to fill the object.

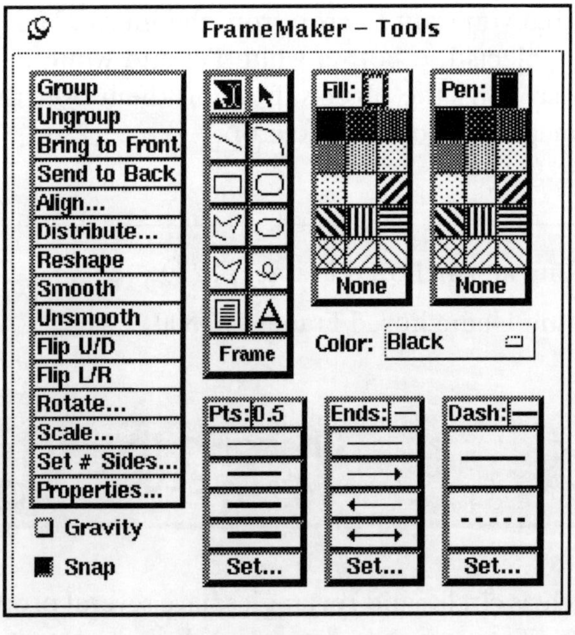

Figure 7.27 The Tools palette.

If you want the object to appear transparent and leave the other objects behind it visible, select **None** as the fill pattern. If you want the object to be opaque without a pattern, select the **White** pattern.

3. Click a pattern in the **Pen** area to select a pattern for the object's border.

   Selecting **None** in the Pen area will leave the object without a border, which may be useful in some figures.

4. Click a line width in the **Pts** (Points) area to select the width of the object's border.

5. Click a line style in the **Dash** area to set the style for the border.

   You can select a solid or dashed line style in this area.

6. Select a color from the **Color** pop-up menu.

What To Do If

- If you want to change the properties of several objects at once, select the objects by **Shift**-clicking each in turn. After doing this, modify the properties as described in this section.

- If you want to view the properties of an object, select the object and press **Shift** while choosing **Pick up Object Properties** in the Graphics menu. FrameMaker will display the properties of the object in the Tools palette.

- If you want to copy the properties of one object to another, select the original object and hold down the **Shift** key while choosing **Pick up Object Properties** in the Graphics menu. Select the objects to which you want to copy the properties, and click the current properties to set them for the destination objects.

See Also

- Drawing Enclosed Objects, p. 294.
- Specifying Line Properties, p. 318.
- Specifying Object Stacking, p. 330.

Specifying Line Properties

By setting the line properties in the Tools palette, you can easily modify the width and style of any line. For example, you can create a solid line, or select from a range of dashed styles to suit the information in the document. In addition, you can add several different types of arrowheads to the end of a line, enabling you to create sophisticated diagrams and pointers.

Assumptions

- You wish to change the width, dash style, or end style of a line.

Exceptions

- None.

Steps

First, select the line you want to modify. Then choose **Tools** in the Graphics menu. FrameMaker will display the Tools palette. The line properties are located in the lower right-hand section of the dialog box.

- Click on a width in the **Pts** area to change the width of the line.
  You can modify the four options that FrameMaker displays in the Pts area of the Tools palette. To do this, click on the **Set** button and enter the new line widths (in any order) in the **Line Width Options** text boxes (see Figure 7.28). You can also revert to FrameMaker's default values by clicking the **Get Defaults** button.

- Click on an end style in the **Ends** area.

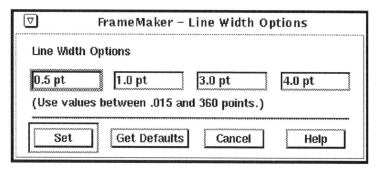

Figure 7.28   The Line Width Options dialog box.

By selecting a line end, you can add arrowheads to either or both ends of the line. You can also specify the line end to assume one of three styles: projecting, round, or butt.

To choose a line end style or to select a new style of arrow, click the **Set** button in the Ends area. FrameMaker displays the Line End Options, from which you can specify the line end style (see Figure 7.29).

- Click on a dash style in the **Dash** area.

  You can select either a solid or a dashed line in the Dash area. You can also specify the type of dashed line by clicking on the **Set** button in the Dash area. FrameMaker displays a dialog box enabling you to choose from several styles, including dash, long dash, dot, and dot-dash.

What To Do If

- If you want to connect two thick lines of the same width at right angles, use a projecting cap with both lines. You can select this cap style by clicking on the **Set** button in the Ends area of the Tools palette.

- If you want to connect two thick lines at any angle other than a right angle, use a round cap with both lines.

- If you want to connect two lines of differing width, select butt cap for both lines.

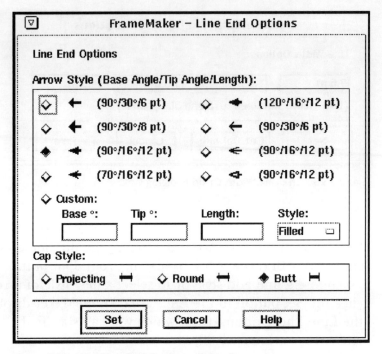

Figure 7.29   The Line End Options dialog box.

See Also

- Drawing Lines, Arcs, and Curves, p. 292.
- Selecting Objects, p. 306.
- Changing the Properties of an Enclosed Object, p. 315.

150 Creating Reverse Text

Certain sections of a page should visually draw the reader's attention to the material. When you need to place special emphasis on small amounts of text on a page, you should consider using reverse text. Reverse text usually is white text appearing on a dark background. It can very effectively catch the eye, especially if it is carefully framed with the right amount of white space.

Assumptions

- None.

Exceptions

- None.

Steps

1. Draw an object that will serve as the background for the text. In most cases, you can use a rectangle as the background object.

2. Select a dark fill pattern for the object using the **Tools** palette. On most printers, a black fill pattern works well for reverse text.

3. Outside the object, create the text line you want to reverse. Make sure that the text line is outside the object, otherwise, you may not see the text you enter.

4. Move the text line so that half of it overlaps the background object.

5. **Control +** click on the text line to select it.

6. Select **White** from the Color pop-up menu in the Tools palette.
   The part of the text line overlapping the background object should now become visible and the rest of the line disappear.

7. Move the text line over the background object to create the reverse text (see Figure 7.30).

> **TIP**
> Select a dark fill pattern to use as the background for the reverse text.

What To Do If

- These steps will not create reverse text out of a text column. Instead, you need to change the color of the text, using the

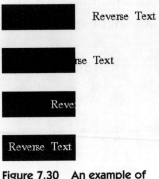

Figure 7.30 An example of reverse text.

Character or **Paragraph Designer**. For more information, please refer to "Changing the Color of a Paragraph."

See Also

- Changing the Color of a Text Range, p. 82.
- Changing the Color of a Paragraph, p. 84.

151 ▽ Flipping Objects

When you insert a graphic into a document, its orientation may not work well with the objects surrounding it. You can create a mirror image of an object by flipping it left, right, or upside down using a simple command. Using this feature, you can also easily create symmetrical objects by drawing half of the image and having FrameMaker flip it to create a perfect mirror image.

Assumptions

- You have an object in a document that you want to flip.

Exceptions

- You cannot flip frames, equations, text lines, or text columns.

Steps

1. Select the object you want to flip.

2. Choose **Flip Left/Right** in the Graphics menu to flip the object horizontally.
   FrameMaker flips the object using an imaginary center line running vertically through the center of the object.

3. Choose **Flip Up/Down** in the Graphics menu to flip the object vertically.
   The object is flipped upside down about an imaginary line vertically centered on the object (see Figure 7.31).

What To Do If

- None.

See Also

- Selecting Objects, p. 306.
- Reshaping Objects, p. 311.
- Rotating Objects, p. 324.

> **TIP**
>
> If you want to create a symmetrical object, you can use FrameMaker's flipping feature to create a perfect image, saving you extra work. Draw half of the graphic that will form the final symmetrical object, then make a copy of it. Using either of the Flip features described above, flip the object and move the copy next to the original.

> **TIP**
>
> Make a copy of the object before flipping if you want both mirror images.

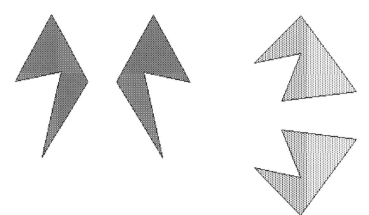

Figure 7.31   Examples of flipped objects.

Rotating Objects

FrameMaker gives you the flexibility to rotate most objects any number of degrees, with the exception of frames and equations. You can quickly rotate an object by selecting it and dragging its handle, or, if you need more control, you can specify the object's exact angle of rotation. When you specify the angle of rotation, FrameMaker asks you to enter an angle from the object's current position, or from its unrotated position. With FrameMaker you can edit most of these rotated objects in much the same way as unrotated objects.

Assumptions

- You have an object in a document you want to rotate.

Exceptions

- Objects snap to multiples of the angle specified in the View Options dialog box when **Snap** is turned on in the Graphics menu.

- FrameMaker rotates most objects around their center points. Text lines and equations, however, are rotated around their alignment points.

- FrameMaker enables you to rotate frames and equations only in 90-degree increments.

- You cannot edit equations, anchored frames, and rotated text columns until you restore them to their regular, unrotated orientation.

Steps

1. Select the object you want to rotate.
   FrameMaker displays the handles of the object by which you can rotate it.

2. Drag a handle with the right mouse button while holding down the **Control** key.

Move the mouse in the direction that you want to rotate the object. When you have finished, release the mouse to complete the rotation.

3. To specify an exact rotation, select the object and choose **Rotate** in the Graphics menu.

FrameMaker displays the Rotate Selected Objects dialog box (see Figure 7.32). You can rotate several ungrouped objects at once by **Shift +** selecting each and specifying the rotate information in this dialog box.

4. Specify the direction and the amount of rotation in degrees. You can rotate an object in a clockwise or counterclockwise direction.

5. Click **Rotate**.

What To Do If

• If you want to know an object's current rotation angle, select the object and choose **Object Properties** in the Graphics

TIP

If you want to rotate a frame or equation, select the object and choose **Rotate** in the Graphics menu. Specify the rotation angle in the dialog box and click **Rotate**. Remember, you can rotate frames and equations only in 90-degree increments.

TIP

To rotate in 45-degree increments, hold down **Shift + Control** while dragging the object's handle using the right mouse button.

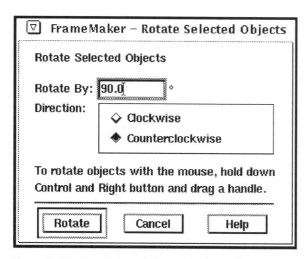

Figure 7.32   The Rotate Selected Objects dialog box.

menu. The Angle text box contains the rotation angle of the object.

- If you want to specify the exact rotation angle of an object starting from its unrotated position, select the object and choose **Object Properties** in the Graphics menu. Enter the exact angle in the Angle text box and click **Set**.

See Also

- Selecting Objects, p. 306.
- Flipping Objects, p. 322.
- Aligning Objects, p. 334.

153 Smoothing Objects

FrameMaker provides a set of tools to smooth out harsh corners. Using this feature, you can smooth polylines, polygons, and rectangles that you create using the FrameMaker drawing tools. You can also increase the curvature of rounded rectangles. If you find that your illustration is becoming too smooth, you can unsmooth the curves and restore angles in it.

Assumptions

- None.

Exceptions

- FrameMaker changes the current drawing properties to the corner radius you specify. Any new rounded rectangles you draw after this will use these new properties until you exit FrameMaker or change the radius using the **Object Properties** option.
- If you unsmooth and later resmooth a curve that you've drawn freehand, the resulting curve may be slightly different from the original.

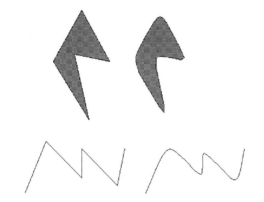

Figure 7.33   Several smoothed and unsmoothed objects.

_____ **Steps**

1. Select the object you want to smooth or unsmooth.
2. Choose **Smooth** in the Graphics menu to smooth the object.
3. Choose **Unsmooth** in the Graphics menu to unsmooth the object (see Figure 7.33).

> **TIP**
> Using a larger value for the corner radius increases the curvature of the corner.

_____ **What To Do If**

- If you want to change the curvature of a rounded rectangle, select the object and choose **Object Properties** in the Graphics menu. Enter the new corner radius, which determines the new curvature, and click **Set**. In most cases, it doesn't make sense to use a radius larger than half the smaller dimension of the rectangle. Thus in a rectangle measuring 4 inches by 6 inches, you should not consider using a radius larger than 2 inches.

_____ **See Also**

- Drawing Lines, Arcs, and Curves, p. 292.
- Drawing Enclosed Objects, p. 294.

- Changing the Properties of an Enclosed Object, p. 315.
- Specifying Line Properties, p. 318.

154 ▽ Measuring Objects

Some drawings, illustrations, and other objects are constrained to appear a certain size or position on the page. When this is the case, you need some way to determine the size of an object and exactly where it is positioned on the page. FrameMaker enables you to get this information using either the mouse or a dialog box.

Assumptions

- FrameMaker calculates the size of an object by the dimensions of the rectangle that encloses the object.
- The position of an object is measured from the upper left corner of the frame or the page containing the object.

Exceptions

- None.

Steps

TIP

To measure the distance between two objects, position the mouse on the object, hold down **Shift + Control**, then drag the mouse to the second object. Look in the status bar for the border dimensions.

To determine the dimensions of an object:

1. Select the object whose dimensions you want to determine.
2. Press the left mouse button while holding one of the object's handles.
   FrameMaker displays the object's dimensions (width and height) in the status bar at the bottom of the document window.
3. Select **Object Properties** in the Graphics menu.
   FrameMaker displays the Object Properties dialog box.

You can see the object's dimensions in the Size area of the dialog box.

To determine the position of an object:

1. Select the object whose position you want to determine.

2. Press the left mouse button while pointing to the object's border.
    FrameMaker displays the distance between the object and the upper-left corner of the frame or the page in the status bar at the bottom of the document window. You can also see the guidelines in the rulers at the edge of the document if you set the rulers to be visible.

3. Select **Object Properties** in the Graphics menu.
    You can see the position of the object by looking in the **Offset From** area in the Object Properties dialog box. These values are the distances from the upper left corner of the frame or page to the upper left corner of all objects except text lines and equations. For equations and text lines, the distance in the dialog box is from the upper left corner of the frame or page to the baseline or alignment point of the object.

_____ **What To Do If**

*   None.

_____ **See Also**

*   Resizing Objects, p. 309.
*   Reshaping Objects, p. 311.

Arranging Objects on the Page

The way you arrange text and graphic objects in relation to one another will have a great effect on how the reader perceives the information you are trying to convey. FrameMaker provides several features to help you manage this relationship and to control the way objects are arranged in the document.

One of the most basic properties that all FrameMaker objects share is the stacking order. You can use this order to specify which objects appear above or below others, enabling you to control which objects obscure or cover others. Also, if you expect to perform several operations on a set of objects, or if the objects naturally belong together, you can group these objects together to form a single unit.

FrameMaker also helps you to align objects horizontally and vertically to one another. This feature can clean up an illustration and make it appear more professional. Likewise, FrameMaker enables you to distribute the objects, to control the spacing between them, and to connect objects.

155 ▾ Specifying Object Stacking

FrameMaker maintains a stacking order for the objects that you draw in a frame or on a page. Whenever you create a new object, by either drawing it or pasting it to a new location, FrameMaker places the new object on top in the stacking order. You can see the result of this, especially if the object has some fill pattern, because the underlying objects become obscured. You can use this feature to your advantage by controlling the stacking order of objects and moving objects in front of or behind others.

Note that clicking in a region on the page where there is more than one object causes FrameMaker to select the topmost object.

Assumptions

- You wish to change the stacking order of objects on the page.

Exceptions

- None.

Steps

First, select the object you want to move to the front or push to the back.

- Select **Bring to Front** in the Graphics menu to move the object in front of others.
  FrameMaker moves the object in front of all other objects.

- Select **Send to Back** in the Graphics menu to move the object behind the others.
  This causes the object to be moved behind all other objects.
  Figure 7.34 shows an example of objects in front and back.

What To Do If

- If you want to create a drop shadow for a rectangle, start by creating two rectangles, one slightly offset from the other and filled black. By sending the filled, shadow rectangle to the back of the foreground rectangle, you create a pleasant drop-shadow effect.

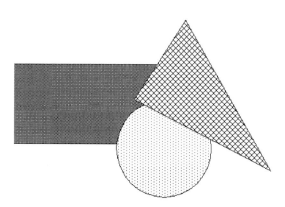

Figure 7.34   Example of objects in front and back.

See Also

- Grouping Objects, below.

156 ⬦   **Grouping Objects**

Illustrations and drawings often consist of several objects that work together to present one single image, so it often makes sense to manipulate them as a single object as well. You can flip, align, move, or resize a group of objects in one step. FrameMaker also lets you extend a group of objects into a larger group by adding new elements. If you need to separate out the objects in the group, you are free to ungroup at any time.

FrameMaker maintains the objects that form a group in a hierarchy to keep object relationships intact even after grouping. For example, if you ungroup an object that was created by a separate object and an existing group, FrameMaker will return the previous group as a unit.

Assumptions

- You have several objects you wish to group together so as to handle them as a single unit.

Exceptions

- FrameMaker doesn't permit you to group frames together.

TIP

Grouping enables you to perform the same operation on several objects in one step.

Steps

Select the objects you want to group together. You can select an object by clicking on it. You can add objects to this selection by **Shift**-clicking. FrameMaker displays handles around each of the objects that you select.

- Select **Group** in the Graphics menu to group the objects. FrameMaker groups the objects together and lets you know that it now treats this as a single object by displaying a single set of handles around all the objects in the group.

- To ungroup objects, select **Ungroup** in the Graphics menu. Make sure that the object you want to ungroup is selected before performing this command. FrameMaker displays the autonomy of each object by giving each its own set of handles (see Figure 7.35).

_____ **What To Do If**

- If you are ungrouping a set of objects that are groups themselves, you may need to perform the ungroup operation several times before each object on the page is separate from the others.

_____ **See Also**

- Selecting Objects, p. 306.
- Rotating Objects, p. 324.

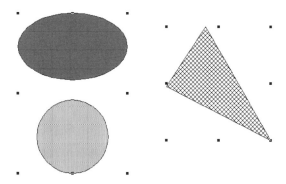

Figure 7.35   Grouped and ungrouped objects.

157 ⟩ Aligning Objects

When you have more than one related object close together on a page or in a frame, you can make them appear better organized by aligning them with each other. With FrameMaker you can align objects horizontally along the top, bottom, or vertical center of an object. Likewise, you can vertically align objects along either the left, right, or left/right center of the objects.

Assumptions

- You wish to align several objects vertically or horizontally with each other.

Exceptions

- FrameMaker uses the last object you select as the reference object for aligning the other objects you select. If you select the objects using the selection border, FrameMaker uses the first object in the stacking order as the reference.

Steps

1. Select the objects you want to align.

2. Select **Align** in the Graphics menu.
   FrameMaker displays the Align dialog box. You can use this dialog box to select how FrameMaker should align the objects.

3. Select an option in the **Top/Bottom** area, if you want to align the objects horizontally, or an option in the **Left/Right** area if you want to align the objects vertically. Each option describes the imaginary line that FrameMaker uses to align the objects. For example, selecting **Tops** will instruct FrameMaker to align the tops of the objects.

4. Click **Align**.

> **TIP**
>
> Select the object you want to align the other objects with last.

FrameMaker aligns the selected objects according to the settings (see Figure 7.36).

What To Do If

- If you want to align a line of text to make it either left-, center-, or right-justified, select the text line, and choose **Object Properties** in the Graphics menu. Using the Object Properties dialog box, select an alignment from the **Alignment Point** pop-up menu. When you are finished, click **Set**.

See Also

- Selecting Objects, p. 306.
- Distributing Objects, p. 336.
- Connecting Objects, p. 337.

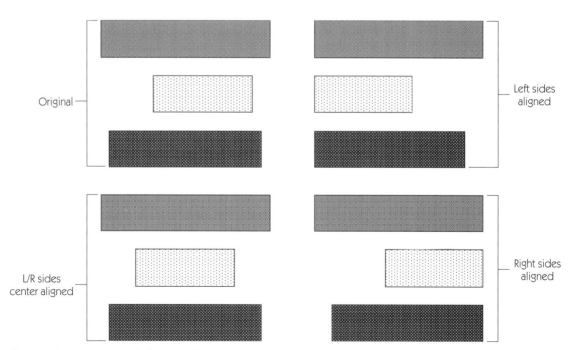

Figure 7.36   Examples of aligned objects.

158 — Distributing Objects

When you have several objects next to each other, the spacing between them can affect the appearance of the frame or the entire page. If the spacing appears haphazard, the effectiveness of the illustration can be reduced. FrameMaker enables you to distribute several objects so that the spaces between the objects are equal.

You can have the objects spaced along either the horizontal or vertical direction. You can also specify whether FrameMaker should measure the distance from the edge of the objects or from the centers.

If you need more control, you can specify the precise gap between the edges. When you specify the edge gap between objects as an exact distance, FrameMaker positions all the objects selected except for the one on the left (or the top if you select a vertical distribution).

Assumptions

- You have several objects you wish to space evenly.

Exceptions

- FrameMaker doesn't move the left and right objects (or the top and bottom objects) when you specify the space between the object centers or edges to be equidistant. Instead it moves the objects between these end objects.

Steps

1. Select the objects you want to distribute.
2. Select **Distribute** in the Graphics menu.
   FrameMaker displays the Distribute dialog box.
3. Choose the spacing in the dialog box.
   You can instruct FrameMaker to make the objects equidistant from the center or from the edges. You can also specify

whether you want the objects to be distributed horizontally or vertically.

4.   Click **Distribute**.

_____ **What To Do If**

- If the objects are moved off the page because you specified too large a value for the edge gap, select **Undo** in the Edit menu immediately.

_____ **See Also**

- Selecting Objects, p. 306.
- Aligning Objects, p. 334.
- Connecting Objects, below.

| **Connecting Objects** | 159 |

You won't always have the need to connect objects together; however, when you do, you can use a FrameMaker feature known as "gravity" to help you. When you turn on gravity, it causes objects to attract each other whenever you move them close to each other. This attraction also applies when you draw a new object or resize and reshape an existing object.

FrameMaker gives an object gravity along its entire path and at its corners. In the case of rectangles and ovals, gravity is also exerted at the center of the object. Since objects are more frequently connected at their corners, FrameMaker assigns greater gravitational pull at an object's corner than at its sides.

_____ **Assumptions**

- You have two or more objects that you want to have snap into exact contact with each other.

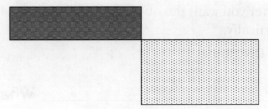

Figure 7.37 Connecting two objects at the corner using gravity.

Exceptions

- None.

Steps

1. Select **Gravity** in the Graphics menu.
   You can determine whether gravity is already on by examining the checkbox beside the Gravity option in the menu.

2. Drag a handle of an object close to the object to which you want to connect it.
   You can also draw a new object and bring it close to an object. When you get close enough to the object, its gravity will cause the object you are dragging to snap to it (see Figure 7.37).

What To Do If

- None.

See Also

- Selecting Objects, p. 306.
- Resizing Objects, p. 309.

Using Color

Color can highlight important information and add a sense of dynamics to an otherwise passive piece of paper; it can even create a path for the eye through a complex page of information. FrameMaker enables you to use a set of predefined colors or to create your own, by combining other colors and assigning these new colors a name.

When it comes time to print the color document, FrameMaker enables you to print either composite plates, which contain all the colors on the same page as you see them on the monitor, or color separations, which consist of multiple sheets for each page. Composite pages are useful for in-house laser printers when you want to print a single, finished sheet for each page in the document.

On the other hand, if you plan to send the output to a commercial printer that requires color separations, you can direct FrameMaker to print separate sheets for the cyan, magenta, yellow, and black components of the colors on the page. The commercial printer can then process these separations when printing the color document on its press. It's a good idea to consult your commercial printer early during the design process of the document. Often they can advise you on how to create outputs that can reduce the printing time and cost.

Specifying a Color Model | 160

In FrameMaker, colors are created by mixing the basic colors that are part of the model you're using. With FrameMaker you can select from four color models, each serving a different purpose:

- CMYK (Cyan, Magenta, Yellow, Black)
- RGB (Red, Green, Blue)

- HLS (Hue, Lightness, Saturation)
- PANTONE (PANTONE Matching System)

The CMYK color model is often used by commercial printers to produce color documents, whereas RGB is used to display screen colors on a color monitor. The HLS model is a more traditional system that is used by artists. Finally, the PANTONE system allows print shops to mix ink colors using precise formulas to match a color.

Each color is stored with the document in a color catalog. This is similar to the way FrameMaker stores formats in character and paragraph formats. You can modify the colors in the catalog, and add new colors that you create. You can add new colors to the catalog from other FrameMaker documents. You can also add new definitions to the color catalog by importing an Encapsulated PostScript (EPS) image that includes Adobe color definitions.

After creating or modifying color definitions, you can assign these colors to text and objects in the document. For example, you may want to assign a certain color to important information in certain table cells. Another option is to use colors to highlight important headers in the document, such as those for the troubleshooting or help sections. You can assign colors to text and objects using the Color pop-up menu in the Tools palette. In addition, you can assign colors to text by selecting a format in the Character or Paragraph Catalog.

Assumptions

- You need to select the color model that is to be used with a document.

Exceptions

- None.

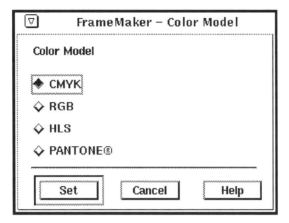

Figure 7.38   The Color Model dialog box.

_____ **Steps**

1. Select **Color:Model** in the View menu.
    FrameMaker displays the Color Model dialog box (see Figure 7.38). You can select a color model using this dialog box.

2. Choose a color model.
    You can select from CMYK, RGB, HLS, and PANTONE.

3. Click **Set**.
    When defining colors for the document, FrameMaker will use the color model you selected.

> **TIP**
>
> To ensure consistency throughout the document, use the character and paragraph formats to apply color to text.

_____ **What To Do If**

• If you want to create color separations for use with a four-color commercial printer, use the CMYK color model. FrameMaker prints each of the four color components on a separate sheet of paper.

• If you want to use color to display information on the workstation's screen, select the RGB color model. This model is ideal for creating online manuals, for example.

- If you want to create colors in a fashion similar to picking a color from a color wheel, select the HLS color model. Artists often use this method to mix colors. You can also define the general look of the color, the shade, and the clarity.
- If you want to use colors that are defined using precise formulas, select the PANTONE color model. The advantage of using this model is that commercial printers can match the colors by using the same formulas given a particular color name.

See Also

- Creating New Colors, below.
- Applying a Predefined Character Tag, p. 66.
- Applying a Predefined Paragraph Tag, p. 71.

161 ⟩ Creating New Colors

Use your creativity to create new colors by mixing the color levels using one of the four models. With this feature, you can create just about any color you can imagine. FrameMaker automatically adds any new colors you create to the Color pop-up menu in the Tools palette. These new colors appear in the Character Designer, the Paragraph Designer, the Object Properties dialog box, and the Custom Ruling and Shading dialog box as well.

Assumptions

- You wish to create a new color.

Exceptions

- Colors are displayed in the Color Definition dialog box only on color monitors. When you are defining colors using a monochrome monitor, every color other than white is displayed as black. Obviously, defining colors by visual feedback on a monochrome monitor is next to impossible.

Steps

1. Select **Color:Definitions** in the View menu.
   FrameMaker displays a dialog box for you to modify the color definitions for the color model you are using in the document. FrameMaker displays a different dialog box for each of the four different color models that it supports (see Figure 7.39).

2. Click **New Color** in the Colors scroll list.

3. Enter a name for the new color.

TIP

When creating new color definitions, name them according to how they will be used as opposed to how they look.

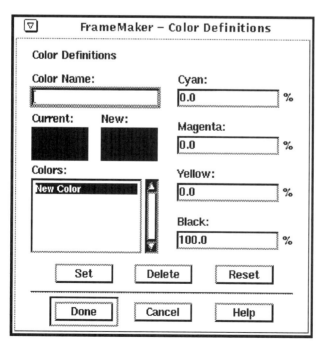

Figure 7.39   The Color Definitions dialog box for the CMYK model.

4.   Enter the values defining the color.

The region below the Color Name text box has two areas to reflect your color definitions. The area labeled Current displays the color as it appeared before you started modifying the color definition. In the case of a new color definition, this area is black.

The area labeled New contains the new color you are creating. As you enter new values to define the color, this area changes to reflect the new color. Use this area to fine-tune your color definition before finally accepting the values.

5.   Click **Set**.

FrameMaker adds the new color, with the name you assigned, to the Colors scroll list. You can repeat steps 2 through 5 to create new colors.

6.   Click **Done**.

FrameMaker adds all the new colors to the Color Catalog for the document. If you modify colors used by text or objects in the document, FrameMaker also applies the new definitions to these objects.

What To Do If

- If you don't like the changes you've just made, click **Reset** before clicking **Set**.

- If you want to rename a color, select the color in the scroll list and enter a new name in the **Color Name** text box. After entering the name, click **Set** to rename the color. You can rename any number of colors by repeating this procedure. When you're finished, click **Done**.

- If you want to delete a color, select the color in the Colors scroll list and click **Delete**. When you are finished deleting colors, click **Done**. FrameMaker doesn't let you delete any of the base colors, such as red, green, blue, cyan, magenta, yellow, black, or white. FrameMaker also prevents you from deleting any colors that are defined in an imported EPS file.

See Also

- Specifying a Color Model, p. 339.

Viewing Colors 162

When you create a document using several colors, you may want to control which colors are displayed at any given time. FrameMaker allows you to create up to six different color views of a document. A view specifies which colors FrameMaker will visibly display.

For example, if you are creating a complex graphic that is composed of many parts, you can assign each component a different color. You can then assign color views that display only the parts of the graphic that are of interest to you. Likewise, color views specify how FrameMaker displays all objects in the document including, of course, text.

Assumptions

- You wish to create a view specifying which colors in the document will be visible.

Exceptions

- On a color monitor, colors in the Normal list appear as expected. The colors in the Cutout list are shown as white when they overlap objects with different colors. FrameMaker will not display the colors in the Invisible list. On a monochrome monitor, all colors in the Normal list, except for white, appear as black.

Steps

1. Select **Color:Views** in the View menu.
   FrameMaker displays the Define Color Views dialog box (see Figure 7.40).

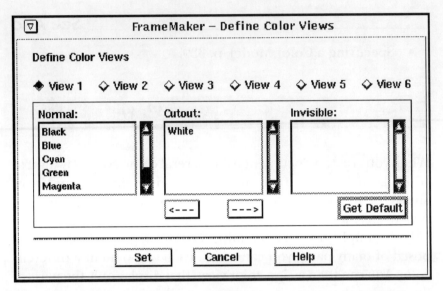

Figure 7.40   The Define Color Views dialog box.

2. Select the view number you want to set.
   Each view specifies which colors will appear as normal, cutout, or invisible in the document. You can instruct which colors FrameMaker should display in each manner by moving the color into the respective list in the Define Color Views dialog box.

3. Click on the color you want to move to a new list.

4. Click on either the left or right arrow to move the color.
   The arrow buttons appear directly below the scrolling lists. Clicking on the arrow moves the selected color to the new list in the appropriate direction. You can return to the default definition of the view by clicking on the **Get Default** button.

5. Click **Set**.
   FrameMaker saves the settings you made for a view and displays the document using the current view.

_____ **What To Do If**

- If you want to select a view without making any changes to the colors that define a particular view, choose **Color:Views** in the Views menu. In the Define Color Views dialog box, click on the view you want FrameMaker to use, and click **Set**.

- If you want to make sure that certain parts of the document, such as a particular level of heading, use the same color, you can test this using color views. To do this, take the color in question and move it to the Invisible list. If any part of the document you are checking for is still visible, you know it's not assigned the proper color.

_____ **See Also**

- Printing Color Separations, p. 351.

Overprinting Objects | 163

When printing objects that overlap, FrameMaker cuts out the part of the object that is being overlapped and prints it as white. This means that only part of the background object is actually printed—the part that isn't overlapped by an object in front. This can introduce a small white gap between the front and back object where FrameMaker has performed the cutout.

You can override this cutout and allow the objects to overprint one another. This means that the front object will be printed on the background object, and where there is an overlap, FrameMaker will blend the colors without any white gaps between the objects.

_____ **Assumptions**

- You want an object to overprint another.

Exceptions

- None.

Steps

1. Select the object you want to overprint another object.
2. Choose **Overprint** in the Graphics menu.
   FrameMaker displays the Overprint dialog box (see Figure 7.41).
3. Turn on the **Overprint** option in the dialog box.
4. Click **Set**.

What To Do If

- If you move the object to another location, you can select **Don't Overprint** to turn this option off, if required.

See Also

- Printing Composite Pages, p. 349.
- Printing Color Separations, p. 351.

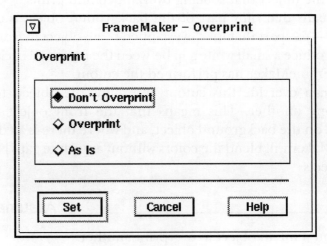

Figure 7.41   The Overprint dialog box.

Printing Composite Pages | 164

When it is time to print the pages of a color document, Frame-Maker lets you choose whether to print all the colors on a single plate for each page, or to print colors on separate plates using color separations. If you have a color or monochrome laser printer, you can print the document using composite pages and achieve high-quality results. However, if you need to produce plates for a commercial printer that requires color separation, you should not print composite pages.

In this section, you'll read about printing all the colors on composite pages; the following section will describe how to print color separations.

When you print a composite plate, FrameMaker prints all the colors that it is currently displaying using the selected color view.

When FrameMaker prints composite plates on a color printer, the resulting pages are also in color. On a black and white printer, the colors will be represented by shades of gray that reflect the density of the colors they are substituting.

Assumptions

- You wish to print a document as composite pages.

Exceptions

- None.

Steps

1. Select **Print** in the File menu (or press **Esc f p**). FrameMaker displays the Print dialog box (see Figure 7.42).

2. Turn off the **Print Separations** option.

3. Select the other print options as appropriate in the dialog box.

> **TIP**
>
> Print composite pages if you only want to output a single sheet per page.

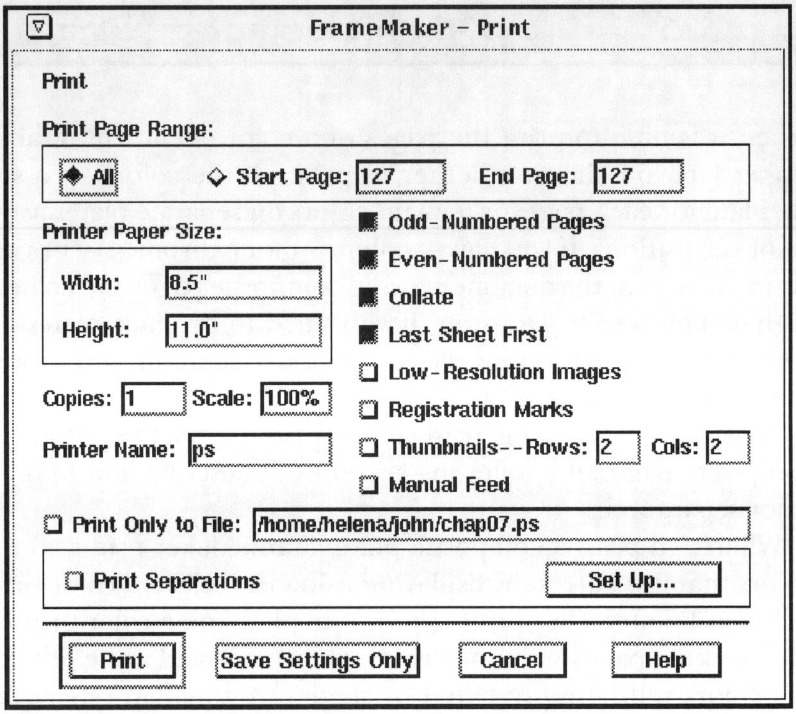

Figure 7.42   The Print dialog box.

For more information about these options, please refer to "Printing a FrameMaker Document."

4.   Click **Print**.

What To Do If

- None.

See Also

- Printing a FrameMaker Document, p. 35.
- Overprinting Objects, p. 347.
- Printing Color Separations, p. 351.

Printing Color Separations | 165

Most color laser printers will produce a high-quality image that is adequate for internal use. However, for publication-quality material, you still need to rely on a commercial printer. In order to print your color documents, many commercial printers will require you to produce color separation plates, which you can easily create on FrameMaker.

When you print color separations, FrameMaker enables you to select which colors should be printed as process colors, which should be printed as spot colors, and which colors shouldn't be printed at all. Using this information, FrameMaker prints the text and the objects for each separation in black, along with the proper color name, displayed outside the registration marks. For each color you include in the Print As Process list, FrameMaker will print four separate plates. Each plate corresponds to one of the CMYK components of the color. This is true even if you defined the color using a model other than CMYK. FrameMaker prints a single plate for each color you include in the Print As Spot list.

Assumptions

- You wish to print document as a set of color separations.

Exceptions

- FrameMaker will not produce any printed plate for the colors you include in the Don't Print list.

Steps

1. Select **Print** in the File menu (or press **Esc f p**).
   FrameMaker displays the Print dialog box.
2. Turn on **Print Separations**.
3. Click **Set Up**.
   FrameMaker displays the Set Print Separations dialog box (see Figure 7.43).

TIP

Check with your commercial printer for any special requirements before printing color separations.

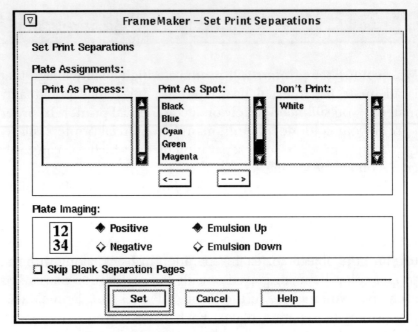

Figure 7.43   The Set Print Separations dialog box.

4.   Select a color and move it to the appropriate list.
     You can move a selected color by clicking on the arrow
     buttons below the lists. If you want to move all the colors
     to another list, select any color in the list and **Shift +** click
     the arrow button.

5.   Select **Positive** or **Negative** in the Plate Imaging area.
     A Positive setting will print objects black on white, as ex-
     pected. Selecting **Negative,** however, will print the reverse.

6.   Select **Emulsion Up** or **Emulsion Down**.
     FrameMaker prints a mirror image of the plate when you
     select **Emulsion Down.** When you select either option, the
     numbers appearing in the box to the left of the selection
     will change to reflect the new setting. Your choice for both
     the Positive/Negative and Emulsion settings depends on
     the requirements of your commercial printer. You may

need to ask your printer for the proper settings before printing the plates.

7. Click **Set**.

FrameMaker returns you to the Print dialog box, and lets you complete setting the options for the print job.

8. Select the other print options as appropriate in the **Print** dialog box.

9. Click **Print**.

What To Do If

- If you don't want FrameMaker to print blank pages without text and graphics, select **Skip Blank Separation Pages** in the Set Print Separations dialog box. This option can save you time and money, since printing color separations can be expensive.

- If you want to display objects online when viewed on the monitor, but you don't want these objects to be output to the printer, assign them a special color that you will only use for this purpose. You can then make the color behave in the desired fashion by defining it as a Normal color in the Define Color Views dialog box, and including the color in the **Don't Print** list in the Set Print Separations dialog box. A better way to do this, however, is to assign these objects the **Comment** condition tag and hide them when printing the document.

See Also

- Printing a FrameMaker Document, p. 35.
- Overprinting Objects, p. 347.
- Printing Composite Pages, p. 349.
- Applying a Condition Tag, p. 438.

Chapter

8

Modifying the Basic Page Properties

Using Master Pages

Working with Text Flows

Creating Headers and Footers

Using Reference Pages

CREATING THE PAGE LAYOUT

355

Modifying the Basic Page Properties

With FrameMaker you can set up and modify the existing basic page properties such as size, page numbers, and number of pages in a document. You can modify any of the settings you specified when you started a new custom document, and you can change any of the default settings that affect pages.

166 ▽ Modifying the Existing Normal Layout

The "normal layout" consists of any of the page settings Frame-Maker allows you to specify when you first open a new custom document. The page size, number of columns, margins, and whether your document is single- or double-sided are all settings that you can modify at any time. When you modify these settings, FrameMaker also adjusts the paragraph and table formats to match the new page size.

Assumptions

- You wish to modify the normal layout.

Exceptions

- You cannot modify the page to a size that will not accommo-date the text columns on custom Master Pages. FrameMaker only adjusts the column size of the Right and Left Master Pages.

Steps

Select **Pages:Normal Page Layout** from the Format menu (see Figure 8.1). If you have the Layout window open, select **Normal Page Layout** from the Basic menu. To open the Layout window, select **Pages:Layout Commands** from the Format menu.

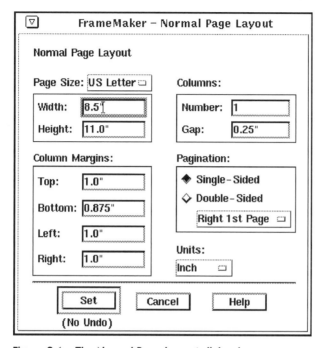

Figure 8.1   The Normal Page Layout dialog box.

- Select the page size from the **Page Size** pop-up menu. The pop-up menu contains the most frequently used standard sizes for the United States and Europe. You can type a custom page size in the **Width** and **Height** text boxes.

- Change your document's pagination to single or double-sided in the **Pagination** area. If the document is double-sided, select the document's starting page side from the pop-up menu in the Pagination area.

- Type the margins in the **Column Margins** text boxes. The text boxes will be labeled differently for single-page documents than for double-page documents. Single-page documents have Left and Right margins, whereas double-page documents have Inside and Outside margins.

- Select the number of columns and the distance between columns from the **Columns** area.
- When done, click **Set**.

What To Do If

- If you want to change the measuring units for your document, make a selection from the Units pop-up menu. The measuring units are reflected throughout FrameMaker's dialog boxes and rulers.
- If you have layout overrides on body pages, FrameMaker gives you the chance to change the layout on those pages as well.
- If you are working on a FrameMaker book, set up the starting page side in the book's **Set Up File** dialog box. The book settings override the file settings.

See Also

- Opening a Custom Document, p. 5.
- Assigning a Layout to Body Pages, p. 363.

Setting Up Page Numbering and Page Count

You can specify the page numbering style for your document, the number with which to start your document, and whether to make your document's page count odd or even. You can set up or modify these properties any time you want.

Assumptions

- You wish to set the page numbering or page count.

_____ **Exceptions**

- You cannot specify different numbering styles for each page in a document. When you assign a numbering style, it is applied to the whole document. If you want to specify a different style of numbering for a specific consecutive set of pages, create a separate file for those pages and create a book that contains all the files for the document.

_____ **Steps**

- First select **Document** from the Format menu (see Figure 8.2).
- Select the page numbering style from the **Page # Style** pop-up menu.

TIP

If you want the second page to be page 1, set the first page to start at zero(0). You can also start at a negative number.

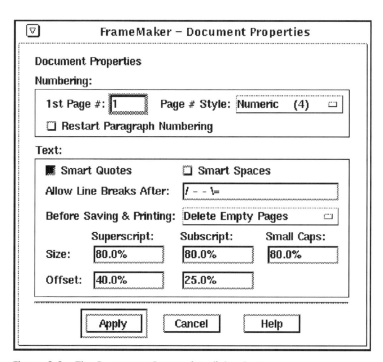

Figure 8.2   The Document Properties dialog box.

- Type the number of the first page in the **1st Page #** text box. You can start with any number.
- Choose a page count from the **Before Saving and Printing** pop-up menu.

After choosing the options you want, click **Apply**.

What To Do If

- If you set your document to delete empty pages, Frame-Maker only deletes pages that use the Left or Right Master Page; it does not delete pages that contain layout overrides.
- If you are working on a FrameMaker book, set up page numbering in the book's **Set Up File** dialog box. The book settings override the file settings.

See Also

- Creating a Book, p. 384.

168 ▾ Adding Pages

Generally you add new, disconnected pages when you are creating or working on the layout of a multiflow document, such as a newsletter. If you add new body pages, they are disconnected from the rest of the flow. You might need to assign a master page to them and connect the flow with the rest of the document.

Assumptions

- You are working with a multiflow document.

Exceptions

- Do not add a page manually if you are working in a regular document; let FrameMaker add pages automatically as you need them. For example, if you want to import a graphic that is larger than the space you have left, merely import it—FrameMaker creates the page automatically.

Steps

1. Select **Add Disconnected Pages** from the Special menu (see Figure 8.3).
2. Select the location of the new page from the **Add** pop-up menu.
3. Type the number of new pages in the **Number of Pages To Add** text box.
4. Select the master page to use in the **Use Master Page** pop-up menu.
5. Click **Add**.

> **TIP**
>
> To keep track of which columns are connected, place the insertion point in the column with the flow you want to check, select **Select All in Flow** from the Edit menu, and reduce the page size to 25%. Everything that is highlighted is connected.

What To Do If

- If you add a page anywhere in a document, connect it to whichever other columns in your document you want. If you do not do this explicitly, the columns will not be connected and your text may not flow in the way you expect it to.

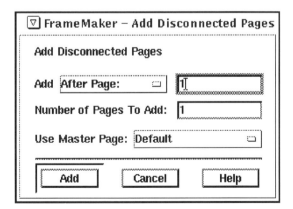

Figure 8.3   The Add Disconnected Pages dialog box.

- If you see a solid line at the bottom of a column, you have added or imported more text than fits in the column, and so there is text that is not appearing anywhere.

See Also

- Creating Master Pages, p. 365.
- Assigning a Flow Name to a Text Column, p. 369.
- Connecting Columns, p. 371.

169 Deleting Pages

Although FrameMaker enables you to delete an entire range of body pages by a single command, you can delete only one master or reference page at a time. Since you cannot undo this command, FrameMaker prompts you to cancel the command before it deletes.

Assumptions

- You know the page numbers you want to delete. The page number is the number of the page within a whole document. If you are working in a multifile document, it is the number at the bottom of the window that is not in parentheses. For example, page 257 of a document could be page 5 of the current file. In this case, you specify page number 257 to delete.

Exceptions

- None.

Steps

1. Select **Delete Pages** from the Special menu.

2. Specify the page range you want to delete, and then click **Delete**.

_____ **What To Do If**

• If you are deleting master or reference pages, FrameMaker deletes the current page. It does not display a dialog box. However, it does prompt you to cancel and lets you know which page you are deleting.

_____ **See Also**

• None.

Using Master Pages

Master Pages offer a variety of layout choices for specific use in your document. Using Master Pages is especially helpful when working on documents with few flows. Master Pages enable you to assign a layout to each page in your document or different layouts for first and other special pages. In addition, you can change the layout of specific pages, or all pages, by just modifying the Master Page or by changing the Master Page associated with specific Body Pages.

| Assigning a Layout to Body Pages | 170 |

The layout of Body Pages is by default based on the Right and Left Master Pages. These pages have a default layout based on the page size and margins you specify when you create a custom document. If you are using a template, the layout of these pages is specific to the template. If you are using a template or have created new Master Pages, you can use different Master Pages for specific pages in your document.

Assumptions

- You created new Master Pages.
- You are displaying the Body Pages.

Exceptions

- If you modify the Right, Left, or other already used Master Page, FrameMaker applies the change to all the Body Pages that use it. You do not need to reapply a Master Page if you modify it.

Steps

> **TIP**
>
> Try to anticipate the different layouts you may need for a specific document, and create the Master Pages in advance. Then you can modify them later without applying and reapplying Master Pages as you go. You can create up to 25 Master Pages for a document.

1. Select **Pages:Master Page Usage** from the Format menu. You can also select **Basic:Master Page Usage** from the Layout window. Figure 8.4 shows the Master Page Usage dialog box.

2. Select the Master Page you want to assign from the **Use** area. If you are applying a Master Page other than Left or Right, select the name from the **Custom** pop-up menu.

3. Select the Body Pages to which you want to apply the Master Page. You can select the current page, a range of pages, all odd or all even pages, or pages that currently use another Master Page.

4. Click **Set**.

What To Do If

- If you apply a Master Page that contains text columns that do not have a flow name, the columns do not appear in the Body Pages.

- If you want to update an existing Master Page with the layout of a Body Page, select **Basic:Update Page Layouts** from the Layout window (select **Pages:Layout** from the Format menu). FrameMaker displays the Update Page Layouts dialog box, where you can confirm the Master Page to update.

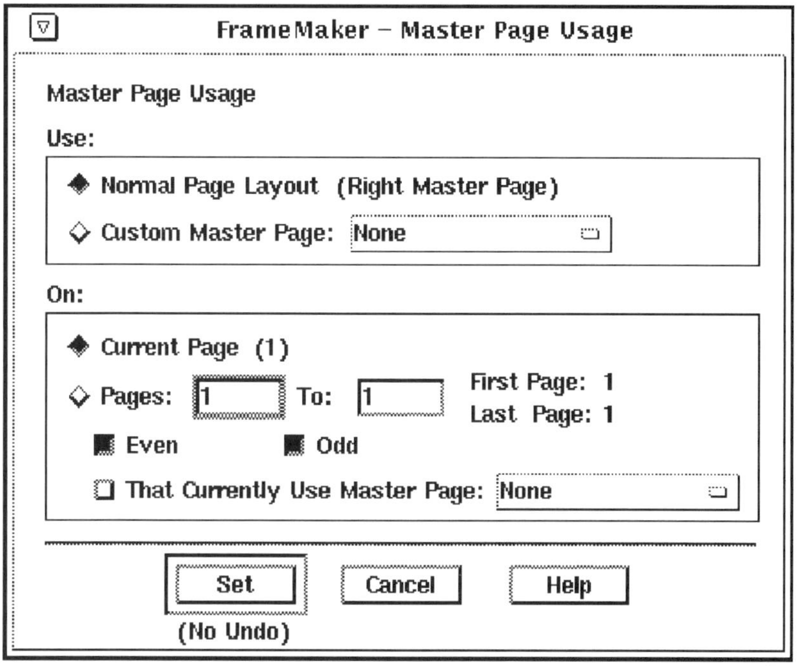

Figure 8.4   The Master Page Usage dialog box.

- If you want to design a Body Page from scratch, you can specify a master page of **None** when applying a Master Page.

_____ **See Also**

- Modifying the Existing Normal Layout, p. 356.
- Creating Master Pages, below.
- Creating Text Columns, p. 367.

Creating Master Pages   171

The Left and Right Master Pages are the default layout for your document. After you modify them to fit your design, you can create any Master Pages you need to use beyond Left and Right. You can define up to 25 Master Pages for a document.

Assumptions

- You are displaying the Master Pages.

Exceptions

- You cannot create or delete the Right and Left pages; you can only modify the existing ones.

Steps

1. Select **Add Master Page** from the Special menu.
2. Type a name in the **Name** text box.
3. Select a default layout from the **Initial Page Layout** area, and click **Add**.

What To Do If

- You can add a new Master Page by creating the layout on a Body Page and selecting **Basic:New Master Page** from the Layout window (select Pages:Layout from the Format menu).

- If you want to create a rotated Master Page that contains un-rotated information, create a new Master Page and add the information you want to appear unrotated. Then open the Layout window and select **Clockwise** or **Counter Clockwise** from the Rotate Page pop-up menu. Add the text columns and other information you want to appear rotated.

See Also

- Adding Pages, p. 360.
- Deleting Pages, p. 362.
- Creating Text Columns, p. 367.

Working with Text Flows

The key to layout in FrameMaker is the text columns and how they connect in flows. Each flow has a name. If you want to create a document such as a newsletter, you are likely to need a multiflow document, whereas if you are working on a book, you are probably working with a single flow. You can have a multicolumn document that is single-flow, as well as a single-column document that is multiflow.

| Creating Text Columns | 172 |

Whenever you create a new Master Page or modify an existing one, you may need to create new text columns for the page. When you create a text column in a Master Page, FrameMaker prompts you for a flow name. When you create a text column in a Body Page, FrameMaker makes it a disconnected column and expects you to explicitly assign it a flow name and connect it to the other columns.

Assumptions

- You are displaying Body Pages, if you are overriding the layout of a page.

- You are displaying the Master Pages, if you are creating or modifying the layout of a Master Page.

Exceptions

- If you create a text column in a Master Page and do not assign it a flow, the column is used for background text only and is not applied to the Body Page.

Steps

1. Open the graphics palette.

2. Select the text column tool (see Figure 8.5).

3. Draw the text column by click-dragging the cursor where you want the column.
   If you are adding a text column to a Master Page, Frame-Maker displays the Add New Text Columns dialog box. Make the appropriate selections.

4. If you are adding a text column to a Body Page, assign a flow name to the new column and connect the column if appropriate.

What To Do If

- If you want to create columns that are the same size, copy and paste the first column you created.

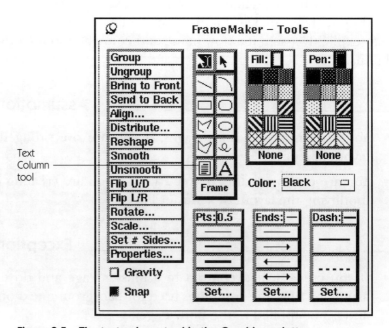

Figure 8.5   The text column tool in the Graphics palette.

- If you want to set up parallel flows, create them in a Master Page and make sure that they have different flow names. If you are working on a double-sided document, make sure that the Right and Left Master Pages have the same flow names for the corresponding columns.

- If you want to set up a multiflow document, create the basic layout in the Master Pages and change the flow names as needed in the Body Pages. Name the flows in the Master Page the same and turn off Autoconnect. FrameMaker considers the changes to the Body Pages to be layout overrides and will prompt you for information any time you modify the Master Pages.

See Also

- Adding Text Columns, p. 304.
- Splitting and Merging Columns, p. 373.

Assigning a Flow Name to a Text Column   173

Each column in the Master Pages needs a flow name for use in the Body Pages. Since the columns in the Left and Right Master Pages need to connect to one another as you are working on a document, they both should have the same flow name and should be set up to autoconnect. Any two Master Pages that are used alternately need to have text columns with the same flow name assigned to them.

Assumptions

- The insertion point is placed in the column to which you are assigning a flow name.

- The column does not have a name already, or you want it to become a separate flow from the rest of the document.

Exceptions

- If a column in a Body Page does not have a flow name assigned to it, FrameMaker does not create a new page automatically when you get to the end of the column.

Steps

1. Select **Flow** from the Format menu (see Figure 8.6).
2. Type the name of the flow in the **Flow Tag** text box.
3. Turn on **Autoconnect**, and then click **Set**.

What To Do If

- If you are working on a multicolumn document and want to align text lines with each other in neighboring columns,

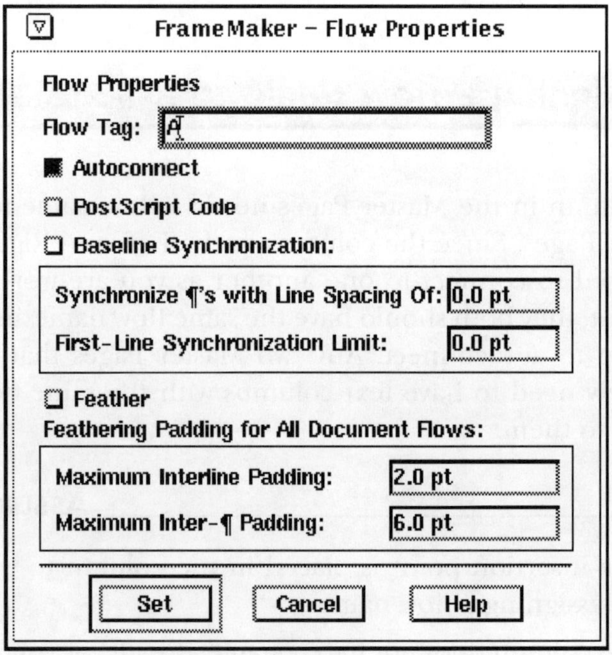

Figure 8.6   The Flow Properties dialog box.

select **Baseline Synchronization** and make sure **Feather** is turned off.
Specify the value for the grid spacing in the **Synchronize ¶** text box, and specify the largest font size to align at the top of a column in the **First Line Synchronization** text box.

- If you want to make sure the whole column is used by text, turn on **Feather**. Specify the value for the maximum space to add between paragraphs in the **Inter-¶ Padding** text box and the maximum space to add between lines in the **Interline Padding** text box.

- If the flow names in the Master Pages are set up incorrectly for alternating pages, such as for the Left and Right Master Pages, FrameMaker still creates the new page with connecting flow, but it may not be using the correct Master Page.

See Also

- Connecting Columns, below.

Connecting Columns | 174

When you create one or two flows to use in a document in the Master Pages, FrameMaker will create new pages to accommodate new text or graphics as you go along. When FrameMaker creates the new page, the columns in the page are automatically connected to the ones in the previous page. However, when you create Master Pages for multiflow documents, the Master Page columns are set up with the same flow name, and you have to change the flow names for the columns in the body pages to match your need for text flow. In this case, connect each column manually as you work on the content of your document.

Assumptions

- The Layout window is open (press **Esc o g l** to open it).

Exceptions

- You cannot connect more than two columns at a time. To connect more than two, connect the first two, then connect the following one to the last column that has the correct flow name.

Steps

1. Select the two columns you want to connect in the order you want the text to flow.
   Note that if the columns are in different pages, and the first column does not remain selected, FrameMaker will remember the first selection.

2. Select **Basic:Connect Columns** from the Layout window.

What To Do If

- If you want to add a column in the middle of a flow, connect the new column to the column that follows it.

- If you want to disconnect a column, select **Disconnect Current Column** from the Layout window.
  You can choose **From Previous**, **From Next**, or **From Both.**

- If you disconnect a column, the Autoconnect setting will be affected for the columns being disconnected. For example, if you disconnect columns that are on the same page, Autoconnect will be off for both columns.

Disconnect Choice	Flows Affected	New Autoconnect Setting
Previous	Previous	Off
	Current	On

Disconnect Choice	Flows Affected	New Autoconnect Setting
Next	Current	Off
	Next	On
Both	Previous	Off
	Current	Off
	Next	On

See Also

- Creating Text Columns, p. 367.
- Assigning a Flow Name to a Text Column, p. 369.

Splitting and Merging Columns 175

FrameMaker lets you split columns vertically or horizontally. You can turn a one page layout into two or more parallel columns, or you can split a column to insert a graphic in the middle or to start a new flow.

Assumptions

- You selected the column you want to split.
- The Layout window is open (press **Esc o g l** to open it).

Exceptions

- These steps are for splitting and merging columns vertically, not horizontally. For information on splitting columns horizontally, see "What To Do If."

Steps

1. Select **Replace Columns** from the Basic pop-up menu (see Figure 8.7).

2. Specify the number of columns and the gap between them in the **Replace with Columns** area. To merge columns, select the columns you want to merge, and specify one column in the **Replace with Columns** area.

3. Specify the margins in the **Column Margins** area, and then click **Replace**.

What To Do If

*   If you want to split a column horizontally, click on the line where you want the column to split, and select **Below Selection** from the Split Current Column pop-up menu in the Layout window.

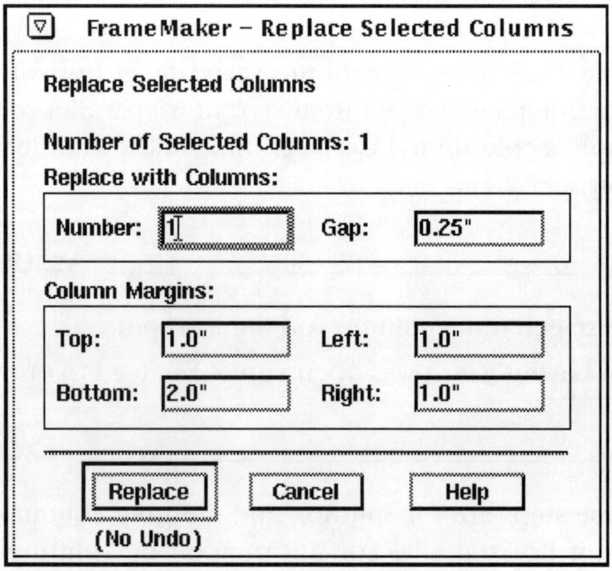

Figure 8.7   The Replace Selected Columns dialog box.

- If you want to place a nonanchored graphic in your page, split the column and resize it to leave space for the graphic between them.

- If you want text to flow around a graphic, place the graphic where you want it on top of the text. Split the column above and below the graphic. Click on the column in the middle— the one that still overlaps the graphic—and select **Into Lines** from the Split Current Column pop-up menu. You can now resize each line so that it flows around the graphic and each line is now an individual column.

_____ **See Also**

- Creating Text Columns, p. 367.

Creating Headers and Footers

When you create a custom document, FrameMaker creates header and footer columns, with center and right tab stops, in the Left and Right Master Pages. The header and footer columns are background columns, so they do not have a flow name. The format of the text is defined by a Header or Footer paragraph tag, respectively. These tags do not appear in the Paragraph Catalog and are lost if you apply a different tag.

When you create a Master Page, you may want to add header and footer columns and specify the format and content for them. Header and footer columns are just like any other column. However, you set them up as background text only, and you generally use variables and running headers and footers to specify the content.

Setting Up Header and Footer Columns | 176

Setting up header and footer columns for a new Master Page consists of either drawing the text column yourself or copying and pasting one from the existing Master Pages. If you are working on a double-sided document, you may want to create left and right versions of the new Master Page.

Assumptions

- You are displaying the Master Pages.
- You added a new Master Page.

Exceptions

- None.

Steps

1. Go to the Master Page that has the basic layout you want for the new Master Page.
2. Select the header and copy it to the FrameMaker clipboard.
3. Go to the new Master Page.
4. Paste the header.
5. Repeat these steps for the footer.

What To Do If

- If you want to draw the columns yourself, FrameMaker prompts you to give the column a flow name or to make it background text. Select background text. Place the header or footer within the top or bottom margin, and draw it margin to margin.
- If you want to format the header and footer, use the paragraph designer to modify or create the header and footer tags. The tags do not have to display in the Paragraph Catalog. When you create the tags, do not select Add to Catalog.

See Also

- Creating and Updating Format Tags, p. 104.
- Creating Text Columns, p. 367.

Creating Running Headers and Footers

177

Once you create the header and footer, you can specify the content. FrameMaker enables you to create running headers and footers based on the document's content. For example, if you want the header to be the name of the chapter or section, you can set up a Running Header/Footer variable and insert it where you want that information to appear.

Assumptions

- You are displaying the Master Pages.
- The insertion point is placed where you want to insert the variable.

Exceptions

- You cannot insert a Running Header/Footer in Body or Reference Pages.

Steps

1. Select **Variable** from the Special menu to open the Variable dialog box.
2. Select a **Header/Footer** variable.
3. Click **Edit Definition**, and then select the building block appropriate for the information you want to display.
4. Click **Edit**.
5. Click **Insert** in the Variable dialog box.

What To Do If

- None.

TIP

When you add a Header/Footer variable for chapter or section names that are long, create a Header/Footer marker for the heading, type a shorter name for the heading, and display the marker instead of the heading.

See Also

- Modifying System Variables, p. 190.
- Using System Variables, p. 192.

178 ⟩ Adding Page Numbers and Other Variables

Page numbers, page count, file name, and date and time of creation or modification are all variables frequently used when working with a document. While you will use some of these variables for work in progress, such as the file name, others will be part of your final document, such as page numbers.

Assumptions

- You are displaying the Master Pages.
- The insertion point is placed where you want to insert the variable.

Exceptions

- You cannot insert the Current Page variable in Body or Reference Pages.

Steps

TIP
Edit the variable definition to match your specific needs. FrameMaker displays the building blocks available to you in the Edit Variable dialog box.

1. Select **Variable** from the Special menu.
2. Select a variable.
3. Click **Edit Definition**, and then select the building block appropriate for the information you want to display.
4. Click **Edit**.
5. Click **Insert** in the Variable dialog box.

_____ **What To Do If**

- None.

_____ **See Also**

- Modifying System Variables, p. 190.
- Using System Variables, p. 192.

Using Reference Pages

Reference Pages are special pages you use to store information that FrameMaker uses for special purposes or to store boilerplate graphics. The advantage of using Reference Pages for this type of information is that it allows you to control both the material FrameMaker uses and some of the material you use.

FrameMaker uses the Reference Pages to store formatting and other information for generated files, such as indexes and tables of contents. It also contains frames that contain the rules or other graphics you can specify to use above or below a paragraph. You can use the Reference Pages not only to store graphics but also to store them in the exact position you want them to appear on a page. When you cut and paste from a Reference Page to a Body Page, FrameMaker positions the graphic in the same place it was in the Reference Page.

Creating Reference Pages   179

FrameMaker automatically adds the Reference Pages it needs for a file and for generated files. You can also add your own.

_____ **Assumptions**

- You are displaying the Reference Pages.

Exceptions

- None.

Steps

1. Select **Add Reference Page** from the Special menu.
2. Type a name in the **Name** text box, and then click **Add**.

What To Do If

- None.

See Also

- Adding Pages, p. 360.
- Deleting Pages, p. 362.
- Creating Reference Frames, below.
- Chapter 10, "Creating Generated Files."

180　Creating Reference Frames

The graphics you use as part of a paragraph format are in the Reference Pages on an unanchored frame called a reference frame. If you want to add more graphics or rules that you can use with your document, you can add reference frames with the appropriate graphics inside. The length and width of the frame and the position of the graphic inside the frame determine how it appears in the Body Page.

Assumptions

- You are displaying the Reference Pages.

Exceptions

- None.

Steps

1. Draw an unanchored frame.
   FrameMaker displays the Frame Name dialog box.

2. Type a name for the frame.
   This is the name that appears in the Above and Below pop-up menus in the Paragraph Designer's Advanced Properties window.

3. Place the graphic in the frame.
   The width of the frame determines the distance between the paragraph and the graphic. The frame is positioned in exactly the same way you created it in the Reference Page to use in the Body Page, so make sure to align the left and right edges where you want them to be on the page.

4. Type in the name above the frame. This is for your own reference.

> **TIP**
>
> Apply the reference frame you are creating or modifying to a paragraph tag while you are still working on it. Going back and forth between the Reference Page and the Body Page with the paragraph tag displays the result immediately, and allows you to make any necessary adjustments.

What To Do If

- If you want to rename a reference frame, click the frame's name in the status bar at the bottom of your document window. Change the name in the **Frame Name** dialog box. Make sure also to change the name above the frame.

See Also

- Creating Graphics, p. 289.

Setting Up Boilerplate Graphics 181

When you use graphics frequently and in the same place on a page, a Reference Page can be very useful. You can place the graphic exactly where and how you want it to appear on the page.

Assumptions

- You are displaying the Reference Pages.

Exceptions

- None.

Steps

1. Create a new Reference Page with the same layout as the type of Body Page where the graphic will appear.

2. Create an anchored frame and position it exactly where you want the graphic to appear.

3. Place the graphic in the frame.

What To Do If

- If you copy a graphic that uses an anchored frame from the Reference Pages to a Body Page, select the anchored frame, not the graphic. Then copy and paste it where you want it anchored in the Body Page.

- If you want to use a graphic without an anchored frame, draw the graphic on the page where you want it to display in the Body Page. Then copy and paste it to a Body Page.

See Also

- Creating Graphics, p. 289.

Chapter
9

Creating a Book

Updating a Book

CREATING
BOOKS

Creating a Book

One of the strengths of FrameMaker is its ability to handle multi-file documents. Most large publications are divided into chapters or sections, which may be authored by different people. You can maintain a unified look and feel, numbering scheme, and indexing for a document like this by using the Book function.

The Book function allows you to link files together to form books. You can control features such as page and paragraph numbering and cross-references across groups of files. You can standardize the formats for a series of related documents, such as the chapters in a book, or the sections of a report, and generate book-level table of contents, lists, and indexes. The book feature also allows you to easily add, rearrange, and reformat files when necessary.

When you create a book, you set up a list of existing files and place them in a specific order. The book is a file that keeps track of the document files, their order, and any special numbering or pagination settings you specify for each file within a book or for the whole book. FrameMaker book files contain a .book extension as part of their file name.

Once you set up a book, you may add as many files as you want. You can set up the starting page side for each file and the page and paragraph numbering. You can also save the book settings and the files, and you can print the whole book or a number of specific files from the book.

182 ◢ Setting Up a Book

Setting up a FrameMaker book is a fairly straightforward process. Once you create the book file, you can add the rest of the files that belong to that book and specify the settings you want. FrameMaker allows you to share files between books and to set up a book for each different version of a document. For more information

on setting up books for multiple versions of a document, see
Chapter 11.

Assumptions

- You have a set of files that are part of a larger document,
  such as the chapters of a book.

- One of the files is open.

Exceptions

- You cannot set up a book made up of book files. For example,
  if you have a library of books, volume 1 to volume 10, where
  each book is a FrameMaker book, you cannot group the
  volumes in a book that contains each volume's book file.

Steps

1. Select **Generate/Book** from the Book File menu.
2. Turn on **New Multifile book**.
3. Click **Generate**.
   The Book File window appears (see Figure 9.1). The book
   inherits the name of the file, with a .book extension.
4. Rename the book by selecting **Save As** from the Book File
   menu and saving it with a new name.

> **TIP**
> If you use a file
> in more than one
> book, update the
> book you are using
> before you print or
> make any changes
> to it. Keep in mind
> that any change in
> a file common to
> several books also
> affects the other
> books.

What To Do If

- If you want to create a master index, list, or table of contents
  for a library of books, create a book that contains the generated files for each of the books and generate the master.
  For more information, see Chapter 10, "Creating Generated
  Files."

- If you want to set up books for multiple versions of a book,
  set up a book for each version. Each version should contain
  the Conditional Text settings specific for each version of
  the book. For more information, see Chapter 11, "Creating
  Conditional Documents."

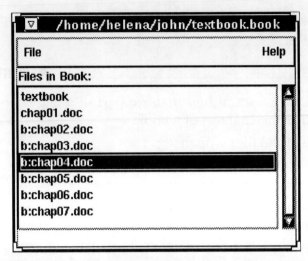

Figure 9.1   The Book File window.

See Also

- Adding Files to a Book, below.

Adding Files to a Book

You can add as many files to a book as you need. However, the more files you add, the longer it takes to perform functions to the entire book, such as applying a new template or creating generated files such as a table of contents or index.

Assumptions

- A book is open.
- The book window is selected.

Exceptions

- Individual files do not have to be open to add files to a book.

- Files generated for a book are not added using these steps.
- You cannot add selected multiple files to a book. You add either one file at a time, or all files displayed at once.

--- **Steps**

1. Select **Add File** from the Book File menu.
   The Add File to Book dialog box will appear.
2. Select the file you want to add to the book.
3. Select the location of the file within the book, and then click **Add**.

--- **What To Do If**

- If you add files by accident, select **Rearrange Files** from the Book File menu and delete the file from the book. This removes the file from the book.
- If you add a file in the wrong place, select **Rearrange File** from the Book File menu and move it.

--- **See Also**

- Updating a Book, p. 396.

> **TIP**
> If you want to use a template for a book's generated files, add the template for the files using the names they will take when you generate them from the book. For example, if you generate a table of contents for a book called Reference.book, the name of the generated table of contents will be ReferenceTOC. In this case, you would add a file named ReferenceTOC to the book that contains the template you want to use for the table of contents.

Setting the Starting Page Side for Each File in a Book   184

FrameMaker lets you choose whether a file begins on a right or left page for a double-sided document. This book setting overrides settings at a file level, such as making the page count odd or even or deleting extra pages when saving. For example, if you want a book to start each chapter on the right page but you have the files set to delete extra pages when saving, the chapters may all start on different sides of the page. To correct this, you use the Set Up File book function for each file to specify that each chapter should start on the right page. This setting overrides the file setting and would add an empty page where necessary.

On the other hand, if you have a book where not all files are chapter files, you can specify each file that is the beginning of a new chapter to start on the right page, and have the rest of the files to start on the next available side.

Assumptions

- A book is open.
- The book window is selected.

Exceptions

- Individual files do not have to be open to have this setting specified.

Steps

1. Select a file from the book window.
2. Select **Set Up File** from the Book File menu.
3. Choose a setting from the **Starting Page Side** pop-up menu.

> **TIP**
>
> The selection you make in the pop-up menu overrides any individual file settings for pagination.

What To Do If

- If you want to keep the setting from the file, select **Read From File**.
- If you want to start on a side based on the side of the last page of the previous file, select **Next Available Side**.
- If you select Read From File and your files are not starting on the side you want, reset the file to start on that side. Otherwise, open the file and reset the **Pagination** setting for that file in the Document Format dialog box.

See Also

- Specifying the Page Count in a Document, p. 132.

Setting Page Numbering for Each File in a Book

185

The type of numbering for each chapter or section in a book is controlled by specifying whether the page numbering restarts for the chapter or continues incrementing from the previous chapter. For example, generally the page numbering for a book begins with Chapter 1, but the front matter of the book is also numbered. In this case, you would start the page numbering in the front matter, restart numbering on Chapter 1, and set each chapter after that to continue. This is particularly useful if you are numbering your book by number-by-folio.

Assumptions

- A book is open.
- The book window is selected.

Exceptions

- Individual files do not have to be open to have this setting specified.
- You cannot specify two automatic page numbers for the same document.

Steps

1. Select a file from the book window.
2. Select **Set Up File** from the Book File menu.
3. Choose a setting from the **Page Numbering** pop-up menu.

What To Do If

- If you want to continue incrementing the page numbering from the previous file, select **Continue.**

TIP

The selection you make in the pop-up menu overrides any individual file settings for page numbering. For example, a file can be set up to restart the page numbering in the Document settings of that file, but if you use the Set Up Files menu in the book file to set it to continue the page numbering, the numbering will increment from the previous file.

- If you want to retain the setting from the file itself, select **Read From File**.

- If you select Read From File and the numbering of your file is not what you expected, open the file and check the Numbering setting in the Document Format dialog box.

- If you want to set the chapter or section number as a prefix, such as for number-by-folio, type the number in the **Page # in Generated Files Prefix** text box. You can also add a suffix to your page numbers if you type text in the **Suffix** text box.

See Also

- Specifying Spacing and Pagination, p. 120.

Setting Paragraph Numbering for Each File in a Book

Specifying whether paragraph numbering restarts or continues incrementing from the previous file enables you to control the type of numbering for each chapter or section in a book. For example, you can use paragraph numbering to number your chapters or sections in a chapter. To number the chapters, you can choose to continue the paragraph numbering from file to file. Autonumbering chapters also allows you to rearrange the files without having to worry about correcting the sequence.

Assumptions

- A book is open.
- The book window is selected.

Exceptions

- Individual files do not have to be open to specify this setting.

- You cannot control paragraph numbers for different levels of numbering with this function. For information on numbering levels and sequencing, see Chapter 4, "Creating the Formats."

Steps

1. Select a file from the book window.
2. Select **Set Up File** from the Book File menu.
3. Choose a setting from the **Paragraph Numbering** pop-up menu (see Figure 9.2).

What To Do If

- If you want to continue incrementing the paragraph numbering from the previous file, select **Continue**.

- If you want to restart the numbering for the file, select **Restart**.

- If you do not use the same paragraph tag for a specific numbered paragraph from one file to the next, the numbering for that paragraph will be off. For example, to number your figures consecutively through a book, use a paragraph tag named "Figure" for the caption in Chapter 1. Then use the same paragraph tag for the figure captions in Chapter 2 and beyond. This way the figure numbers are consecutive throughout.

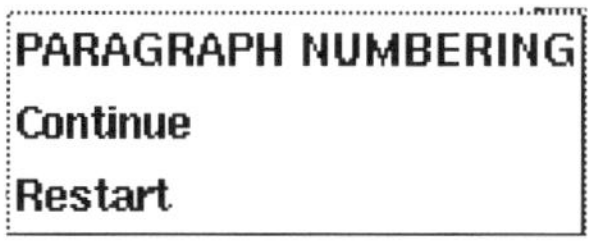

TIP

When you use autonumbering in a book, make sure the numbering is working for each file first. This will avoid problems in making the numbering work throughout the book and in generating the table of contents, index, or other generated files. If you make changes to the book, such as moving, adding, or deleting files, make sure you update the book.

```
┌──────────────────────┐
│PARAGRAPH NUMBERING   │
│Continue              │
│Restart               │
└──────────────────────┘
```

Figure 9.2   The Paragraph
              Numbering
              pop-up menu.

- If you want to restart the numbering in a numbered list, use a tag specific to the first item on the list each time you restart. Otherwise, the numbering will be off.

- If your numbering is off from file to file anyway, check that all columns are connected. A disconnected flow that contains numbered paragraphs will set the paragraph numbering off for the book.

See Also

- Creating Numbered Lists, p. 163.

Saving and Closing a Book

When you close a book file, FrameMaker gives you the option of saving the book file and any book-related files that were open. If any of your files are open, you should save them before you close them to ensure that you don't lose any information. If you have many files open, this may take a considerable amount of time. If you want to avoid saving all the files at the time you close the book file, save and close them individually as you are done working with them.

Assumptions

- A book is open.
- The book window is selected.

Exceptions

- Individual files do not have to be open to save settings set at the book level.
- You cannot save any open files that are not part of the book.

_____ **Steps**

1. Select **Save** or **Save As** from the Book File menu.

2. Type the name of the book, if necessary, and then click **Save**.

3. Select **Close Book** from the Book File menu.

_____ **What To Do If**

- If you want to save all the files in a book without saving the book file, press the **Shift** key and select **Save All Files** from the Book File menu.

- If you want to close all the files in a book without closing the book file, press the **Shift** key and select **Close All Files** from the Book File menu.

_____ **See Also**

- Updating a Book, p. 396.

Printing from a Book File | 188

Printing from a book file gives you the flexibility of choosing which files you want to print. The printing options from a book file are very similar to the printing options from an individual document. You can select single-sided or double-sided if available in your printer. You can print drafts or camera-ready copy, and you can print several copies of your book.

_____ **Assumptions**

- A book is open.
- The book window is selected.

Exceptions

- You cannot print specific pages from a document using these steps.
- You cannot print thumbnails from a book file.
- You cannot specify manual paper feed from a book file.
- Individual files do not have to be open to print them from a book.

Steps

1. Select **Print** from the Book File menu.
   All the files in the book are listed in the Print scroll list (see Figure 9.3).
2. Move the files you do not want to print to the **Don't Print** scroll list.
3. Click on **Print**.
4. Turn on the printing options you want in the Print dialog box (see Figure 9.4).

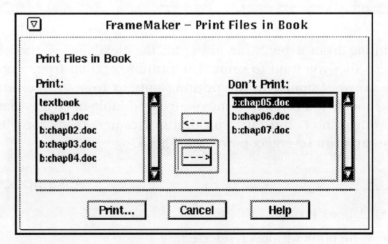

Figure 9.3   The Print Files in a Book dialog box.

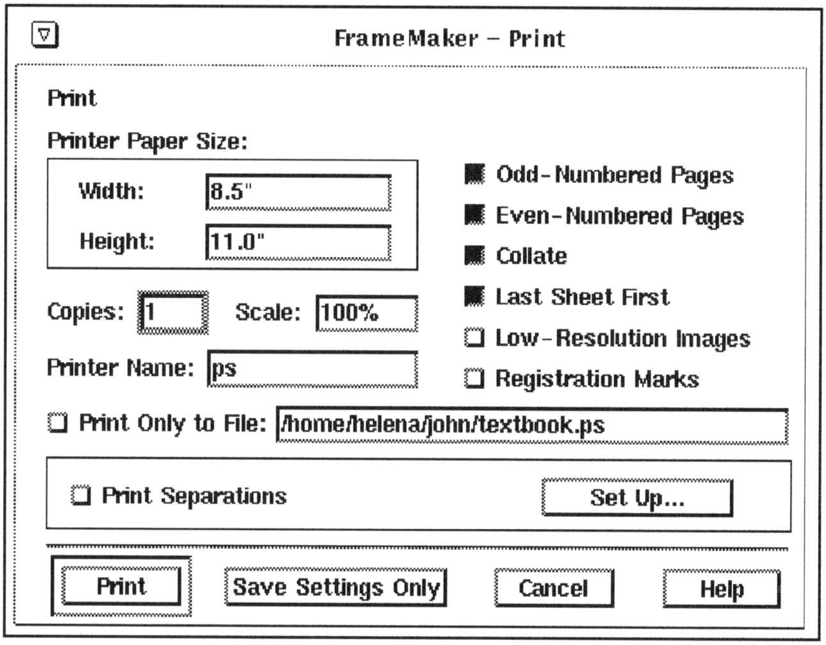

Figure 9.4   The Print dialog box.

5.   Check that the **Printer Paper Size** values match the size of the paper in the printer.

6.   Specify the number of copies you want to print in the **Copies** text field.

7.   Specify the name of the printer in the **Printer Name** text field.

_____ **What To Do If**

•   If you want to print an enlarged or reduced version of your book, type the scaling factor in the **Scale** text field.

•   If your printer prints pages facing up, turn on **Last Sheet First**. If it prints pages facing down, turn **Last Sheet First** off.

•   If you want to print double-sided without a duplex printer, turn **Even-Numbered Pages** off and print. Then turn the pages over, turn **Even-Numbered Pages** on, **Odd-Numbered Pages** off, and print.

- If you want to print camera-ready copy, turn **Registration Marks** on and make sure that **Low-Resolution Images** is turned off.

- If you want to output to a PostScript file instead of a printer, type the name of the file in the **Print Only to File** text box.

See Also

- Printing a Document, p. 35.
- Printing Color Separations, p. 351.

Updating a Book

Once you set up a book in FrameMaker, you can update the order of the files or the format of the whole book or of individual files, and you can compare two versions of the same book. You can also rearrange any of the pagination and numbering settings as well as add new files at any time. If you change or rearrange the original settings, some changes take effect immediately, but you have to regenerate the book for all of the changes to take effect.

If you share files between books, any changes you make to the file to work in one book will affect how it appears in the other. For example, if a chapter is shared between Book A and Book B, applying a new template to it in Book A will make it show up with the same template in Book B.

189 ▽ Moving Files within a Book

FrameMaker enables you to rearrange the files in a book easily by just pointing and moving them up or down. Thus you can create a book and reorganize it or set it up early, even before you know the exact order of the files.

_____ **Assumptions**

- A book is open.
- The book window is selected.

_____ **Exceptions**

- Individual files do not have to be open for you to rearrange their order within a book.
- If you share a file between books, rearranging its position in one book does not affect its position in the other books.

_____ **Steps**

1. Select **Rearrange Files** from the Book File menu.
2. Select the file you want to move.
3. Click **Move Up** to move the file above the previous file or **Move Down** to move the file below the next file.

_____ **What To Do If**

- If you want to move a file several places up or down the list, keep clicking **Move Up** or **Move Down** until the file reaches its new place in the list.
- Once you finish reordering the files in your book, regenerate the book to update the numbering and table of contents.

_____ **See Also**

- Adding Files to a Book, p. 386.

Updating the Formats for a Book | 190

You can apply a template to an entire book or to selected files in a book. When you apply a template to a file, the tags and formats that have the same name as the ones you are importing will change to the template formats. Any tags and formats with names not shared by the ones in the file are merged into the catalog. If you do not want to change a specific format, make sure that either the template you are applying does not include a format of the same name, or that the format or tag having the same name has the characteristics you want.

When you apply a template to the entire book, the files do not have to be open. FrameMaker opens each file, applies the new template, and then saves and closes the file. You do not see this actually happen, but a message at the bottom of the book file window shows the name of the file and whether it is being opened or saved.

Assumptions

- A book is open.

- The document from which you are importing the formats is open.

- The existing files do not have formats you want to keep, so you can override the existing formats by importing new ones.

- The book window is selected.

Exceptions

- You cannot specify exactly which tags or specific master pages to import using these steps.

- You cannot import the content of a document using these steps.

- You cannot undo or reverse these steps.

- Individual files do not have to be open to update the formats for files in a book.

Steps

TIP

Names are case-sensitive, so if you are importing tags or other formats with the same name but different case, your document will contain both. For example, you can have a BodyText tag and a bodytext tag.

1. Select **Import:Formats** from the Book File menu (see Figure 9.5).

2. Select the file from which you are importing these formats.

3. Turn on the **Format Specifications** you want to import.

4. Turn the format overrides on or off, as appropriate.

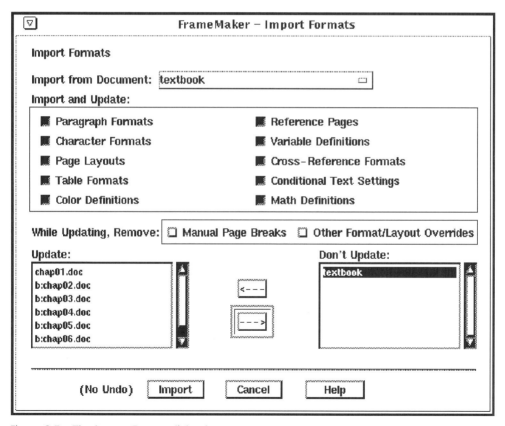

Figure 9.5   The Import Format dialog box.

5. Move the files you do not want to update to the **Don't Update** scroll list.

6. Click on **Import**.

What To Do If

- Importing formats causes the imported tags, pages, and settings to merge with the existing ones. If the formats in your document have the same names as the formats being imported, they will be replaced by the imported ones.

- If you import Paragraph Formats, the settings imported include the footnote properties, Allow Breaks After setting, and Feather settings.

- If you import Page Layouts, the settings imported include the character properties, the First Page properties, and the View option settings.

- If you import Table Formats, the Table Catalog and Ruling Styles merge with the existing ones.

- If you import Reference Pages, FrameMaker removes any reference frames with a name different from the imported ones.

- If you import Cross-references, FrameMaker updates the internal cross-references.

- If you import Conditional Text, the Show/Hide settings are imported as well.

- If you import Math Definitions, FrameMaker copies the equation size and font settings into your document.

See Also

- Chapter 4, "Creating the Formats."

Updating the Changes in a Book   191

Whenever you make any major changes to the settings in a book—such as rearranging, adding, or deleting files—you need to regenerate the book to update the numbering and any generated lists you have set up for the book. Regenerating a book is also a good practice for spotting any problems with numbering, flow connections, and file ordering as you make changes to a book.

Assumptions

- The book window is selected.

Exceptions

- Individual files do not have to be open to update the changes in a book file even though they are affected.

Steps

1. Select **Generate/Update** from the Book File menu.
2. Move the files you do not want to generate into the **Don't Generate** scroll list. The scroll lists only list generated files.
3. Click **Update.**

What To Do If

- If you want to update a generated list, such as a table of contents, keep the list in the **Generate** scroll list. This way you can either generate the lists or update them all at once.
- If a file is open, the changes made in it are not automatically saved. You need to save the file explicitly to keep the changes.
- If a file is not open, the changes made in it are automatically saved.

TIP

When you update a book, you can select which generated files to update. FrameMaker updates all the non-generated files in the book each time you regenerate it. If you are using a file in more than one book, the file saves the settings from the last book that was updated.

- If you have unresolved cross-references, FrameMaker displays an error message. Fix the unresolved cross-references and update the book.

- If conditional text settings differ from file to file in the book, FrameMaker displays an error message. You can fix the settings throughout the book by importing the Conditional Text Settings using Import Formats.

See Also

- Chapter 10, "Creating Generated Files."
- Updating Cross-References, p. 182.

192 Comparing Books

With FrameMaker you can compare two versions of a book and produce reports that outline the differences. This capability is useful when you are working with conditional books or when you are updating documents for new versions of the same product or story.

FrameMaker creates two types of documents when you compare books: a report showing the setup differences between the books and a composite document of the books you are comparing. The composite document displays everything common to the documents in the normal manner, and it displays everything different between the documents with a condition tag for each version.

Assumptions

- You have two versions of the same book.
- The books that you are comparing are both open.
- You are in the newer version of the book.

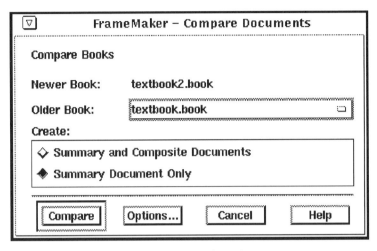

Figure 9.6   The Compare Documents dialog box.

Exceptions

- FrameMaker does not compare two different books, only different versions of the same book.

Steps

1. Select **Compare Books** from the Book File menu of the newest book. Figure 9.6 shows the Compare Documents dialog box.

2. Select the older version of the book from the **Older Book** pop-up menu.

3. Select the document you want to create.

4. Click on **Options** to set up the comparison options. Figure 9.7 shows the Comparison Options dialog box.

5. Click **Compare**.

What To Do If

- If you want to list the differences in book setup information, select **Summary Document Only**. The document

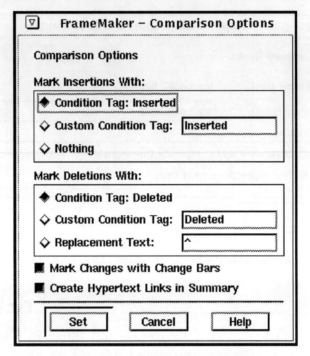

Figure 9.7   The Comparison Options dialog box.

with this information is saved in the file named <newbook> Summary.doc.

- If you want to list the differences in each file, select **Summary and Composite Documents**. The document with this information is saved in the file named <filename>CMP.doc.

- If there are no differences, FrameMaker displays an alert box with this information and does not create the report documents.

See Also

- None.

Chapter
10

CREATING GENERATED FILES

Creating a Table of Contents

A table of contents is one of the two most commonly used lists in publishing, and FrameMaker makes them easy and painless to generate. You can generate a table of contents and either format it yourself or use an existing template to format it. A table of contents is generated into a file separate from the rest of your document, and it can also be added to, and generated from, a FrameMaker book.

193 — Generating a Table of Contents

Generating tables of contents is easy and quick. Once you have a document in place and are clear on the use of paragraph tags, particularly for the document's headings, you can generate a table of contents.

Assumptions

- The headings in your document have a paragraph tag assigned to them that reflects their function and heading level.
- You have a table of contents template in place that you can use to format it.
- You are in the document for which you want to generate a table of contents.

Exceptions

- You cannot create a table of contents for documents that do not use paragraph tags.
- You cannot create an accurate table of contents if you do not use the paragraph tags consistently. Do not use one heading tag and format it manually for each type of heading.

Steps

1. Select **Generate/Book** from the File menu.
2. Choose **Table of Contents** from the List pop-up menu. The Set Up Table of Contents dialog box (see Figure 10.1) will appear.
3. Click **Generate.**
4. Select each paragraph tag you want to include in the table of contents and move it to the **Include** scroll list. FrameMaker reads each paragraph tagged with the tags in the Include list and places the content of the paragraph in the list.
5. Set the **Create Hypertext Links** check box.
6. Click **Generate.**
   FrameMaker creates a new file with the same name as the source file, but with a suffix of TOC.

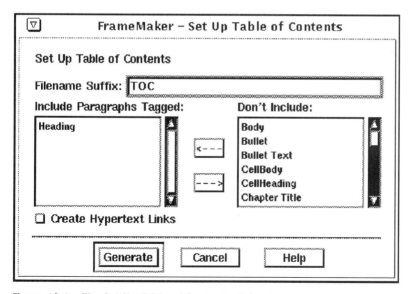

Figure 10.1   The Set Up Table of Contents dialog box.

What To Do If

- If you want to generate hypertext links for your table of contents entries, turn **Create Hypertext Links** on.

- If you want to trace a table of contents entry to its source, use the right mouse button to **Control +** click the entry in the table of contents. FrameMaker opens the source document on the page with the source information and highlights the heading.

See Also

- Formatting the Table of Contents, below.

194 Formatting the Table of Contents

When you generate a table of contents, FrameMaker does not format the list unless you are using a template. The table of contents is generated using default building blocks and formats. To format the table of contents, you have to modify the paragraph tags to format the entries, then use the table of contents building blocks in the Reference Pages to specify the content that appears for the entries. In addition, you can create a Master Page for the first page and change the headers and footers for the file.

When FrameMaker generates a table of contents, it also generates paragraph tags for it. For example, an entry generated from the tag named Heading has a tag named HeadingTOC.

Assumptions

- You have generated a table of contents for a document or as a starting point for a TOC template.

- You are at the Reference Pages of the table of contents. The Reference Pages should contain a special text column with a flow name of TOC. The column should contain a paragraph for every tag you included in the list and one for the hypertext links.

Exceptions

- None.

Steps

1. Click on a paragraph. You can see which level of entry you are on by the name of the paragraph tag on the tag bar at the bottom of the window.

2. Modify the building blocks to display the information you need in the order you want. Table 10.1 presents building blocks available to you.

3. Repeat the previous step for each entry paragraph in the flow.

4. Regenerate the table of contents.
   The entries should now contain the information you specified, in the order you specified it.

5. Open the Paragraph Designer.

6. Click on an entry.

7. Make any modifications you want to the entry's format. Remember, an entry should always use the TOC tag.

> **TIP**
>
> Once you try these steps once, you probably won't want to regenerate the table of contents every time you make a change. Just remember that any changes you make using the Reference Pages do not show until the file is regenerated, including adding tabs.

Table 10.1   Building Blocks for the Table of Contents

Building Block	Displays	Example
<$paratext>	The paragraph text	Creating Generated Files
<$paranum>	The paragraph autonumber	Chapter 10
<$pagenum>	The entry's page number in the source document	300

Otherwise, when you regenerate the table of contents, it will not retain the format you specify.

8. Repeat the previous two steps for each entry you want to format.

9. Make any changes you want to the Master Pages.

10. Save the table of contents.
    Do not change the name of the table of contents unless you are creating a template.

What To Do If

- If you want to align the page numbers to the right, add a tab or tab symbol (\t) between the <$paratext> and <$pagenum> building blocks. Go back to the Body Pages and add a tab stop to the corresponding paragraph tags. Regenerate the table of contents.

- If you want to add leader dots or other leader characters, turn the leader dots on when you create the tab stop for an entry's paragraph tag.

- If you want to specify a character tag for a specific part of an entry, such as the autonumber, insert the name of the tag in angle brackets in front of the building block to which you want to apply it. To change back to the default font, insert <Default Para Font> after the building block you are modifying. For example:

```
<Emphasis><$paranum><Default Para Font>
                    \t<paratext>\t<$pagenum>
```

- If you want to keep the number with the paragraph text, insert a nonbreaking space or another kind of space, such as an em space or an en space.

- If you insert the paragraph autonumber, insert a tab or space between the number building block and the text building block to line up the text.

- If you want to place special text in the entries, insert it in the Reference Pages where you want it to appear. For example, if you want an em dash to follow the paragraph autonumber, place it after the <$paranum> building block.

- If you want to use special headings for sections, add them after you finalize the table of contents. Otherwise, they will be placed at the beginning of the file each time you regenerate the file.

- If you want to use a special first page in the table of contents, create a new Master Page and apply it to the first page. When you regenerate the file, it will use the first Master Page just as you assigned it.

- If you use a first Master Page, make sure that the flow of the first page in the Body Pages is connected to the rest of the document.

- If you want to create a template for the table of contents, first generate a table of contents. Format it using the steps outlined in this section, and save it. You can name the template anything you want.

  When you use a template to create a table of contents, open it as a new document, and save it with the name you expect the table of contents to take. For example, for Chapter10.doc, name the template Chapter10TOC.doc. When you generate the table of contents for Chapter10.doc, the table of contents will use the template's formats.

  Note that in order to use a template, your paragraph tags have to match the ones in the template. For example, for Heading tags, the table of contents contains HeadingTOC tags, which it uses to format the Heading entries. If your headings are tagged with a format called Head instead, FrameMaker generates a HeadTOC tag for its entry and does not use the HeadingTOC formatting.

- If you want to use a template but have already generated the index, use the **Import:Formats** command from the File menu to import the template. Make sure that Paragraph

Formats, Character Formats, Reference Pages, and Master Pages are selected before you import. Then regenerate the table of contents.

See Also

- Creating and Updating Format Tags, p. 104.
- Specifying the Position and Alignment of Tabs, p. 115.
- Using Master Pages, p. 363.

Creating an Index

Indexes are the second most commonly used lists in publishing. With FrameMaker you can implement your index design by using tools to create the index markers, and generate it based on these markers. To create an index for your document, first you design the index and mark the index entries throughout the document; then you generate the index. The index is generated into a file separate from the rest of your document and can be added to, and generated from, a FrameMaker book.

You can format the index once it is generated, or you can use a template to format it. When you format an index or create a template for it, you can specify the information FrameMaker uses for the entries, their order, their look, and their location, as well as the sort order and paragraph format for each type of entry.

195 ▼ Marking Index Entries

Inserting the markers for index entries is a fairly straightforward process. Designing the index and deciding the types of entries to use and how many levels to use make index creation more complex. In addition, deciding what constitutes a good index entry and guessing what readers look for to find a specific subject are difficult and demanding tasks for the index creator.

FrameMaker's index-generating feature makes creating, order-ing, and formatting the index a relatively minor issue once the basic framework is built, allowing you to spend more time on the actual content of the index.

Assumptions

- You've already made design decisions about your index, such as how many levels of entries the index will have and whether you are using See and See Also entries.

- The insertion point is placed where you want to insert a marker.

Exceptions

- You cannot insert index markers in text created with the Graphics tool.

Steps

1. Select **Marker** from the Special menu (or press **Esc s m**). Figure 10.2 shows the Marker window.

2. Select **Index** from the Marker Type pop-up menu.

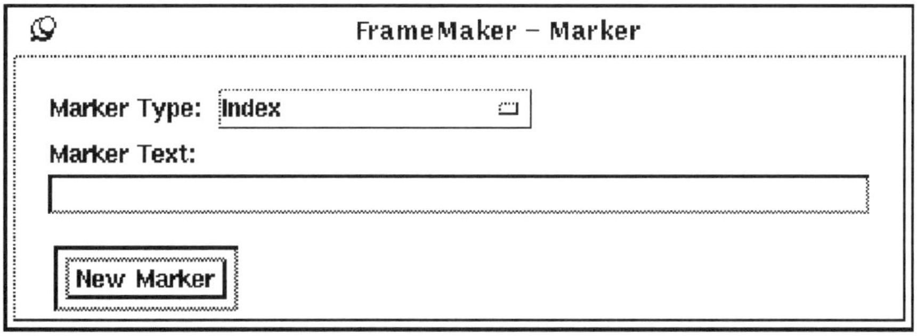

Figure 10.2 The Marker window.

TIP

Place the index marker at the beginning of a paragraph to make the document easier to edit. Generate the index once in a while to see how it is going. This helps you to find errors such as double entries or misplaced entries. Double entries occur when entries for the same topic are typed with different capitalization styles. Misplaced entries occur when a colon or semicolon is mistyped in the entry.

3. Type the index entry. Table 10.2 presents the building blocks available to you.

4. Click **New Marker.**

What To Do If

- If you want to include a colon, semicolon, bracket, angle bracket, or backslash in an index marker, precede it with a backslash.

- If you do not enter any text in the index marker, the word to the right of the marker becomes the index entry.

- If you want to place more than one entry in a marker, separate each entry with a semicolon.

- If you want to make subentries to subentries, separate them with a colon. You can have as many levels of subentries as you want. Each subentry separated by a colon is subordinate to the preceding entry.

- If you want to specify a page range, insert a start marker at the beginning of the information you are indexing and an end marker at the end.

- If you want to use See or See Also entries, enter the information directly into the Marker Text text box. For See references, suppress the page number of the entry. For a See Also entry, create it as a subentry to the main topic. For example:

Index Marker Entry	Result
<$nopage>RAM. See memory	RAM. See memory

<$nopage>hard drives:See
    also storage media
	hard drives 25, 47
	    See also storage media

- If you want to specify that an entry appear in a specific place in the index, use brackets to specify the sorting information. The sorting information consists of the text you want FrameMaker to take into consideration when sorting the index. For example, if you want to sort a number by

Table 10.2   Building Blocks for the Index

Building Block	Action	Example Index Entry	Sample Results
Colon (:)	Separates entry levels	index:building blocks	index building blocks 95

Semicolon (;)	Separates entries in a marker.	index:building blocks; building blocks:index	building blocks
			    index 95
			
			.
			.
			.
			
			index
			    building blocks 95

brackets ([])	Specifies an entry's sort order	2nd Street [second]	seals 234 2nd Street 15 songwriting 135
<$startrange>	Starts a page range	<$startrange> memory: allocation	memory allocation 35–75
<$endrange>	Ends a page range	. . . <$endrange> memory: allocation	
<$nopage>	Indicates an entry with no page number	<$nopage> New Wave; <$singlepage> New Wave:Erasure; Erasure	Erasure 55 . . .
<$singlepage>	Restores the page number for an entry following another one with no page number.		New Wave Erasure 55
Charter tags	Changes the character format of an entry or a page number	music:latin, <Emphasis>See<Default Para Font> Salsa	music latin, *See* Salsa

its name rather than its number, type the number's name between the brackets, such as:

2nd street [second]

FrameMaker uses the word "second" for sorting the entry, but displays the actual entry. In this case, "2nd street" would appear under S.

You can also specify which parts of an entry to consider for sorting, such as

memory allocation:for PCs [memory allocation:PCs]
memory allocation:in Macs [memory allocation:Macs]

In this case, FrameMaker considers PC and Mac as the words to sort, but it displays the whole entry:

memory allocation
in Macs
for PCs

- If you want to change the character format of an entry or its page number, use the character tag between angled brackets as a building block. To change the format back to normal, use the <Default Para Font> building block. To change the format of the page number, place the character tag building block at the end of the entry.

See Also

- Generating an Index, below.
- Formatting the Index p. 419.

196 ▽ Generating an Index

Generating the index is easy and quick. Once you place all the markers you want to see, you can generate the index. Usually you generate the index several times to check specific parts before you decide to generate for a complete edit. If you are indexing a FrameMaker book, you can generate separate indexes for the files you are marking before you generate a complete index.

Assumptions

- You created index markers from which to generate the index.

- You have an index template in place that you can use to format it.

- You are in the document for which you want to generate an index.

Exceptions

- You cannot index text created with the Graphics tools.

Steps

1. Select **Generate/Book** from the File menu (or press **Esc f g**).

2. Choose **Standard Index** from the Index pop-up menu. The Set Up Standard Index dialog box (see Figure 10.3) will appear.

3. Click **Generate**.

4. Select the index marker type and move it to the **Include** scroll list.
   FrameMaker reads the contents of the index markers, and translates the building blocks and text into entries for the index.

5. Set the **Create Hypertext Links** check box.

6. Click **Generate**.
   FrameMaker creates a new file with the same name as the source file, but with a suffix of IX.

TIP

- If you want the index to be formatted right away, create and use an index template. Open the template and save it with the file name you expect the index to have. For example, for an index for a file called Chapter10.doc, name the index template **Chapter10IX.doc**, then generate the index.

- If you decide to use a template after you generate the index, you can use the **Import:Formats** command in the File menu to import the template. Make sure that Paragraph Formats, Character Formats, Reference Pages, and Master Pages are selected before you import. Then regenerate the index.

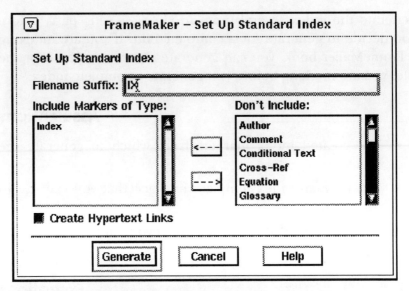

Figure 10.3   The Set Up Standard Index dialog box.

What To Do If

- If you want to generate hypertext links for your index entries, turn **Create Hypertext Links** on.

- If you want the generated file to have another suffix, type the suffix in the **Filename Suffix** text box.

- If you want to trace an index entry to its source, use the right mouse button to **Control +** click the entry in the index. FrameMaker will open the source document on the page with the source information and highlight the marker. You can then open the Marker window and edit the marker.

See Also

- Formatting the Index, p. 419.

Formatting the Index | 197

When you generate an index, FrameMaker does not format it unless you are using a template. The index is generated by using default building blocks and formats, in addition to the ones you used in the markers. To format the index, you have to modify the paragraph tags to format the entries, and you have to use the index building blocks in the Reference Pages to determine more specifically the contents of each entry and the sorting order of the index. In addition, you can create a Master Page for the first page, and change the headers and footers for the file.

When FrameMaker generates an index, it also generates paragraph tags for it. The paragraph tags are named after each level of entry and have an IX suffix. For example, a first-level entry has a tag named Level1IX.

Assumptions

- You have generated an index for a document, or as a starting point for a template.
- You are at the Reference Pages of the index.
  The Reference Pages should contain a special text column with a flow name of **IX**. The column should contain a paragraph for the following items:

Item and function	Paragraph tag associated with it
Each entry level	Level1IX, Level2IX, and so on
Hypertext links	Active IX
Sort order	SortOrderIX
Page number separators	SeparatorsIX
Title for each index grouping, such as A,B, and so on	Group TitlesIX
Characters to ignore	IgnoreCharsIX
The marker types, in this case Index	IndexIX

When you click on any of these paragraphs, you can see the name of its paragraph tag in the tag bar at the bottom of the document window. These tags also describe the function of the paragraphs.

Steps

1. Click on the **Index** paragraph.

   You can see the paragraph you are on by the name of the paragraph tag on the tag bar at the bottom of the document window.

2. Modify the building block to display the information you want. You can display either the page number of an entry or the number of the paragraph that contains the marker. Table 10.3 presents the building blocks available to you for this type of paragraph.

3. Click on the separator paragraph.

4. Change any of the separators. You must always use the numbers 1, 2, and 3.

   You can specify a separator to precede the first page number, one to separate multiple page numbers, and one to appear between a range of numbers. For example:

   1, 2–3

Table 10.3	Building Blocks for the Index	
Building Block	**Displays**	**Example**
<$paranum>	The paragraph autonumber of the paragraph that contains an index marker	Chapter 10
<$pagenum>	The entry's page number in the source document	350

In this case, a tab is placed between an entry and the first page number, a comma is placed between page numbers, and an en dash between a range of numbers.

5. Click on the sort order paragraph.

6. Change the sort order to match your needs. Table 10.4 presents the building blocks available to you for this type of operation.
    You can reorder these building blocks or replace them with your own set of characters in the order you want them to sort. Separate the letter groups with a space.

7. Click on the **Group Titles** paragraph.

8. Change the groupings and group titles to match your needs.

9. Save and regenerate the index.
    The entries should now contain the information you specified, and should be in the order you specified.

10. Go to the Body Pages, if you are not there already.

11. Open the Paragraph Designer (press **Esc o p d**).

12. Click on the type of paragraph you want to format.

13. Make any modifications you want to the paragraph format.

Table 10.4	Building Blocks That Specify the Sort Order of an Index	
Building Block	**Sorts**	**Example**
<$numerics>	Numbers	0123456789
<$alphabetics>	The alphabet of the language you are using	Aa Bb Cc Dd Ee and so on
<$symbols>	All other ASCII symbols	$°\Delta \sqrt{\ } \mu$ and so on

TIP

Once you try these steps, you probably won't need to regenerate the index every time you make a change. Just remember that any changes you make using the Reference Pages do not show until the file is regenerated, including adding tabs.

Do not apply a different paragraph tag to an entry or any other generated paragraph; otherwise, when you regenerate the index, it will not retain the format you specify.

14. Repeat the two previous steps for every type of paragraph you want to format, such as the group titles.

15. Make any changes you want to the Master Pages.

16. Save and regenerate the index.
     Do not change the name of the index unless you are creating a template.

What To Do If

- If you make modifications to any of the paragraphs in the Reference Pages, regenerate the index to see the results.

- If you want to right-align the page numbers, add a tab before the number 1 in the separators paragraph. Go back to the Body Pages and add a right-aligned tab stop to every level of entry's paragraph tag.

- If you want to add leader dots or other leader characters, turn the leader dots on when you create the tab stop for an entry's paragraph tag.

- If you want to include a paragraph's autonumber instead of the page number for index entries, replace the <$pagenum> building block with the **<$paranum>** in the Index paragraph.

- If you want to change the format of the page numbers, type the character format in angle brackets at the beginning of the **IndexIX** paragraph in the Reference Pages.

- If you want to create a page range automatically every time FrameMaker encounters the same entry in consecutive pages, insert **<$autorange>** at the beginning of the Index paragraph in the Reference Pages.

- If you want FrameMaker to ignore certain characters when sorting the index, include them in the **IgnoreChars** paragraph in the Reference Pages. The default setting is to ignore hyphens, nonbreaking hyphens, en dashes, and em dashes.

- If you want to sort the index letter by letter as opposed to word by word, include a regular space in the **IgnoreChars** paragraph in the Reference Pages.

- If you replace the <$alphabetic> building block with your own set of characters, do not create separate paragraphs for each line of characters. Let the lines wrap automatically, placing the character set in one paragraph.

- If you replace the <$symbols> with your own set of characters, insert a backslash before angle brackets (< or >).

- If you specify a letter pair for sorting, such as "ch," place the pair between angle brackets.

- If you change the group titles for the index, edit the **Group-Titles** paragraph in the Reference Pages.

- If you want to specify which letter to start a grouping with, type the letter in brackets after the corresponding group title. For example:

  Symbols [\ ]; Numerics [0]; a-f[a]; g-l[g]; m-r[m]; s-z[s]

- If you want to create an index without group titles, place all the letters in brackets and remove any titles from the GroupTitles paragraph. The information in the brackets ensures that the list is sorted in the right order.

- If you want to use a special first page for the index, create a new Master Page and apply it to the first page. When you regenerate the file, it will use the first Master Page just as you assigned it.

- If you use a first Master Page, make sure that the flow of the first page in the Body Pages is connected to the rest of the document.

- If you want to create a template for the index, first generate an index. Format it using the steps outlined in this section, and save it. You can name the template anything you want. When you use a template to create an index, open it as a new document, and save it with the name you expect the index to take. For example, for Chapter10.doc, name the template **Chapter10IX.doc.** When you generate the index for Chapter10.doc, the index will use the template's formats.

See Also

*   Generating an Index, p. 416.

Creating Generated Lists

A table of contents in FrameMaker is a paragraph tag-based list, and an index is a marker-based list. A paragraph tag-based list is a list that FrameMaker generates from paragraphs having specific tags. A marker-based list is one that you generate by inserting markers throughout the document and then specifying the type of marker FrameMaker should read to build the list.

You can create a variety of lists and indexes with Frame-Maker, and they all fall in one of the two categories above. Each one requires that you prepare the source document, generate the list, and format it. For detailed information on each of these tasks, see "Creating a Table of Contents" and "Creating an Index" earlier in this chapter. For the overall information on generating these types of lists, see the tasks in this section.

198   Generating Paragraph Tag-Based Lists

You can create the following tag-based lists using FrameMaker: Table of Contents, List of Figures, List of Tables, List of Paragraphs, and Alphabetical List of Paragraphs. Each of these lists can be created through any paragraph tag you choose. You can create a list of any paragraph type you want, except an alphabetical list of paragraphs, by choosing **Table of Contents** from the List pop-up menu. However, FrameMaker gives each list its own distinguishing prefix, making it easier to deal with each list separately if necessary.

Assumptions

- The headings in your document have a paragraph tag assigned to them that reflects their function.
- You have a list template in place that you can use to format.
- You are in the document for which you want to generate a list.

Exceptions

- You cannot create a list for documents that do not use paragraph tags.
- You cannot create an accurate list if you do not use the paragraph tags consistently. Do not use a tag and format it manually for each different function.

Steps

1. Select **Generate/Book** from the File menu (or press **Esc f g**).
2. Choose the type of list you want to create from the **List** pop-up menu.
3. Click **Generate**. FrameMaker displays a Set Up dialog box for the type of list you are creating (see Figure 10.4).
4. Select each paragraph tag you want to include in the list and move it to the **Include** scroll list.
   FrameMaker reads each paragraph tagged with the tags in the Include list and places the content of the paragraph in the list.
5. Set the **Create Hypertext Links** check box.
6. Click **Generate**.

TIP

- If you want your list to be formatted right away, create and use a template. Open the template and save it with the file name you expect the list to have. For example, for a list of figures for a file called Chapter10.doc, name the template file Chapter10LOF.doc and then generate the list.
- If you decide to use a template after you generate the list, you can use the Import:Formats command in the File menu to import the template. Make sure that Paragraph Formats, Character Formats, Reference Pages, and Master Pages are selected before you import it, then regenerate the list.

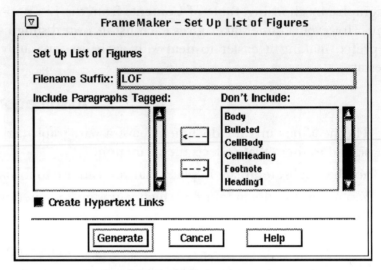

Figure 10.4   The Set Up List of Figures dialog box.

FrameMaker creates a new file with the same name as the source file, but with a different suffix.

Suffix	Type of List
TOC	Table of Contents
LOF	List of Figures
LOT	List of Tables
LOP	List of Paragraphs
APL	Alphabetical List of Paragraphs

What To Do If

- If you want to generate hypertext links for your table of contents entries, turn **Create Hypertext Links** on.

- If you want the generated file to have another suffix, type the new suffix in the **Filename Suffix** text box.

- If you want to trace a table of contents entry to its source, with the right mouse button **Control +** click the entry in the table of contents.

FrameMaker opens the source document on the page with the source information and highlights the heading.

- If you want to format your list or create a list template, see Formatting the Table of Contents (page 408). Substitute the TOC suffix for the one corresponding to your list in the table of contents tasks.

_____ **See Also**

- Formatting the Table of Contents, p. 408.

Generating Marker-Based Lists 199

You can create the following tag-based lists using FrameMaker: List of Markers, Alphabetical List of Markers, List of References, Standard Index, Author Index, Subject Index, and Index of Markers. Each of these lists is generated by specific types of markers. Each list has its own distinguishing prefix, making it easier to be dealt with separately. The restriction on the markers you can use to generate these lists makes each list very specialized. Some of the lists are meant as tools to help you edit cross-references, indexes, and other types of markers you might be using. Others are meant to enable you to index a variety of items independently of each other. For example, an index of authors can be created separately from a document index.

_____ **Assumptions**

- You have created markers from which to generate the list.

- You have a template in place that you can use to format.

- You are in the document for which you want to generate the list.

Exceptions

- You cannot list text created with the Graphics tools.
- If you generate a marker list chosen from the List pop-up menu, the building blocks you use are as described in the tasks in Creating a Table of Contents. You also handle any modifications in the Reference Pages in the same way as in the Table of Contents.

  In addition, marker lists generated from the List pop-up menu use the <$markertext> building block instead of the <$paratext> building block.

Steps

1. Select **Generate/Book** from the File menu (or press **Esc f g**).
2. Choose the type of list you want to create from the **List** or **Index** pop-up menu.
3. Click **Generate**. FrameMaker displays a Set Up dialog box for the type of list you are creating (see Figure 10.5).

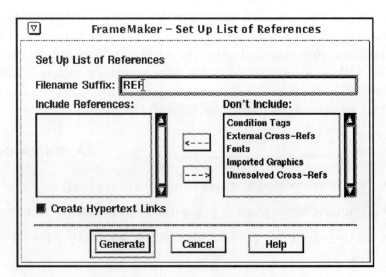

Figure 10.5   The Set Up List of References dialog box.

4. Select the marker type and move it to the **Include** scroll list.
   FrameMaker reads the contents of the markers and translates any building blocks and text into entries for the list. Not all marker-based lists use building blocks.

5. Set the **Create Hypertext Links** check box.

6. Click **Generate**.
   FrameMaker creates a new file with the same name as the source file but with a different suffix.

Suffix	Type of List
LOM	List of Markers
AML	Alphabetical Marker List
LOR	List of References
IX	Standard Index
AIX	Author Index
SIX	Subject Index
IOM	Index of Markers

What To Do If

- If you generate a marker list you have chosen from the Index pop-up menu, the building blocks you use are as described in the tasks in Creating an Index. You also handle any modifications in the Reference Pages in the same way as in a Standard Index.

- If you want to generate hypertext links for your list entries, turn **Create Hypertext Links** on.

- If you want the generated file to have another suffix, type the suffix in the **Filename Suffix** text box.

- If you want to trace a list entry to its source, use the right mouse button to **Control +** click the entry in the index. FrameMaker opens the source document on the page with the source information and highlights the marker. You can then open the Marker window and edit the marker.

- If you want to format your list or create a list template, see "Formatting the Index" (page 419).
  Substitute the IX suffix for the one corresponding to your list in the index tasks.

See Also

- Formatting the Table of Contents, p. 408.
- Marking Index Entries, p. 412.
- Formatting the Index, p. 419.

Creating Generated Lists from a Book

Any list you can generate from a source document, you can generate for a whole book. FrameMaker enables you to generate lists for all the files in your book, using the page numbers and paragraph numbers as you specify them for each file in the book. When you generate lists from books you go though a two-step process: you add the file to the book, then you generate it. After that, you can update it and regenerate the list as often as you need.

200

Adding a Generated List to a Book

Before you can generate a list for a FrameMaker book, you need to add it to the book. The file added to a book is really a placeholder, for the file does not yet exist. However, once the placeholder is there, you can generate the file.

Assumptions

- A book is open.
- The book window is selected.

- You have prepared the files in the book by adding markers or using paragraph tags consistently.

Exceptions

- The files in the book do not have to be open for you to perform this operation.
- You cannot add the same type of list twice unless you change the suffix of the generated file.

Steps

1. Select **Add File** from the book File menu (see Figure 10.6).

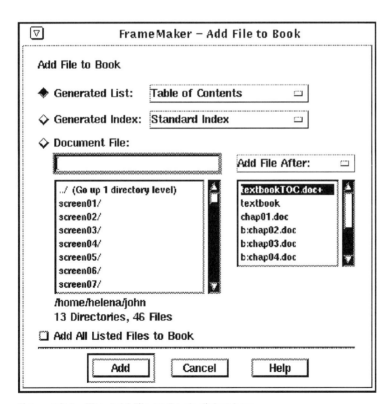

Figure 10.6   The Add File to Book dialog box.

2. Select the type of list you want to add to the book from the **Generated List** or the **Generated Index** pop-up menus.

3. Select the location of the file within the book.

4. Click **Add**.
   FrameMaker adds the generated file to your list. However, it is just a placeholder for now; the file does not exist until it is generated.

What To Do If

- If you want to change the location of a generated file in the book, reorder the files by using the Rearrange Files dialog box.

- If you want to remove a generated file from the book, delete it by using the Rearrange Files dialog box.

- If you generate a file that has the name of an existing file, when you click on the file in the book, FrameMaker displays the existing file.

- If you want to see the contents of the file, generate it and then open it.

See Also

- Creating a Book, p. 384.
- Creating Generated Lists, p. 424.

201   Generating a List from a Book

Once you add the placeholder for the file in the book, you can generate it. When you generate a list from the Book File menu, FrameMaker reads each file in the book and extracts the information you want to display in the list. All of the paragraph and page numbers are based on the choices you made when setting up the files for the book.

Assumptions

- A book is open.
- The book window is selected.
- You have prepared the files in the book by adding markers or using paragraph tags consistently.

Exceptions

- The files in the book do not have to be open for you to perform this operation.
- You cannot generate a file if it hasn't been added to the book first.

Steps

1. Select **Generate/Update** from the book File menu (see Figure 10.7).
2. Move the files you do not want to generate into the **Don't Generate** scroll list. The scroll lists only generated files.

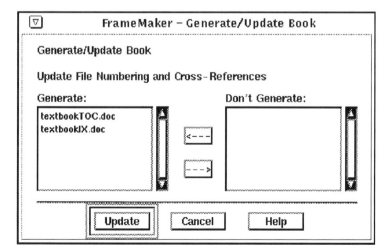

Figure 10.7   The Generate/Update dialog box.

3. Click **Update**.

FrameMaker generates the files in the Generate scroll list.

What To Do If

- If you want to use a template to format generated lists, you can use an existing file that has the name you expect the generated file to have. You can also use the Import:Format command from the File menu to apply the template to the file once it is generated.

- If you want to update generated files, make the modifications, save the file, and regenerate the file using the preceding steps.

See Also

- Creating a Book, p. 384.
- Creating Generated Lists, p. 424.

Chapter

11

Using Condition Tags

Displaying and Printing Conditional
Documents

CREATING
CONDITIONAL
DOCUMENTS

Using Condition Tags

Sometimes you need to create different versions of one document to be used for different purposes. For documents that share a great amount of information, you can use FrameMaker to create conditional documents. A conditional document takes advantage of the information your documents have in common and enables you to keep all versions separate but in one file. This chapter shows you how to create and manipulate conditional documents.

Conditional text is matter that is specific to one version of a document. Any FrameMaker element can be conditional, such as text, graphics, and tables. Unconditional text is common to all versions of the document. You can format conditional text to look different from unconditional text, in order to recognize it easily on the screen. For example, you might display the conditional text of one version as underlined text and that of another version in a different color, such as red or green.

FrameMaker can merge versions of your document into one conditional document. FrameMaker merges the versions by comparing them and creating a composite conditional document. When you decide to make a document conditional, you have to create condition tags for each version of the document. When you create a condition tag, you can specify a distinguishing property, such as underline or color, to differentiate between condition tags. When you apply condition tags to the content of a document, you can view, format, and print them separately or together or apply them to and remove them from any part of your document.

You can also create condition tags for annotation purposes. For example, you can use the default Comments condition tag to annotate a document as you review it or write it. If you are using annotation condition tags, you can view and print the annotations either separately from the document or with the rest of the document.

Creating Condition Tags   202

Before you can make a document conditional, you have to create the condition tags that the document requires. For example, if you have three versions of a document, one for marketing, one for sales, and one for training, you might create Marketing, Sales, and Training condition tags.

Assumptions

- You have identified the different versions of the document that you need.

Exceptions

- None.

Steps

1. Select **Conditional Text** from the Special menu.
2. Click **Edit Condition Tag** in the Conditional Text window (see Figure 11.1).

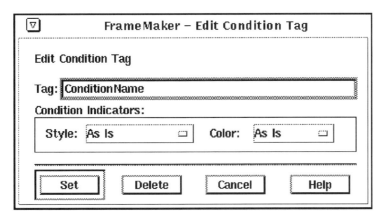

Figure 11.1   The Edit Condition Tag dialog box.

3. Type a name for the new conditional tag in the Tag text box.

4. Choose a character style and color for the conditional text from the Style and Color pop-up menus.

5. Click **Set**.

What To Do If

- If you want to use another document's conditional tags and settings, import them into the current document. Open the other document and use the **Import:Formats** command from the File menu. Make sure that only the Conditional Text Settings are turned on before you import the tags or settings.

- If you want to change any of the settings of a condition tag, click on the tag name in the Conditional Text window, select **Edit Condition Tag**, and make the changes you want in the Edit Condition Tag dialog box.

- If you want to find out which condition tags are used in a document, generate a list of references for condition tags. The report will list the condition tags used in each page of a document.

See Also

- Removing a Condition Tag from the Text, p. 440.

Applying a Condition Tag

Applying a condition tag is almost as simple as selecting the item. You can make any FrameMaker element conditional. However, make sure that it is the items that versions do not have in common that you tag. Everything that your conditional versions have in common should remain unconditional.

When you select the items to be made conditional, keep in mind that in some cases selecting the object alone does not make it conditional. For items such as frames, tables, graphics, and markers you need to select anchor and marker symbols.

Assumptions

- You have created or imported the condition tags for use with the current document.
- You have selected the items to be made conditional.

Exceptions

- You cannot apply condition tags to table columns.

Steps

1. Select **Conditional Text** from the Special menu (see Figure 11.2).

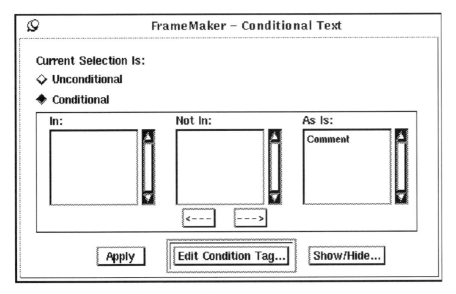

Figure 11.2 The Conditional Text window.

2. Select the condition tag you want to apply from the **Not In** scroll list and move it to the **In** scroll list. If the text is already conditional, the Conditional button will be on. However, you can apply more than one condition tag to an item.

3. Click **Apply**.

What To Do If

- If you want to apply more than one condition tag to an item, use the previous steps. The identifying character styles of both condition tags are used. For example, if one tag underlines and another overlines, text tagged with both will have both an overline and an underline. Similarly, if you combine a tag that is blue with one that is red, the text you tagged will be purple.

- If you want to apply a condition tag to text you haven't typed yet, place the insertion point where you are going to start typing, apply the condition tag, and start typing. The condition tag will turn itself off when you press **Return**.

- If you apply a tag that is hidden, the items will disappear.

- If you are updating cross-references, make sure all text is visible. FrameMaker cannot find cross-referenced sources if they are hidden and declares cross-references to them unresolved.

See Also

- Choosing the View of a Conditional Document, p. 444.
- Choosing Templates for Conditional Documents, p. 445.
- Printing Conditional Documents, p. 447.

204 ▽ Removing a Condition Tag from the Text

At some point you may want to make conditional text common to all versions of your document or eliminate a whole version of your document. With FrameMaker you can remove a condition tag from text to make it unconditional again or delete a condition tag and all the text tagged with it.

If you want to delete a condition tag, select the tag, go to the Edit Condition Tag dialog box, and click **Delete**. Deleting a condition tag does not automatically delete the text tagged by it.

Assumptions

- You have selected the text from which you want to remove a condition tag.
- The Conditional Text window is open (**Esc s C** to open it).

Exceptions

- None.

Steps

1. Select the condition tags you want to remove.
2. Move them to the **Not In** scroll list. To remove all condition tags from a selection, turn **Unconditional** on.
3. Click on **Apply** to remove the tag from the selected items.

> **TIP**
> When you delete a condition tag, deletion of the text tagged by it applies to your whole document, not just a selection.

What To Do If

- If you want to delete the tag, click on **Edit Condition Tag**. Then decide whether to delete the items tagged with it or make them unconditional.
- If you remove the last tag in a selection, the Remove Condition Tags dialog box opens. The dialog box is the same as the Deleting Condition Tag dialog box. Make the same selections as described in the previous bullet.

See Also

- Choosing the View of a Conditional Document, p. 444.

Comparing and Merging Documents

You can also compare two versions of a document and produce reports that outline the differences. This capability is useful when you want to merge two similar documents to make them conditional or when you are updating documents for new versions of the same product or story.

FrameMaker creates two documents when you compare documents: A composite of the documents you are comparing and a report showing the setup differences between them. In the composite everything that is different between the documents is marked by a condition tag.

Assumptions

- You have two versions of one document.

- The documents that you are comparing are both open.

- You are in the newer version of the document.

Exceptions

- FrameMaker does not compare two different documents, but compares only different versions of the same document.

Steps

1. Select **Compare Documents** from the Book File menu of the newest document (see Figure 11.3).

2. Select the older version of the document from the Older Document pop-up menu.

3. Select the document you want to create.

4. Set up the comparison options.

5. Click **Compare**.

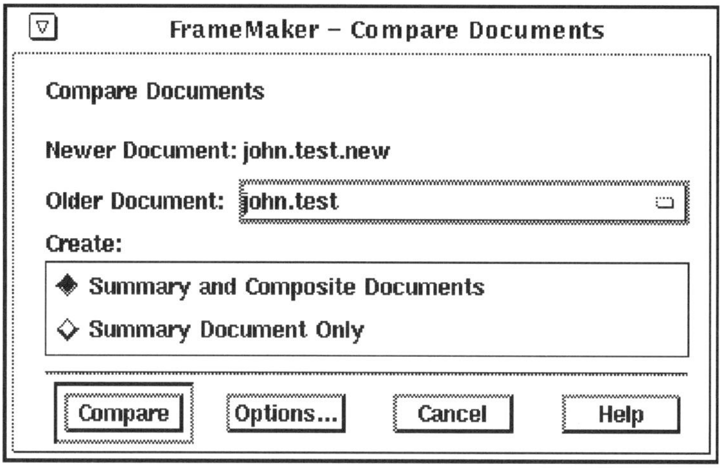

Figure 11.3   The Compare Documents dialog box.

What To Do If

- If you want to list the differences in document setup, select **Summary Document Only**. The document with this information is saved in the file <newbook>Summary.doc.

- If you want to list the differences between the files, select **Summary and Composite Documents**. The document with this information is saved in the file <filename>CMP.doc.

- If there are no differences, FrameMaker displays an alert box saying so and does not create the report documents.

Displaying and Printing Conditional Documents

Once you have created a conditional document, you may want to print each version or print or display the composite version. You can do both of these tasks.

FrameMaker ignores hidden conditional text, so you can assign each version a different look before you display or print it.

Anything that you do to a document affects only the displayed part of the document. So you can make changes in formats, variables, and layout to each version of a document separately.

Choosing the View of a Conditional Document

You can display any version of a conditional document, or you can display a combination of versions at one time. You can make changes in the appearance of the open version of the document and in settings such as variables. These changes will not affect the hidden versions.

Assumptions

- The Conditional Text window is open.

Exceptions

- None.

Steps

1. Click **Show/Hide** (see Figure 11.4).
2. Select the condition tags for the versions you want to display and move them to the **Show** scroll list. To display more than one version, click all the ones you want. To display only one version, make sure all other versions are in the Hide scroll list.
3. Turn on the **Show Condition Indicators** button.
4. Click **Set**.

What To Do If

- If you do not want to display the condition indicators, turn the **Show Condition Indicators** button off before you click **Set**.

TIP

If you display a conditional document for editing, display the condition indicators to make sure you are editing the right version.

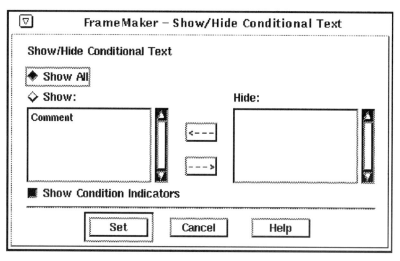

Figure 11.4   The Show/Hide dialog box.

_____ **See Also**

- Applying a Condition Tag, p. 438.
- Choosing Templates for Conditional Documents, below.
- Printing Conditional Documents, p. 447.

Choosing Templates for Conditional Documents

207

If you apply a different template for each version of your document, you can include everything from format and layout to variable definitions and cross-reference formats. Each version of your document should use the same set of formats, such as paragraph, character, and table formats. If you create a different set of formats for each version within the document, the common items might not take the formats you want when you apply the template for a version.

Importing formats to apply a template affects the whole document. The hidden text is also changed to fit the template. If each version of your document has a different format, you have to apply the appropriate template each time you want to print a different version of your document.

Assumptions

- You have a basic template for the conditional document. You use this template for viewing and editing the whole document, and it defines the condition tags for the document. All condition tags appear in this template.

Exceptions

- None.

Steps

1. Set up a template for each version of your document.
2. In the Show/Hide Conditional Text dialog box of each template, move the condition tag that applies to that version only. All other condition tags should be in the Hide scroll list. Also, turn off the **Show Condition Indicators** button.
3. Apply the template for the version you want to view or import it to your document by using the **Import:Formats** command in the File menu.

What To Do If

- If you want to use different variable definitions for each version, make sure that the template for each version contains the appropriate definitions.

See Also

- Chapter 3, "Formatting Text."
- Creating and Updating Table Formats, p. 236.

- Chapter 8, "Creating the Page Layout."
- Creating Cross-References, p. 172.
- Using Variables, p. 186.

Printing Conditional Documents 208

Once you specify the format for a version, you are almost ready to print the specific version. There are a few things you have to double-check before printing.

Assumptions

- You have applied the right template to the version you are going to print.
- The condition indicators for the specific version are off.

Exceptions

- None.

Steps

1. Check that the variable definitions are correct.
2. Update the document's cross-references. If there are cross-references to hidden text, they will show up as unresolved cross-references. You shouldn't have references to hidden text.
3. Save a copy of this version separately from the master document.
4. If you are working with a book, update the book and its generated files.
5. Check generated lists, such as the index, for unresolved markers.
6. Print the document.

What To Do If

- None.

See Also

- Printing a Document, p. 35.

Chapter
12

Creating Online Documents

Using Hypertext Commands

AUTHORING
ONLINE
DOCUMENTS

Creating Online Documents

Online documentation is becoming more pervasive in the delivery of information for computer users of all levels. From the online help systems usually provided with software packages to complete reference manuals and large databases of information, the online medium is providing a plausible alternative for retrieving and displaying large amounts of information effectively and efficiently.

Authoring online documents consists of designing and writing the information and creating the links to access and navigate through the document. Writing for online requires knowledge of the capabilities of the authoring environment. This is akin to finding out the kind of book you're writing, the physical constraints of the format, and the audience's knowledge level and working environment.

The main differences between online and hard-copy documents are the lack of feedback as to where the reader is in the structure of the document and the lack of visible depth of the material the reader has to cover. This implies that you need to chunk the information; have multiple and clear points of entry to each chunk; and not make assumptions as to what the user has seen first. In addition, you should have logical navigation points between the chunks, as well as some way of showing users where they are in the structure you've provided.

FrameMaker enables you to create online documents by using hypertext links, which allow you to structure online documents in any way you want. These documents can be created as easily as hard-copy publications. This chapter discusses the process of creating and editing online documents, using hypertext markers, and locking and viewing the online documents once they are done.

To create online documents using FrameMaker, you need to decide what kind of links or commands you want to use and where to place them in the document. You should design a basic structure for your document before you start designing the links.

The basic structure provides you with a hierarchy you can link together before you start writing. Once you write the chunks of information, you are ready to create the hypertext markers that complete the document's structure and navigation tools.

Creating Active Areas | 209

When you create links, you need to make an area active as a link. An active area can be a word, a group of words, a paragraph, or a graphic. When you create an active area, you should make it distinct from the rest of your text or graphics, to enable users to recognize it as an active area. You can distinguish the active text area by giving the text a different character style. If you make an area active using graphics, make your icons clear and purposeful. For example, you can use arrows to imply forward or backward movement within a set of screens.

Once you create an active area and insert the hypertext marker in it, users can click on the area to activate the command you specified in the marker. When a user clicks the active area, FrameMaker highlights the text for an instant, and then performs the command.

Hypertext markers have to be inside a text box. Therefore, when you want to use an icon or graphic as the active area, you need to place a text box on top of the graphic.

Assumptions

- You want to make some words an active area.

Exceptions

- If you make a whole paragraph an active area, the paragraph should not contain a character format change. FrameMaker stops searching for the hypertext marker when it finds the character change.

Steps

1. Highlight the words you want to make active and insert a hypertext marker in the paragraph.

2. Draw a text column over the graphic you want to make active.
    Make it slightly larger than the graphic.

3. Make sure that the text column is in front of the graphic. Otherwise, FrameMaker will not find the marker.
    To move it to the front, select the column and choose **Front** from the Graphics menu.

4. Make it transparent by selecting the **Pen** and **Fill** patterns to None.

5. Insert a hypertext marker in the text box.
    When a user clicks on the active area, the whole text box over the graphic is highlighted. This reverses the colors of the graphic, providing users with the feedback they need to "see" that a command is being carried out.

What To Do If

*   If you want to create active areas for use in every screen of your document, such as navigation links, Go To buttons, or Close buttons, create them in the Master Pages used by your document.

*   If you use the Master Pages to place links, make sure that there isn't anything in the Body Pages that is placed in front of the link, such as a text column or graphic.

*   If there is a type of link or icon that you use frequently, place it in the Reference Pages and copy and paste into the Body Pages when necessary.

*   If you want to override a Master Page link in one screen but not on the others, create a text column and place it in front of the link you want to override. You can then either leave it

blank, to override any link, or you can create a replacement link in the new text column.

- If you override a Master Page link, you can either make it clear so the icon underneath still shows, or you can make it opaque to cover up the icon completely.

_____ **See Also**

- Creating Text Columns, p. 367.
- Inserting Hypertext Markers, below.

Inserting Hypertext Markers | 210

There are a variety of ways to link and present information in an online document. For this reason, FrameMaker provides you with a simple, yet flexible set of hypertext commands to help you implement your document design.

For example, you can insert markers that take you from one screen to another within the same window, or in another window. You can create an alert or information box for footnotes or short comments. You can even create matrices and pop-up menus that perform other hypertext commands from within.

To decide what kinds of links you need to implement your document, keep in mind the underlying structure and design of your document. Table 12.1 lists the commands available in FrameMaker.

_____ **Assumptions**

- You have chosen the type of link or command you want to use.
- If you are inserting a link to a specific place or page, you already inserted the newlink to mark the spot.

Table 12.1 Hypertext Commands

Command	Action
alert	Displays an alert box.
gotolink	Displays a destination screen using the current window.
gotolink firstpage	Displays the first page in a document.
gotolink lastpage	Displays the last page in a document.
gotopage	Displays a specific page using the current window.
matrix	Displays a matrix of items that contain hypertext tags.
message	Sends a message to another application that is running.
message system	Executes a UNIX shell command.
newlink	Is the destination link for a gotolink or openlink command.
nextpage	Displays the next page in a document.
openlink	Displays a destination screen using a separate window.
opennew	Opens an existing document as a new document using a separate window.
openpage	Displays a specific page using a separate window.
popup	Displays a pop-up menu of items that execute other hypertext commands.
previouslink	Displays the last page the reader viewed.
previouspage	Displays the previous page in the current document.
quit	Closes the current hypertext document.
quitall	Closes all open hypertext documents.

Exceptions

- You do not need to place destination links to use commands such as previouspage or previouslink. These commands take you to the previous page or link in the stack automatically.

Steps

1. Select **Marker** from the Special menu.
   The Marker window will appear (see Figure 12.1).

2. Select **Hypertext** from the Marker Type list.

3. Type the hypertext command in the Marker Text field. When you open the Marker window, you see the highlighted words in the Marker Text field.

4. Replace the words in the Marker Text field with the hypertext command.

5. Click **New Marker**.

What To Do If

- If you want to make a whole paragraph an active area, place the insertion point anywhere in the paragraph, preferably at the beginning, and insert the hypertext tag.

> **TIP**
>
> - Use no more than five to seven links from each screen, aside from straight navigation links, such as backward, forward, and goto links.
>
> - Keep a catalog of all your marker names and what they are associated with. You can generate a list of your hypertext markers that gives you the type of link, the name of the link, and the page number in the current document where the link is located.

FrameMaker – Marker
Marker Type: Hypertext
Marker Text:
New Marker

Figure 12.1   The Marker window.

- If you delete the words using the delete key and then write in the tag, FrameMaker designates the whole paragraph as the active area.
- If you want to insert a destination marker use the newlink marker.
  Remember that the marker has to be inside a text column. This marker has the following format:

  newlink linkname

  where linkname is the name of the marker.

See Also

- Creating Generated Lists, p. 424.
- Creating Navigation and Direct Links, p. 459.

211 ▽ Editing Hypertext Markers

Once you create links, you will want to test them. Some of them may not work right away for a variety of reasons. Maybe you didn't use the right destination link name, perhaps you misspelled some. In some cases, you may find that you change your mind about some links altogether and will want to remove them. In addition, you may be revising existing documents, or the structure of your information is changing.

In any of these cases, you will have to either modify or delete links throughout your document. The process for editing and removing links is fairly simple; however, make sure you keep track of existing links and where they take you. Otherwise, you might lose important links as you edit your structure and your links.

Assumptions

- You have a list of the existing hypertext markers.

- You have a map of the links.
- You unlocked the document.

_____ **Exceptions**

- None.

_____ **Steps**

1.   Select the marker you want to change.
2.   Choose **Marker** from the Special menu (or press **Esc s m**).
3.   Edit the text in the Marker Text field.
4.   Click **Edit Marker**.

> **TIP**
>
> If you have links to other documents, you can create a list of existing lists throughout all the documents involved by creating a book of those documents and generating the marker list from the Book File menu.

_____ **What To Do If**

- If you want to remove a hypertext marker, select it and press **Delete**.

_____ **See Also**

- Creating Generated Lists from a Book, p. 430.
- Locking and Unlocking Online Documents, below.
- Chapter 9, "Creating Books."

Locking and Unlocking Online Documents | 212

Once you finish creating links, you can test them right away by locking your documents and clicking on the links. Locking and unlocking the documents lets you edit the links as you test. For example, if you lock the document and a link doesn't work, you can unlock it and check whether there is a problem with the name of the link or whether the destination marker is still there.

Assumptions

- None.

Exceptions

- None.

Steps

- To lock a document, press **Esc Shift + f l k**.
- To unlock a document, press **Esc Shift + f l k**.

What To Do If

- You can also lock a document by saving it as a View Only document using the Save As menu item.

See Also

- Editing Hypertext Markers, p. 456.

Using Hypertext Commands

Hypertext links and commands enable you to navigate through a document, create paths to specific information, and design the look and feel of your online document. Each online authoring tool provides a variety of tools and types of links and commands you can use to create paths and structure for your online system.

FrameMaker provides the following categories of links and commands:

- Direct or navigation links.
- Matrices of links or commands.
- Pop-up menus.
- Alert boxes.

- Commands to close documents and quit the online system.
- Commands to external programs.

Creating Navigation and Direct Links | 213

Direct links and navigation links differ in their destinations. Navigation links enable users to navigate linearly, go back and forth in the "linear" structure of your document, jump back where they came from, or go to the beginning or end of the document. Five commands help you build navigation tools within your document:

- gotolink firstpage.
- gotolink lastpage.
- nextpage.
- previouspage.
- previouslink.

Direct links let users move around a document by jumping from one place to another. They can navigate through topics they choose, without paying attention to the linear structure or hierarchy of the document. Five commands help you insert direct links to provide different paths through your document:

- gotolink.
- gotopage.
- openlink.
- opennew.
- openpage.

Once you identify your destination markers, you can create direct links to them from anywhere else in your document.

Assumptions

- You created the newlink markers for every destination screen.
- You have a list of all the destination markers available.
- You created any text columns necessary to place hypertext links.

Exceptions

- None.

Steps

1. Choose the hypertext command that will take you to a specific destination. Create an active area for your hypertext marker.

2. Insert the marker using the following format:

   ```
   gotolink filename:linkname
   ```

   Use the filename part only if the destination link is in another document file.

3. Test the links.

What To Do If

- If you want users to be able to retrace their steps, use the previouslink command. FrameMaker keeps a stack of the most recent jumps. The stack can go back up to 69 steps, which are stored according to the rules shown in Table 12.2.

- If you want to display a specific page in a document, use the gotopage or the openpage command with the appropriate file name and page number.

- If you want to display the first or last page in a document, use the gotolink firstpage or the gotolink lastpage command.

Table 12.2 The Hypertext Stack

Hypertext Command	Stack Behavior
alert	Does not stack.
gotolink	Stacks.
gotolink firstpage	Stacks.
gotolink lastpage	Stacks.
gotopage	Stacks.
matrix	Commands in the matrix stack according to their individual stacking properties.
message	Does not stack.
message system	Does not stack.
newlink	Does not stack.
nextpage	Does not stack.
openlink	Starts a new stack for its window.
opennew	Does not stack.
openpage	Starts a new stack for its window.
popup	Commands in the pop-up menu stack according to their individual stacking properties.
previouslink	Navigates the stack.
previouspage	Does not stack.

- If you want to display the next or previous page in a document, use the nextpage or the previouspage command.

- If you want to display a specific screen, use the gotolink or the openlink command with the appropriate destination link.

- If you want to display a different document using a separate window, use the opennew command.

- If you want to display a specific page using a separate window, use the openpage command.

See Also

- Inserting Hypertext Markers, p. 453.

214   Creating a Matrix of Links

You can create matrices of links or commands to manage some of your frequently used choices when you use icons or graphics for your buttons. Using matrices lets you edit the hypertext markers once and use them many times, similarly to using Master Pages to place links in all screens.

With a matrix, however, you can create a group of commands and use them selectively, rather than everywhere as with Master Pages. You can also place the graphic matrix anywhere in the page, as opposed to a specific place all the time as with Master Pages. In addition, you can create one matrix that is used in several instances of a graphic matrix. For example, if you create a matrix composed of the following commands:

gotolink firstpagegotolink lastpagepreviouspagenextpagequitquitall

you can build different sets of icons to use with the same matrix.

Assumptions

- The matrix is composed of equal-sized buttons or cells.
- You created a graphic of equal-sized buttons in your document.

Exceptions

- None.

Steps

1. Place a single text column over the whole graphic.
2. Go to the Reference Pages and create a new text column. Assign the column a flow name.

3. Type the hypertext commands in the text column. Each command should be in a separate paragraph.

4. Go back to the Body Pages.

5. Insert a hypertext command in the flow, using the following syntax:

matrix rows columns flowname

where rows and columns are the number of each in the matrix, and flowname is the name of the flow that contains the matrix of commands. FrameMaker assigns the hypertext commands to the flow left to right, top to bottom.

What To Do If

• If you want to use the same hypertext command matrix with a different set of icons, repeat the previous steps. Make sure you know the name of the flow that contains the commands.

See Also

• Creating Active Areas, p. 451.
• Creating Navigation and Direct Links, p. 459.

Creating a Pop-Up Menu | 215

With FrameMaker you can create a pop-up menu to help you navigate to specific spots in your document or to launch a command to exit the document or execute an external command.

Assumptions

• You have a list of related topics you want your readers to be able to access, or a group of commands you want users to be able to execute.

Exceptions

- None.

Steps

1. Make an area active for the user to click to access the pop-up menu. This can be a graphic, a word, or a paragraph.

2. Go to the Reference Pages and create a new text column. Assign the column a flow name.

3. Type the name of the pop-up menu in the text column. The first line in the flow is always the name of the pop-up menu and should not contain a hypertext command.

4. Type the menu items in the text column. Each menu item should be in a separate paragraph.

5. Insert the hypertext command you want to use for each menu item.

6. Go back to the Body Pages.

7. Insert a hypertext command using the following syntax:

   popup flowname

   where flowname is the name of the flow that contains the list of commands for the menu.

What To Do If

- If you want to use this pop-up menu somewhere else, just insert the hypertext marker and use its name for the popup command.

See Also

- Creating Active Areas, p. 451.
- Inserting Hypertext Markers, p. 453.

Creating an Alert Box | 216

FrameMaker enables you to create information or alert boxes by using the **alert** hypertext command. These are useful when you want users to have important information about a topic without leaving the screen they are on.

Assumptions

- None.

Exceptions

- None.

Steps

- Insert a hypertext command using the following syntax:

  alert message

  where message is the content of the information or alert box. You can type up to 249 characters.

What To Do If

- None.

See Also

- Inserting Hypertext Markers, p. 453.

Executing Commands to Close Documents | 217

You can create buttons enabling users to exit from the online documents. The commands you use to exit behave the same way as the File menu Close command. For example, if a user has un-locked the document, changed it, and locked it again, Frame-Maker prompts the user to save before exiting.

Assumptions

- None.

Exceptions

- None.

Steps

1. Make an area active for the user to click to exit the document.

2. Insert a quit or quitall hypertext command. Quit enables the user to close the current document, and quitall enables the user to close all open online documents.

What To Do If

- None.

See Also

- Inserting Hypertext Markers, p. 453.

218 ▾ Executing External Commands

You can also use hypertext commands to start other applications or to perform UNIX commands. This is very useful if you want to enable users to access programs such as a spreadsheet or database, or to access UNIX shell scripts from within the online document.

_____ **Assumptions**

- You know UNIX.
- You have access to the *FDK Programmer's Guide* to send messages to other applications.

_____ **Exceptions**

- You cannot use the **message** command without FrameMaker API clients.

_____ **Steps**

Insert a hypertext command using the following format:

message system command

where command is the UNIX command you want to execute.

_____ **What To Do If**

- If you want to send messages to another application, use the message command. For more information on using this command, refer to the *FDK Programmer's Guide* included in the Frame Developer's Kit.

_____ **See Also**

- Inserting Hypertext Markers, p. 453.

Index